IMAGES
of America

MUNCY

On the Cover: This lookout tower stood on Muncy Hill around the beginning of the 20th century. Lookout towers were a vital part of firefighting efforts in rural parts of turn-of-the-century America. The tower was named McMichael Lookout in its heyday; according to the *Williamsport Gazette*, the tower was named for its patron, R.R. McMichael. He was a retired capitalist who sat on the board of directors of the First National Bank of Montgomery, a position that no doubt afforded him the wealth to equip the area with picnic tables and other amenities. (Courtesy of Bill Ritter.)

IMAGES
of America

MUNCY

Maggie S. Rymsza and M. Earl Smith
with the Muncy Historical Society
Introduction by Bill Poulton

ARCADIA
PUBLISHING

ISBN 978-1-4671-2871-1

Published by Arcadia Publishing
Charleston, South Carolina

Printed in the United States of America

Library of Congress Control Number: 2017962889

For all general information, please contact Arcadia Publishing:
Telephone 843-853-2070
Fax 843-853-0044
E-mail sales@arcadiapublishing.com
For customer service and orders:
Toll-Free 1-888-313-2665

Visit us on the Internet at www.arcadiapublishing.com

To the people of Muncy, both past and present, for making Muncy what it is and what it will be

Contents

Acknowledgments

The opportunity to write about a town such as Muncy literally comes along once in a lifetime (or twice if we do a volume for Images of Modern America), and therefore, a Herculean effort is required on all sides to do such a town justice. This volume would not be a fraction of what it is without the timely and thorough input of the Muncy Historical Society, especially that of Linda Poulton, who dedicated time out of her busy schedule to allow a couple of college kids to scan the pictures needed to complete this book.

A special thanks must be given to the Rymsza-Sleboda family (E.J., Lisa, Max, Noah, and Bella) for the insights they provided into living in a place as wonderful as Muncy and for the room and board they provided during our research trips. Special thanks go to Lisa for her tireless efforts at providing local connections and review.

We would be remiss if we did not thank the following people and entities for providing both images and research material: Bill Ritter, Malcolm Barlow of Muncy Farms, Janet Woodside Shoemaker, and the Church of the Resurrection, which has served as Maggie's spiritual home since her early childhood.

As always, the team at Arcadia Publishing has done a delightful job in bringing our vision and heritage to life. A special thanks must be given to both Erin Vosgien and Caroline Anderson; without their tireless work, this volume would not be as wonderful as it is.

Finally, though there are too many names to mention, Maggie and M. Earl would like to thank, aside from each other, the following people: John Pollack and the crew at the Kislak Center for Special Collections and Rare Books at the University of Pennsylvania, Nayeli Riano, Nicole Flibbert, Izzy Korostoff, and especially Breanna Himschoot. As always, M. would like to thank his children: Lydia, Nicholas, and Leah.

INTRODUCTION

The selected images that follow represent our past. Enjoy them for what they are. It is our future, however, which will determine how and for what we will be remembered.

While I am not a Muncy native, I am extremely proud to call Muncy my home. Although not reared in Lycoming County, much less Pennsylvania, in my heart, they are home to me.

I am a Connecticut Yankee and will hold its memories close to my heart. Brought up in a small town along the coast, my formative years were spent sailing (I could sail out to Faulkner's Island and back by the age of 15), fishing and crabbing in season, and sledding and ice-skating in the winter. Saturdays at the local theater (35¢) and a wonderful, lively, vibrant downtown entertained my curious mind. Then came the 1960s, and everything changed. There were few jobs for the high school graduate, the amusement park along the waterfront and the theater were closed, and Vietnam happened. To make matters worse, my once-wonderful downtown began to disappear. Almost overnight, a new concept took hold—urban renewal. Many sections of my downtown were completely razed in favor of multiunit housing and parking lots. The big-box stores and shopping strips and malls replaced the local mom-and-pop store, and the candy, hardware, and jewelry stores were now gone.

In a way, my life became a big-box store—the military service aisle, the college aisle, and a variety of job aisles. I wandered its many aisles looking for that one thing I needed but did not know where it was. And then I found myself in New York City, the city that never sleeps; a city with hundreds of built-in small towns; a city to get lost in. Every day was like visiting a new postcard.

But life is strange. At the same time that the downtown of my youth was being bulldozed and as life settled around me in the city, I met my future wife. Working together, we enjoyed the sights and sounds of Thirty-Fourth Street, late night dinners in Chinatown, and walks in the Village. We watched the Twin Towers being built. And it was time to meet our respective families. The original downtown area of my hometown, established in 1642, was gone. I was so disappointed that I could only share my wonderful memories of what once was, and indeed, Faulkner's Island seemed so far away.

Next came my introduction to Muncy. Coming over what turned out to be the Muncy Hills, Interstate 180 West ended here—how fitting! It had been raining for several days, and the night we arrived, it was still raining. Hurricane Agnes had made its way to north-central Pennsylvania. Striking not once but twice, Agnes brought floodwaters from the local creek and the Susquehanna River right into downtown Muncy. The downtown stores and bank, the theater and small businesses, and 40 percent of the homes in the borough flooded. I was enthralled. I fell in love with Muncy that weekend—in spite of its flood mud, building and tree debris, and that assortment of nasty odors.

While New York City was exciting, Muncy was almost perfect. And I stayed! It is like living in a postcard. Even after living here more than half of my life, there is hardly a day that goes by that I don't learn something new about its past. Navigating around town is a history lesson it itself. Aside from Main and Market Streets, most streets are named for a national or local history event or person—Penn, Washington, Lafayette, Lincoln, Sherman, Grant. We even have our own Revolutionary figure, Capt. John Brady; our own Revolutionary War–era historical sites, Fort Muncy and Fort Brady; and our own master spy of the Susquehanna River valley, Samuel Wallis.

Muncy retains its small-town feel in that most of its historic homes are identified by the name of the family that lived there rather than by a street address—the Taggert House, Lowmiller's, the Douglas House, and Rose Hill, to name a few. The McCarty House is one of the oldest homes, named after its builder and one of Muncy's founding fathers. Muncy is like visiting Williamsburg, Virginia, but without the four-hour drive. You can hold up a postcard image from Muncy past and a photograph from today and you'll see the similarities.

Downtown is vibrant, hosting great restaurants and specialty shops. Our streets are as safe as any in small-town America. We have walking trails and parks. And yes, the mall located just outside of town with its big-box stores did hurt many of our small businesses, but guess what? The downtown is coming back. The sense of community is strong, and its residents support its small-town charm.

In sharing this account with you, I hope you can appreciate and understand how Muncy welcomed and adopted me as much as I did Muncy. The best way to fully appreciate Muncy is to live here; the next best is to visit. Walk the streets and alleys. Talk to the merchants and residents. Muncy basks in the glory of its past, all the while looking forward to its future as a small town.

The images, the postcards, and the memorabilia that make up this book are excellent examples of how proud we are of Muncy's past and its current and future potential. We invite you to come, to stay, or just to visit Muncy and help us make its future even better.

—Bill Poulton
President, Muncy Historical Society

One

Rainbow in the Dark

Art and the Arts in Muncy

Given the amount of effort put into making Muncy a town that found its roots in farming and industry, one would think that little time was afforded to artists and the arts. That, however, is not the case, as the artistic community in Muncy shares a vibrant past and present, blending the heritage of the past with modes and methods of the present.

The arts in Muncy owes their history to the rich legacy of Federal, Georgian, and Victorian architecture in the area. Examples of these varied types of building methods date back to before the Revolution and expand past the Civil War era into modernity. Cabinetmaker Benjamin Potts was the forerunner of this type of building; although he started his career as a cabinetmaker, he expanded into framed doorways, masterful pieces of art that survive to this day.

To say that the building arts were the only ones represented would be folly. The New Deal, especially, left its mark on the area. A mural called *Rachel Silverthorne's Ride* was painted on the wall of the post office in 1938 by John W. Beauchamp to honor, through an artistic eye, the role that both women and the area played in the American Revolution. The mural, having stood the test of time, remains today as a nod to the legacy of Roosevelt's Works Progress Administration and its role in Americana.

Oscar Ellis and his chip art have left a more modern legacy on Muncy, even if his style was rooted deep in the past. Such art, produced by a Muncy local, added to the reputation and the lore around the arts in this little industrial enclave. His work, along with the works of other artists, carvers, builders, crafters, and artisans, is preserved faithfully by the Muncy Historical Society.

While far from the highbrow works that populate the Louvre or New York's Metropolitan Museum of Art, these works stand as a timeless testament to Muncy's creative heritage, a heritage that the authors of this book seek to continue with their historical testament.

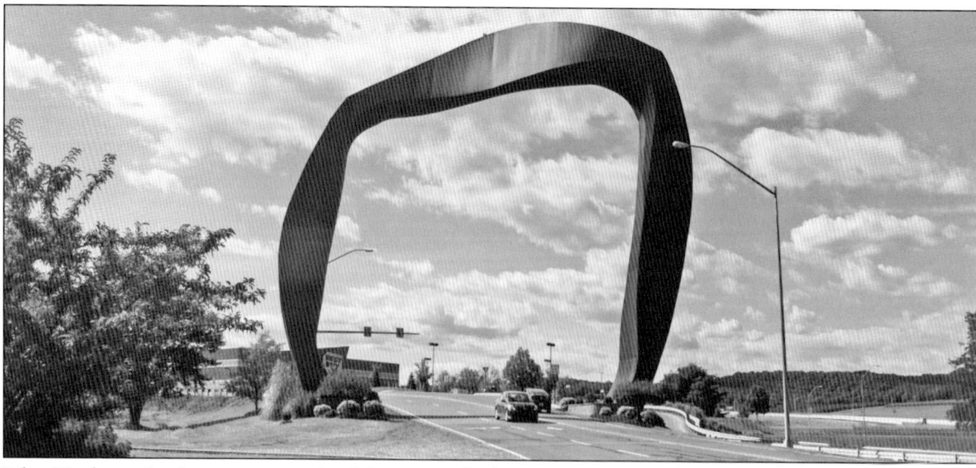

The Hadany Arch is a piece of public artwork that spans Lycoming Mall Circle in Muncy. The arch was installed by internationally renowned sculptor Israel Hadany, who said of it: "I was given the opportunity to build several monumental-sized outdoor sculptures in the United States. One of them, the Hadany Arch, made of [Cor-ten] steel, rises one hundred feet above the road to Lycoming Mall in Williamsport, PA. This sculpture is the tallest I have ever built and is among the tallest in the US." (Author's collection.)

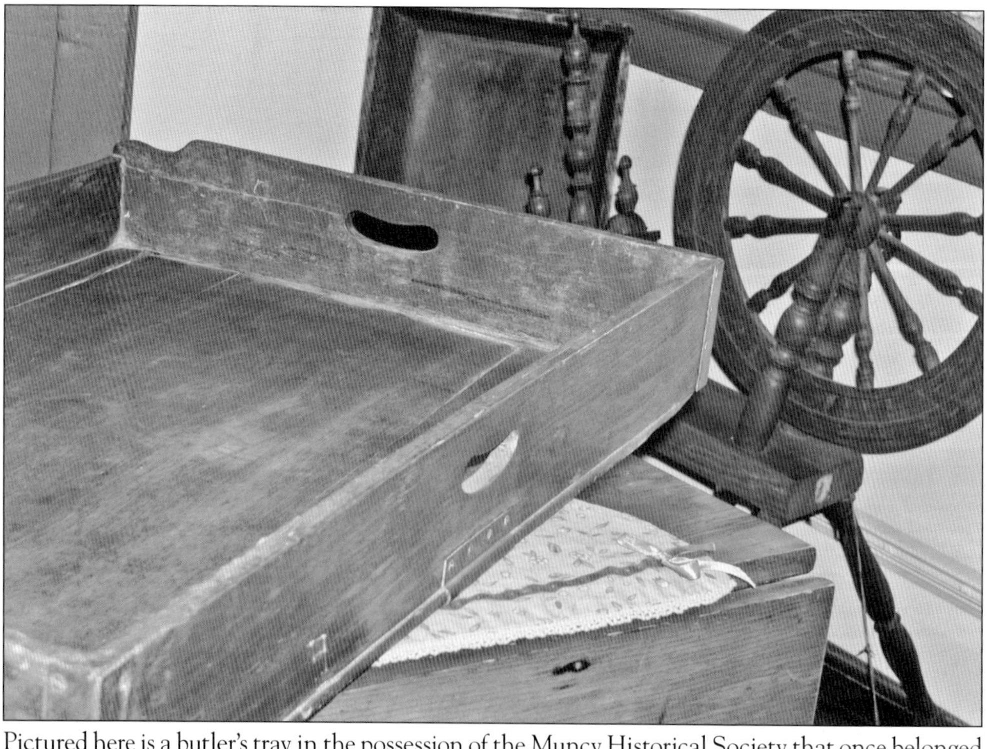

Pictured here is a butler's tray in the possession of the Muncy Historical Society that once belonged to former slave Henry Harris. A butler's tray was originally a two-piece set, with the tray resting on top of a four-legged X-frame pedestal. The style originated in England in the mid-1700s and was brought over by the British bourgeois when they colonized America. This style, with the tray fixed to the stand, was brought into many American homes in the mid-20th century as a part of the Colonial Revival furniture movement. (Courtesy of the Muncy Historical Society.)

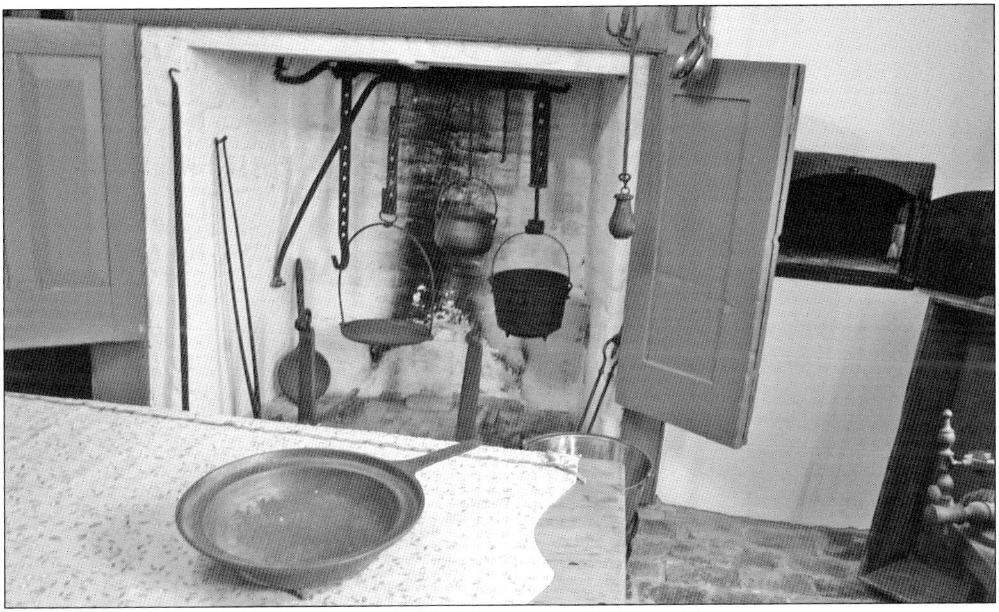

Although the use of cast iron dates to the fifth century BCE in China, its use as a material for cooking rose to prominence in 1707 in London as a cheap alternative to other materials. This artifact, which was owned by Henry Harris, is in possession of the Muncy Historical Society. Despite its age of over 200 years, it looks as if one could put it over a fireplace and enjoy a home-cooked meal today. (Courtesy of the Muncy Historical Society.)

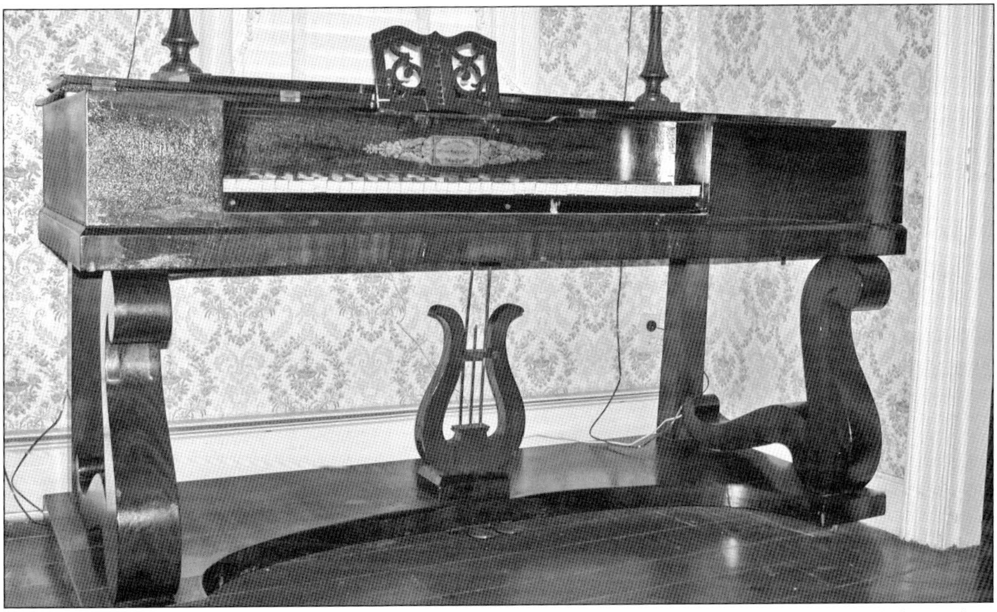

Shown here is the piano of Henry Harris; by all accounts, it was closer to a harpsichord than what one would recognize as a piano today. There is very little doubt that the piano came over from England. After all, the first known American-manufactured piano is dated to Charles Albrecht in 1787, a mere 11 years after the United States claimed independence. Despite the abundance of lumber in the Pennsylvania colony (later state), resources would have been in short supply to build such a masterpiece. (Courtesy of the Muncy Historical Society.)

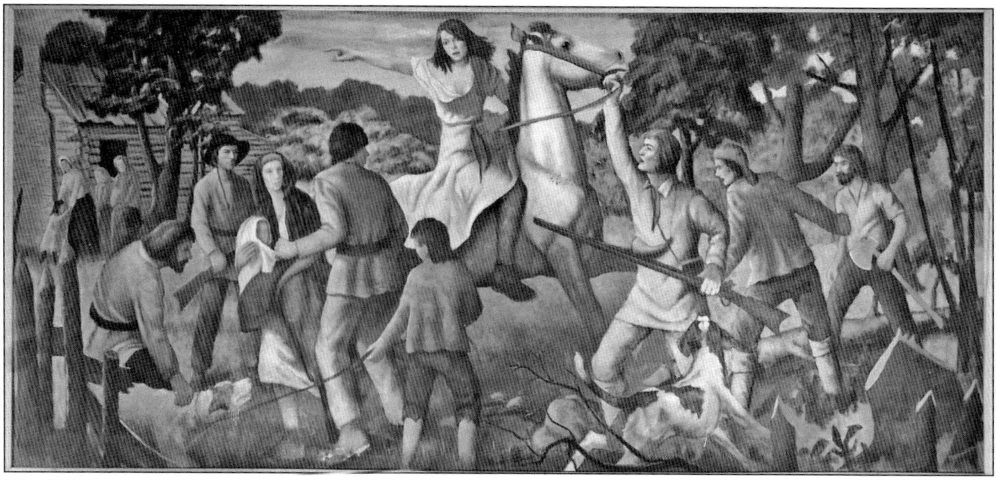

The Works Progress Administration, under Roosevelt's New Deal, was responsible for several arts projects funded through the Treasury's Section of Fine Arts. One such project hangs in the Muncy Post Office. *Rachel Silverthorne's Ride* was painted in 1938 by John W. Beauchamp. Silverthorne, having commandeered Capt. John Brady's horse, is depicted riding back to Muncy to warn settlers of an impending attack by British forces in 1778 during the Revolutionary War. Although her actions allowed most settlers to flee, the property damage from the raid was estimated at $200,000. (Courtesy of the Muncy Historical Society.)

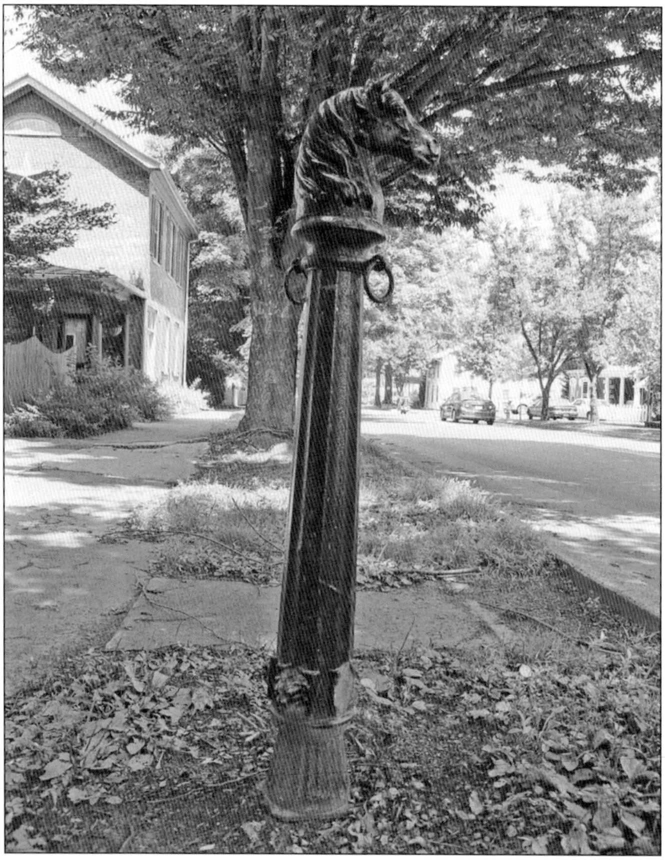

Shown here is one of the many turn-of-the-century hitching posts that stand in Muncy today. The fact that it survived is a miracle, as many were broken and melted down during World War II. The hitching post dates to as early as 1625 in England and was often used to mark distances between towns. The first patent for a hitching post was issued in the United States in 1861 to Charles Bush of Newbury, New York. Today, the posts sell for an average of $1,200 on the antiques market. (Courtesy of the Muncy Historical Society.)

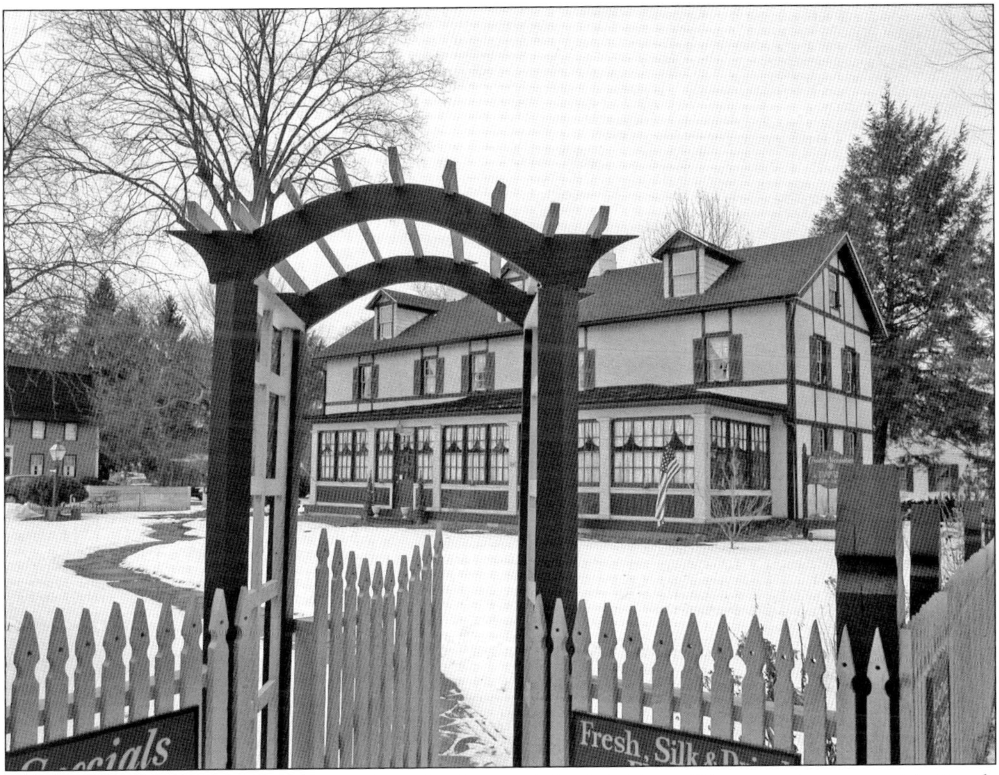

This decorative wooden arch stood at the front of the McCarty-Wertman House at 34 North Main Street in the Muncy Historic District. The property, now a private residence, was most recently occupied by Creative Necessities Florist and Gift Shop. Print ads state that the business specialized in "Fresh silk and dried florals; Weddings; Symphony Arrangements; Parties; Plants; Balloons and gift baskets." These ads give credence to the home's historic value, stating that the shop is located "in the historic McCarty House." (Courtesy of the Muncy Historical Society.)

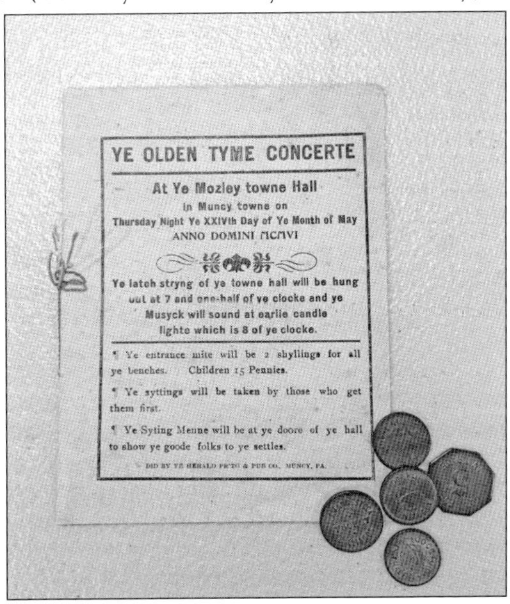

Concerts such as the one advertised on this stub (complete with replica shillings to gain the bearer attendance) were commonplace throughout the early 20th century, as a renewed interest in history and spirituality swept across the United States. This show, hosted by Mozley Town Hall, took place on May 24, 1906. Seating, as the flyer states, was first come, first serve, and the doors opened for seating at 7:30, with the performance to begin at 8:00 p.m. Such performances were a key form of entertainment in a time before radio. (Courtesy of the Muncy Historical Society.)

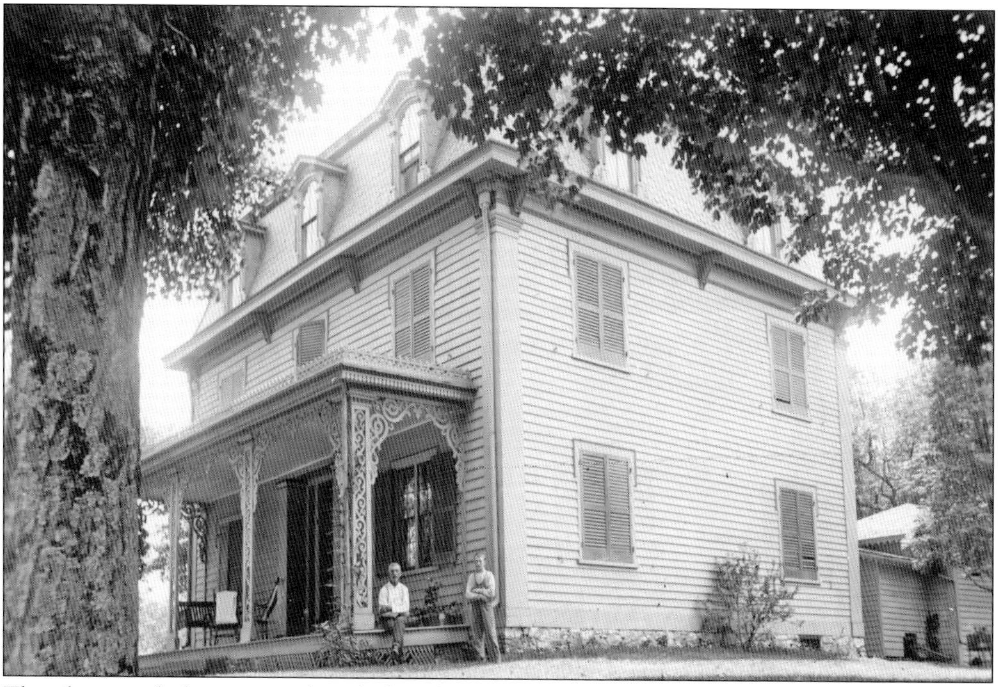

This photograph shows an unidentified residence within Muncy, complete with turn-of-the-century citizens lounging around the porch. This house was built in the Georgian style, which became famous amongst the middle class in Britain between 1714 and 1830. It would be reborn later in the States under the name Colonial Revival. The style features symmetrical lines and columns, with elements of Renaissance styles blended in. The combination provides a classy but affordable aesthetic. (Courtesy of the Muncy Historical Society.)

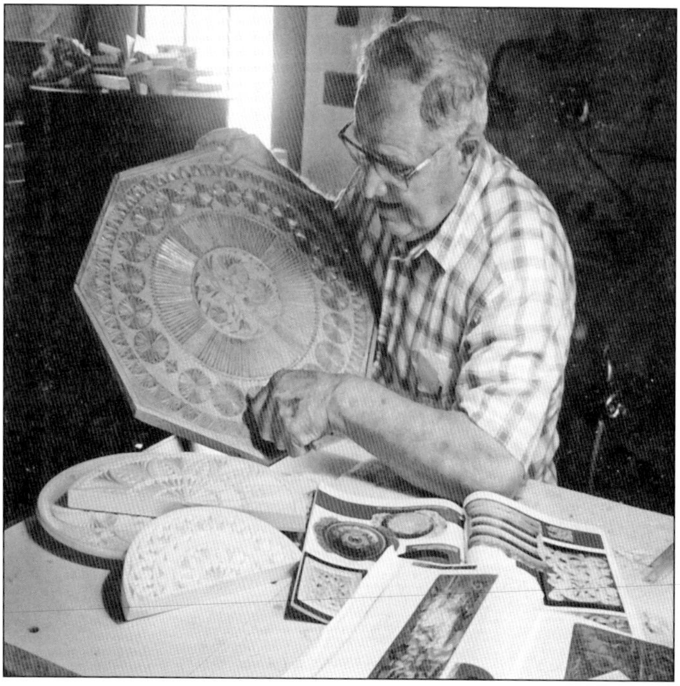

A member of the Lycoming County Woodcarvers, Oscar Ellis, fondly known in the community as "Bud," was one of Muncy's finest woodworkers. A 1943 graduate of Muncy High School, Ellis served in World War II as a supply sergeant with the US Army Air Corps in England. Aside from his art, Ellis was active in the community, serving as his church sexton and as an active volunteer with the Warrior Run–Fort Freeland Heritage Society, where he demonstrated his chip art at the annual Heritage Days Festival. (Courtesy of the Muncy Historical Society.)

These grates pay tribute to the Pennsylvania German immigrants, with the tulips representing the Holy Trinity. For many years, the Pennsylvania Germans were not accepted into mainstream American culture, but these works show how their presence continues to leave a mark on communities across Pennsylvania. The palmette seen on the grate is an ornamental motif resembling the fan-shaped leaves of a palm tree. With origins in ancient Egypt, the palmette is often found in classical architecture and was introduced in Muncy during the Greek Classical Revival period in the 18th and 19th centuries. (Courtesy of the Muncy Historical Society.)

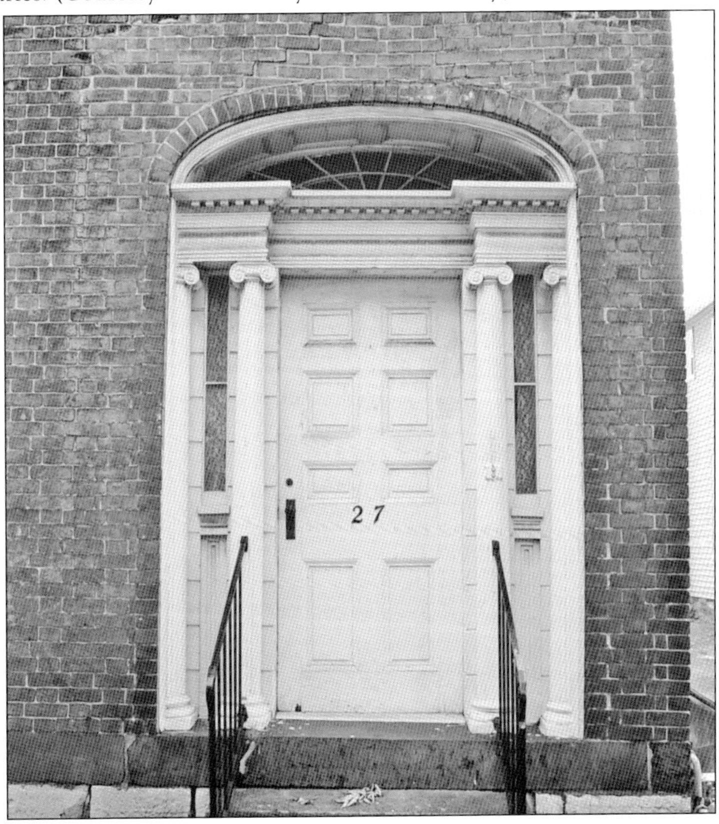

Not only does this doorway on North Main Street showcase Muncy's Pott Doorways, but it was also the entrance to the home of the artist. Benjamin Pott, though a talented cabinetmaker, was more well known in Muncy for his beautiful doorways. Pott left a mark on his home, as he created the doorway and built a novel sidewalk in front of his house in 1877. Pott died on June 24, 1881, but his presence can still be seen throughout the streets of Muncy, as he left an indelible mark on the architecture of the town. (Courtesy of the Muncy Historical Society.)

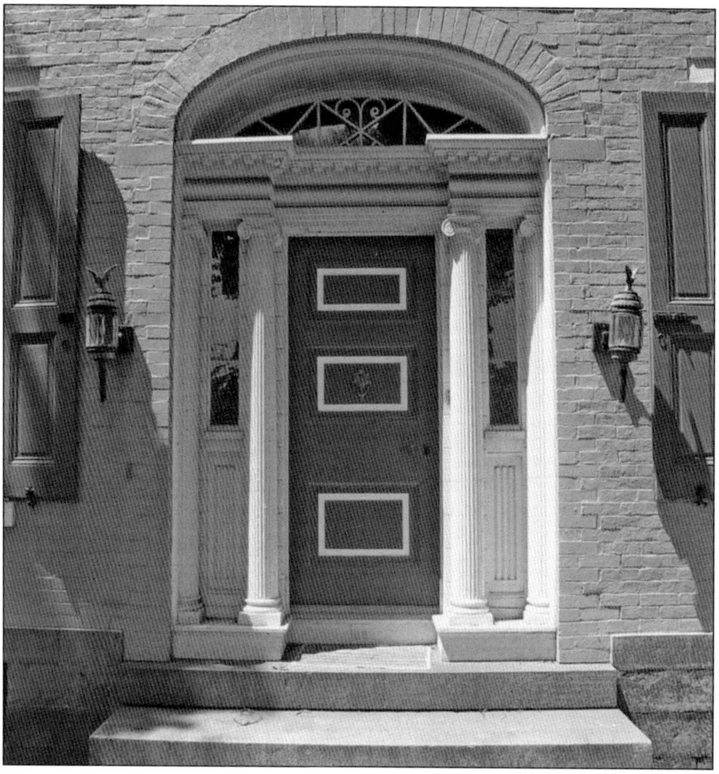

Benjamin Pott was a part of the extensive community of cabinetmakers in Muncy. The McCarty family was also heavily involved in the trade. Lloyd McCarty and his brother, Seth, were born in Muncy in the first decade of the 19th century, and both worked as cabinetmakers. Lloyd worked as an apprentice to Benjamin Pott until moving to Canada in 1836. He returned to the area after two years, and at the time of his passing in 1899, Lloyd was the oldest resident in Muncy. (Courtesy of the Muncy Historical Society.)

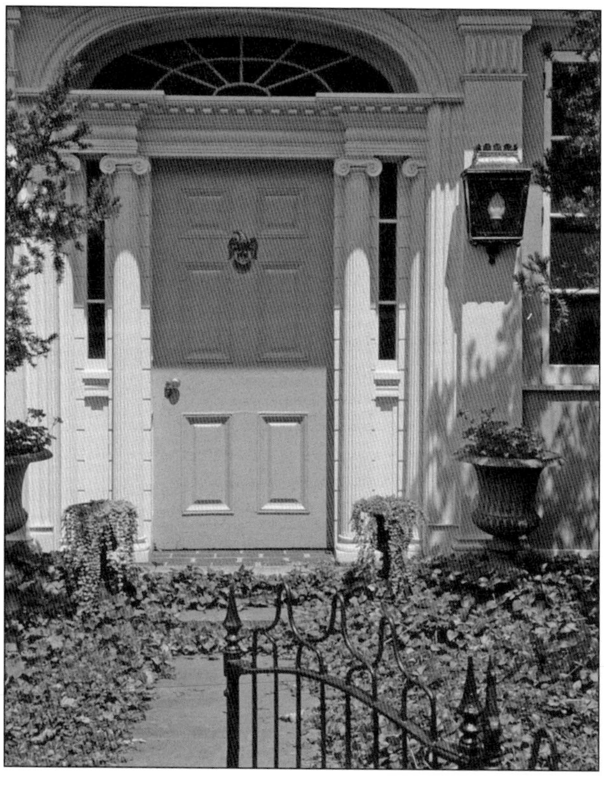

Political thought during the American Revolution was characterized by an emphasis on classical literature and early ideas of republicanism. Similarly, after the Revolution, American architecture was greatly influenced by the ancient buildings of Rome and Greece, initiating what was known as the early Classical Revival style. Born in the early part of the 19th century, Benjamin Pott was greatly inspired by this trend. His doorways feature traits typical of the Roman Classical Revival style, namely a front facade with columns and often an elliptical window at the center of the pediment. (Courtesy of the Muncy Historical Society.)

Two

Sowing the Seeds of Love Houses of Worship in Muncy

Every hour, the bells of St. Andrew's Evangelical Lutheran Church sing throughout the streets of Muncy. For generations, local worship has been an integral part of the town. Many of the community volunteer efforts and local organizations are a result of more than half a dozen churches that dot the streets. As centers for community involvement, many local identities are tied to these houses of worship.

Local denominations include Catholic, Baptist, Methodist, Lutheran, Presbyterian, and Episcopal. Early congregations date back to the 18th century, with St. James Episcopal Church, founded in 1787, and St. Andrew's, established in 1785, serving as two of the oldest houses of worship in the area. Throughout the years, many of the local churches have been improved, renamed, and moved. The Catholic Church of the Resurrection, for example, once located on Main Street, recently expanded and now sits at the top of Musser Lane.

The buildings themselves are imposing structures, as the architecture includes towering steeples, beautiful stained-glass windows, and Gothic Revival architecture. Richard Upjohn—an internationally recognized architect who was partially responsible for the popular Gothic Revival movement in the United States—left his mark on the town in 1859 with his construction of St. James Episcopal Church.

After many years, the local churches have proved to be immensely influential in community life. Catering to Muncy's young residents, many have active youth groups and Sunday school classes. The churches also serve the wider community in different capacities: the Catholic church provides services for over 300 women at the state correctional institution, the Baptist church hosts meeting for Boy Scouts and Alcoholics Anonymous, and the Methodist church's Good n' Plenty program unites the community through monthly suppers. Residents of Muncy continue to see their houses of worship as true homes, as these buildings unite community members, families, and friends through prayer and local activism.

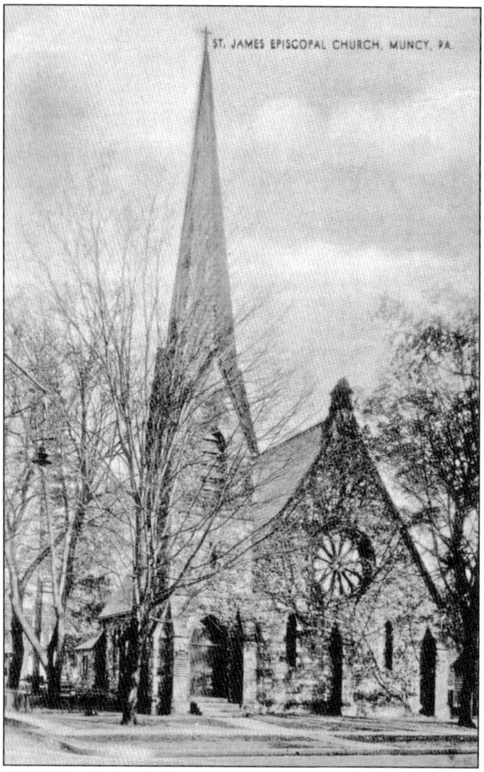

Designed by famed architect Richard Upjohn, the home of the congregation of St. James Episcopal Church at 215 South Main Street in Muncy is shown in this 1910 postcard. Built in the Gothic Revival style, it was constructed between 1857 and 1859 by members of the Muncy community. Capable of seating over 500 people, the building was added to the Pennsylvania Register of Historic Places on July 9, 1979, and to the National Register of Historic Places on November 20, 1979. (Author's collection.)

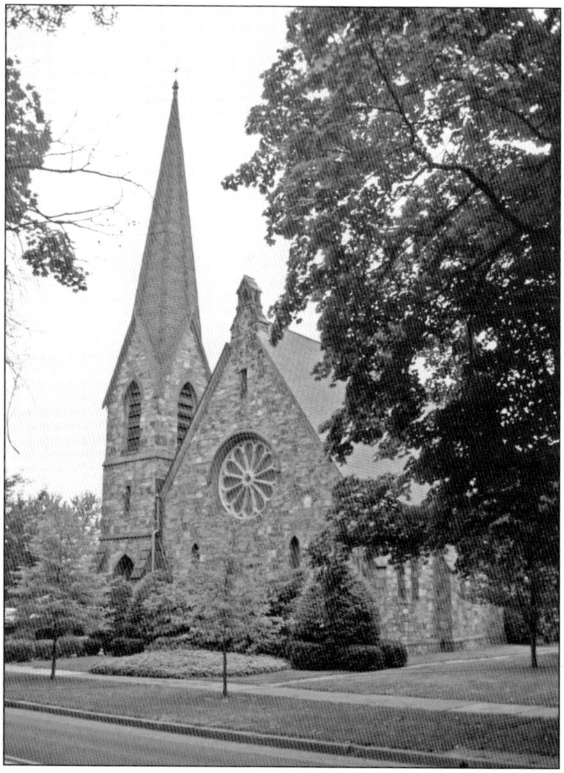

Founded in 1797, St. James Episcopal Church is one of the oldest congregations in Muncy. The church was designed by Richard Upjohn, who also designed Trinity Church on Wall Street in New York. The building of the church is said to have impressed Upjohn so much that he did not charge for his service. After an extensive renovation, thanks to a large endowment from the Margaret Waldron Foundation, the church is still used for Eucharist services to this day. (Author's collection.)

The earliest Lutheran congregation in Muncy was founded in 1785. A Sunday school was founded in 1847, and in 1852, the congregation gathered at the house of Michael S. Russell to organize the Evangelical Lutheran church under the watch of Rev. George Parsons. Expansions included more seating, stained-glass windows, and a parsonage, before the church was named St. Andrew's in 1956. After adding a new pipe organ in 1974, the church expanded again in 2001. Today, Rev. Daniel P. Landin leads the congregation. (Author's collection.)

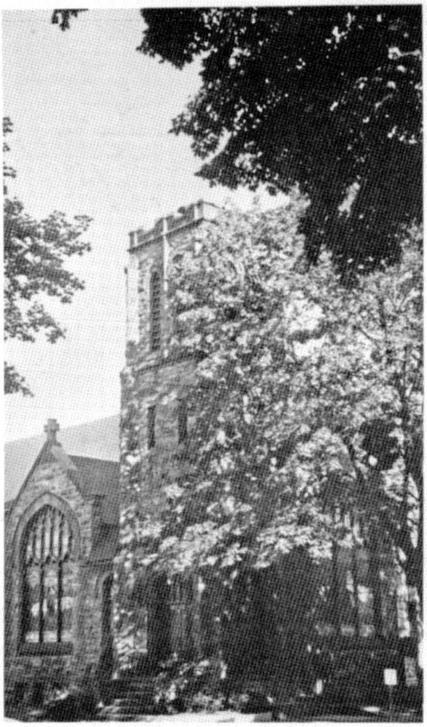

Lutheran Church, Muncy, Pa.

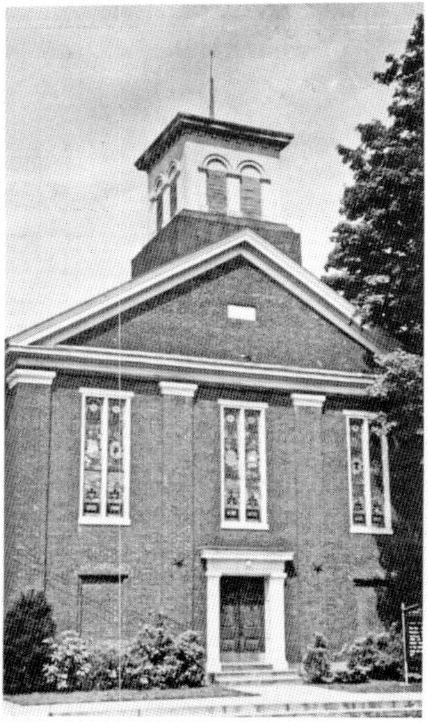

Methodist Church, Muncy, Pa.

Many churches were found just before the 19th century in Muncy, and the First United Methodist Church is no exception. Methodist traveling ministers started including the area in their circuit in 1791, and by 1800, Methodists in the area began to meet in the old Pepper Schoolhouse. The congregation put up its first building in 1830, the first in Muncy used exclusively for worship purposes. In 1967, the church started the building that would become the current site of worship at 206 South Market Street. A bell tower was added in 1998. (Author's collection.)

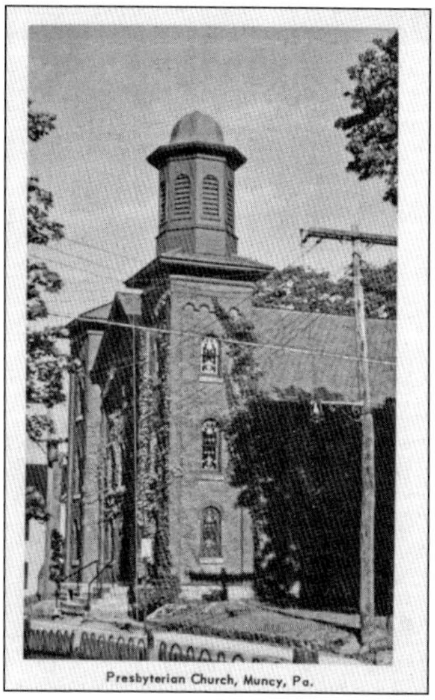

The Muncy Presbyterian Church celebrated its 175th year in 2010. The mission was founded in 1834, and the building was dedicated in 1835. Initially known as Cradle Roll, the church still displays the original charter, which includes 26 members of the community, in the back edifice of the church. The church possesses one of the few Moline Tracker pipe organs known to exist. The organ was installed for $23,997 in today's dollars. The church underwent a complete restoration in 1985, which included installation of a Sunday school room at the back of the church. (Author's collection.)

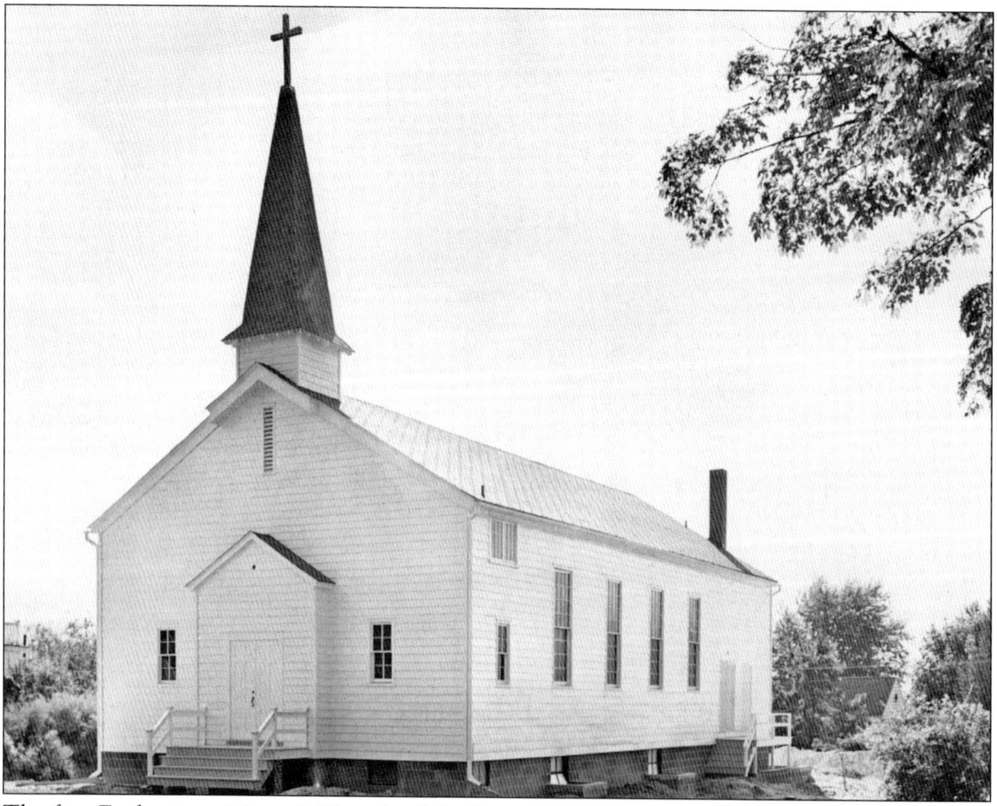

The first Eucharist at Muncy's Church of the Resurrection was celebrated on December 7, 1941. At the time, few Catholics lived in the area; today, the church serves over 600 families. The building pictured, a surplus Army chapel delivered by train from Florida, was dedicated in 1949. In 2008, the Church of the Resurrection moved from South Main Street to Musser Lane, a building project that took over 10 years to complete. Currently led by Fr. Glenn McCreary, the church continues to be a presence in the community through its Social Concerns Committee. (Courtesy of the Church of the Resurrection.)

Highlighting the extensive networks of Muncy's Catholic church, this image of a first holy communion was sent by Bob Wilt, a past resident of the town, to Fr. Philip Sladicaka in 1991. Upon returning from his duties in World War II, Wilt, a member of the church, was hired to print the first edition of the *Muncy Luminary*. He served as editor and publisher until March 1983, when he moved to Santa Barbara, California, after his marriage to Eleanor Murphy. (Courtesy of the Church of the Resurrection.)

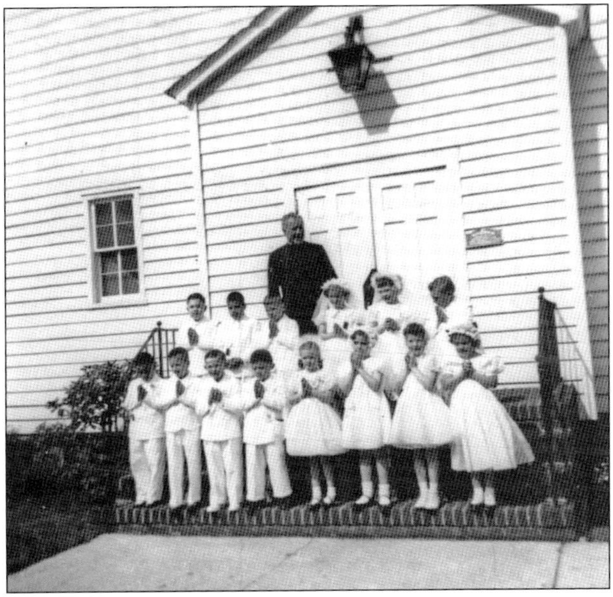

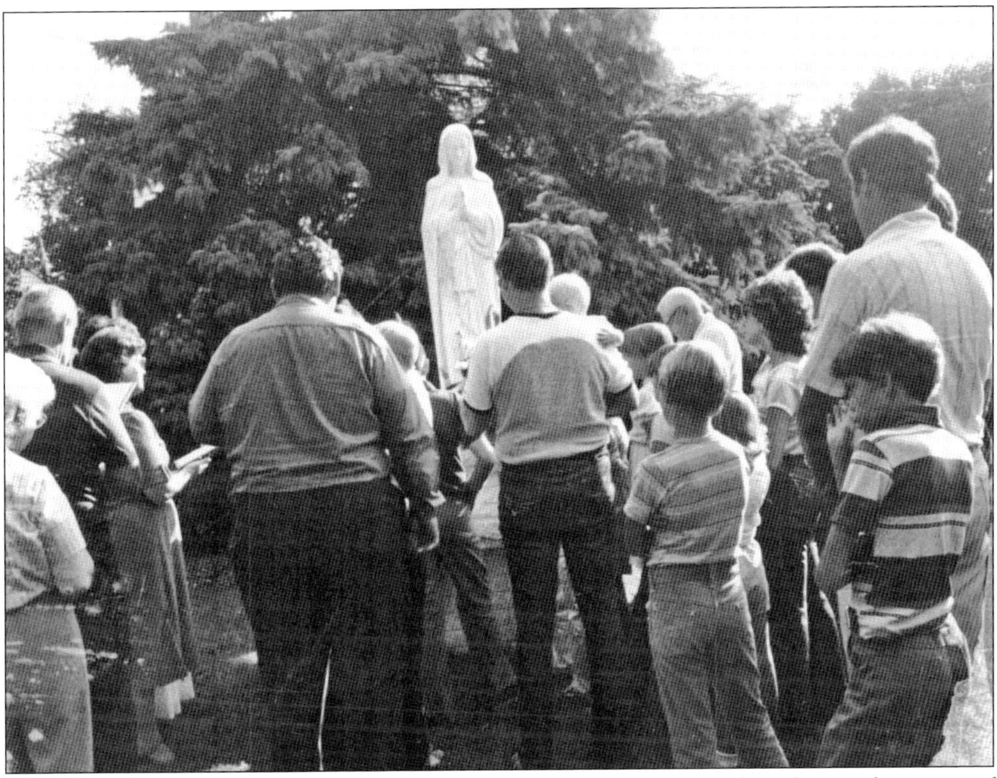

On August 14, 1982, members of the Church of the Resurrection gathered around a statue of the Virgin Mary to celebrate a rosary service, a group recitation of the rosary. Taking about 20 minutes, the service consists of one person leading the group through the first half of the prayer before being joined by all in attendance for the second half. Such a service often precedes a funeral or celebration mass, and one does not need to be Catholic to participate. (Courtesy of the Church of the Resurrection.)

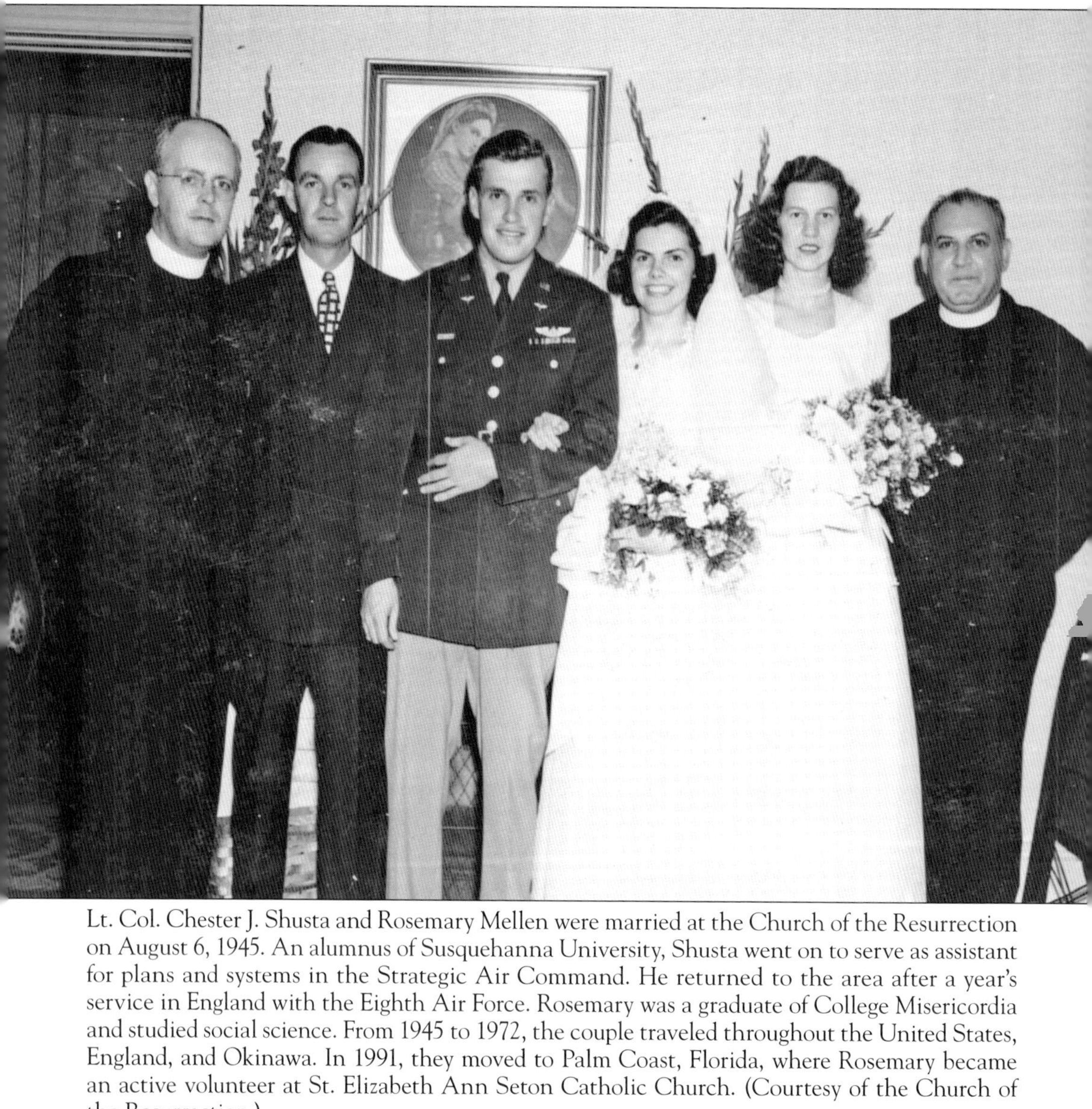

Lt. Col. Chester J. Shusta and Rosemary Mellen were married at the Church of the Resurrection on August 6, 1945. An alumnus of Susquehanna University, Shusta went on to serve as assistant for plans and systems in the Strategic Air Command. He returned to the area after a year's service in England with the Eighth Air Force. Rosemary was a graduate of College Misericordia and studied social science. From 1945 to 1972, the couple traveled throughout the United States, England, and Okinawa. In 1991, they moved to Palm Coast, Florida, where Rosemary became an active volunteer at St. Elizabeth Ann Seton Catholic Church. (Courtesy of the Church of the Resurrection.)

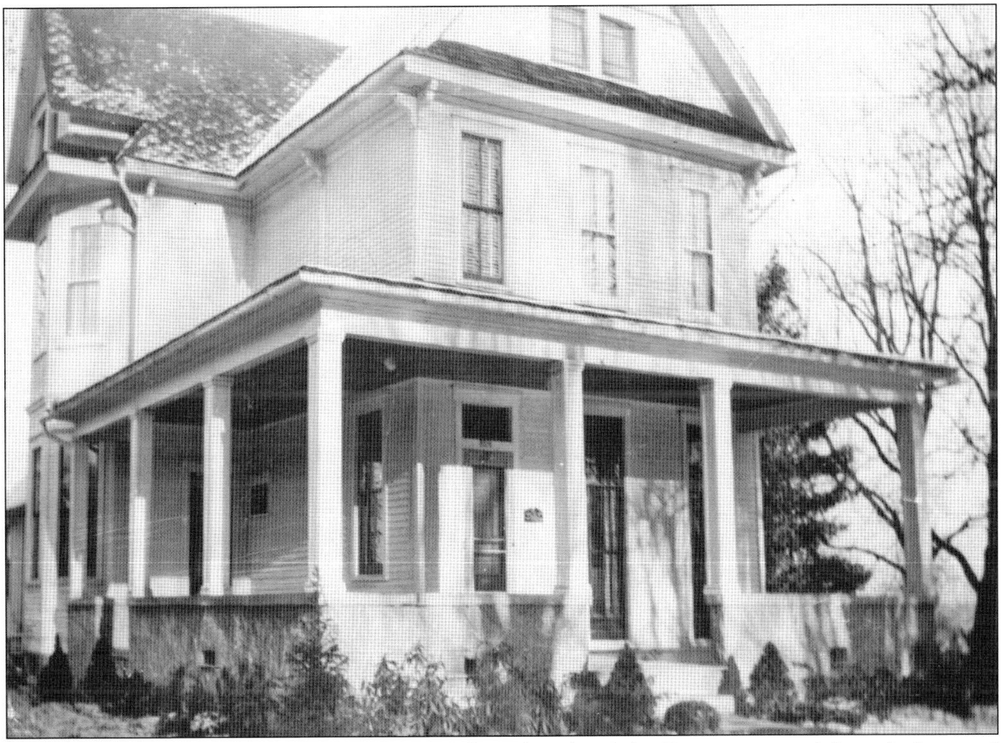

Shown here in 1943 is the first rectory of the Church of the Resurrection, Muncy's first and only Catholic church. The church was founded in 1941 with approximately 65 parishioners; the congregation today stands at 600, not to mention the nearly 300 prisoners at the Muncy women's prison who call the church home. Things moved rapidly for the church; in 1942, it performed its first communion, holy baptism, and marriage. Aside from staffed clergy, the church boasts many lay parishioners in education and service. (Courtesy of the Church of the Resurrection.)

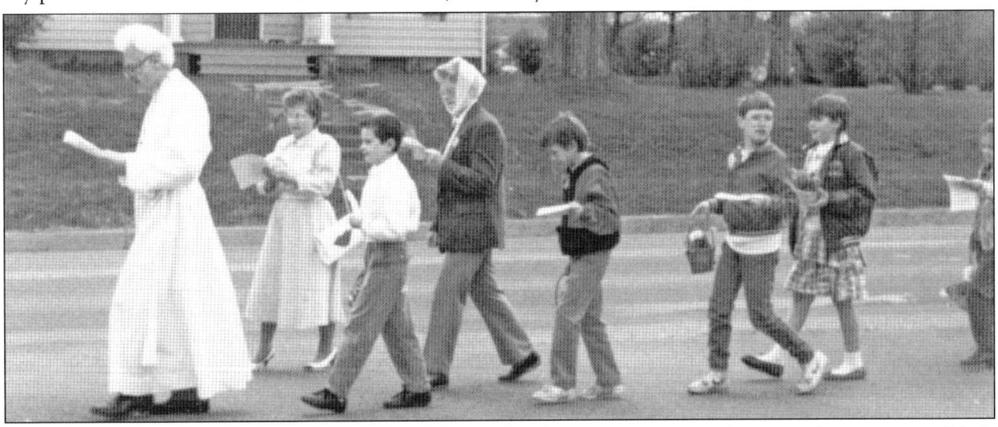

Once the Catholic church finished its structural development on Main Street, it began to establish connections in the local community. In 1958, another building was added to serve as a kindergarten center and convent for the Sisters of the Immaculate Heart of Mary. In 1966, though the sisters departed from the Resurrection building, religious education continued. To this day, the church holds weekly Sunday school classes. The church also has a vibrant youth group program where young parishioners from Muncy and surrounding neighborhoods contribute to local volunteer efforts. (Courtesy of the Church of the Resurrection.)

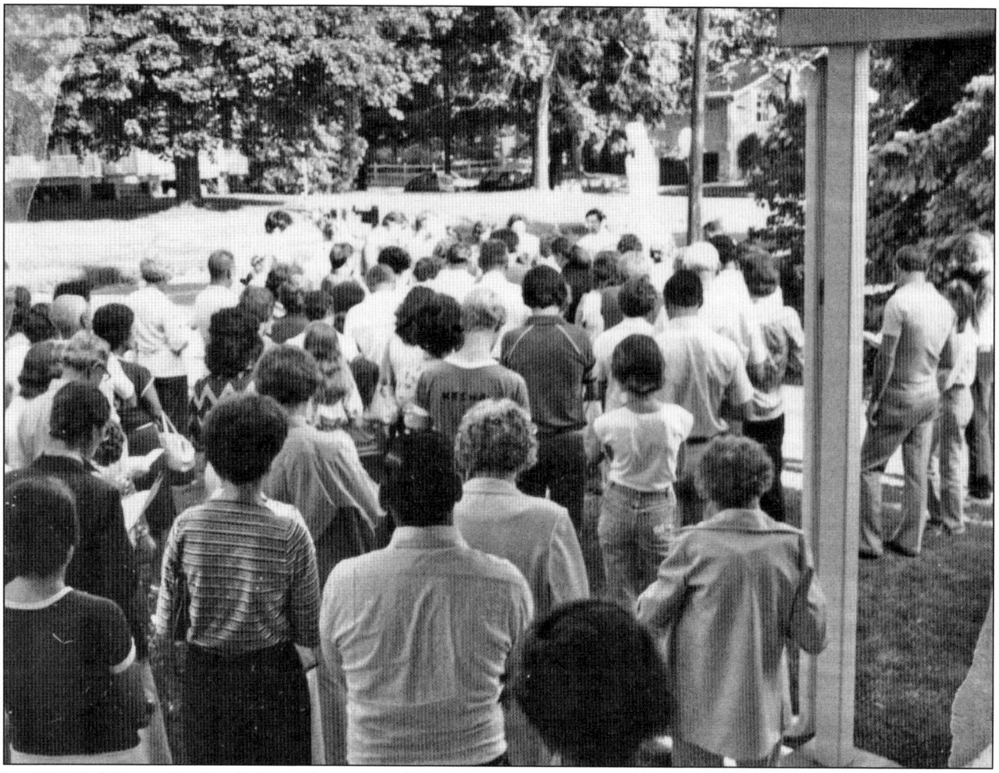

In 2016, Muncy's Catholic church celebrated 75 years of local worship. At the time of the establishment of the Church of the Resurrection, Muncy Catholics had to ride a train to Williamsport. Over the years, families from Hughesville, Montgomery, and Turbotville have joined the parish, creating an extensive network that extends across the Diocese of Scranton. With the addition of so many new members, the church looked to expand. Today, it overlooks the rolling hills of Muncy at the top of Musser Lane. (Courtesy of the Church of the Resurrection.)

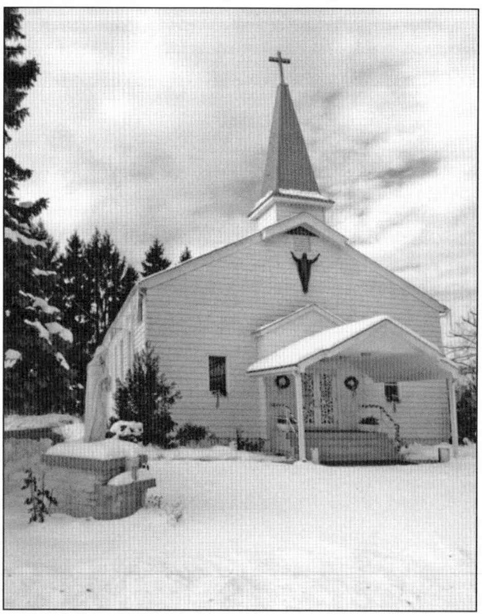

Every year, the Christmas spirit in Muncy is amplified by the strong church presence. For the Church of the Resurrection, Christmas offers many opportunities to interact with the local community. Each December, the youth group spends one evening parading around Muncy to deliver carols to residents. The church also offers many volunteer opportunities during the season, including its annual Giving Tree. On Christmas Eve, the church holds its annual midnight mass, a beautiful candlelit evening. (Courtesy of the Church of the Resurrection.)

Three

Wish You Were Here
Landscapes of Muncy

The West Branch of the Susquehanna River started carving its way through Muncy over 2.6 million years ago, during the Pliocene epoch. As one of the oldest rivers in the world, it carves a pattern through close to 500 miles of watershed in New York, Pennsylvania, and Maryland, emptying into the Chesapeake Bay. The picturesque river is the 16th-longest in the United States and is the largest river in the United States to never have extensive commercial traffic.

Along its meandering, zigzag route, it cuts a path through the Allegheny Plateau and spawns several creeks, runs, and tributaries, including Muncy Creek, along which the Munsee Indians made their settlement. English, German, Dutch, and Irish colonial settlers moved to the area, disrupting the communal tribes that inhabited it while founding the village they would name after these same Indians, Muncy.

While the area owes its existence to the dual destruction of millions of years of water and more modern raids against what was a peaceful group of natives, few can deny the gorgeous scenery that dots the area. Populated by an abundance of fish, wildlife, and native flora, this tiny patch of northeastern Pennsylvania sees more than its fair share of hunters, sightseers, leaf-watchers, and ecotourists. A conscious effort from both locals and environmentalists helps to uphold that tradition, and in each season, Muncy is a sight to behold.

In the spirit of close to three million years of geological, natural, and historic beauty, this chapter presents some of the undeniable beauty of the Muncy Valley and the surrounding area. While a great deal of this is displayed on postcards, photographs taken by locals give an outsider a view of the landscapes that make Muncy's scenes unlike anywhere else in America, both today and in the past. It is a beauty that, no doubt, is worthy of preservation for generations past, present, and future.

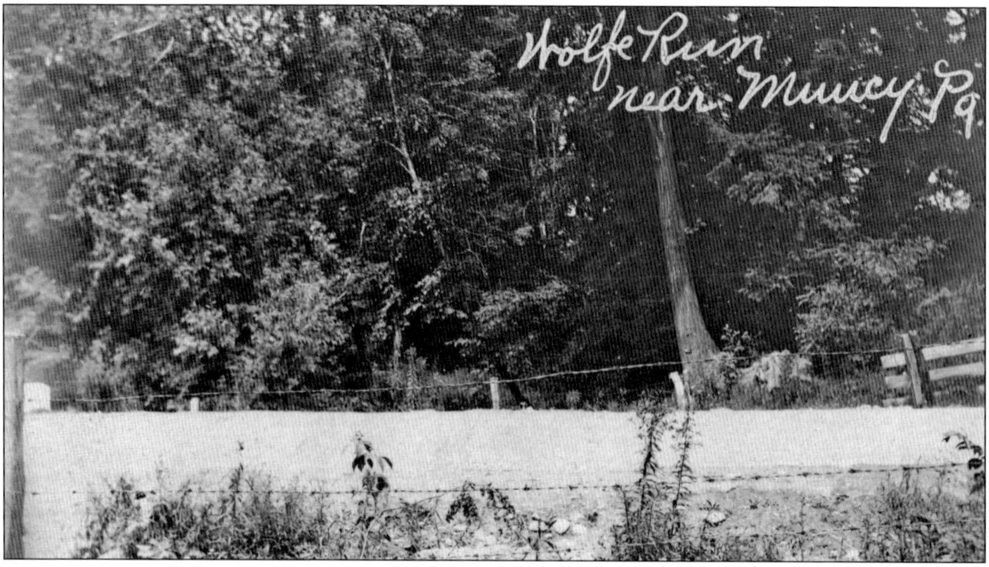

This is a postcard image of Wolf Run. John Adlum, a veteran of the American Revolution and the father of American viticulture, shipped blue marble quarried in Wolf Run to the nation's capital to be used for doorways and window sills. An impressive winemaker, Adlum caught the attention of Thomas Jefferson, who wrote to him praising his grape cultivation and local produce. In his letter to Jefferson, Adlum praises the black grapes along the Susquehanna as proof that "excellent wines may be made in a great many parts of our Country." (Author's collection.)

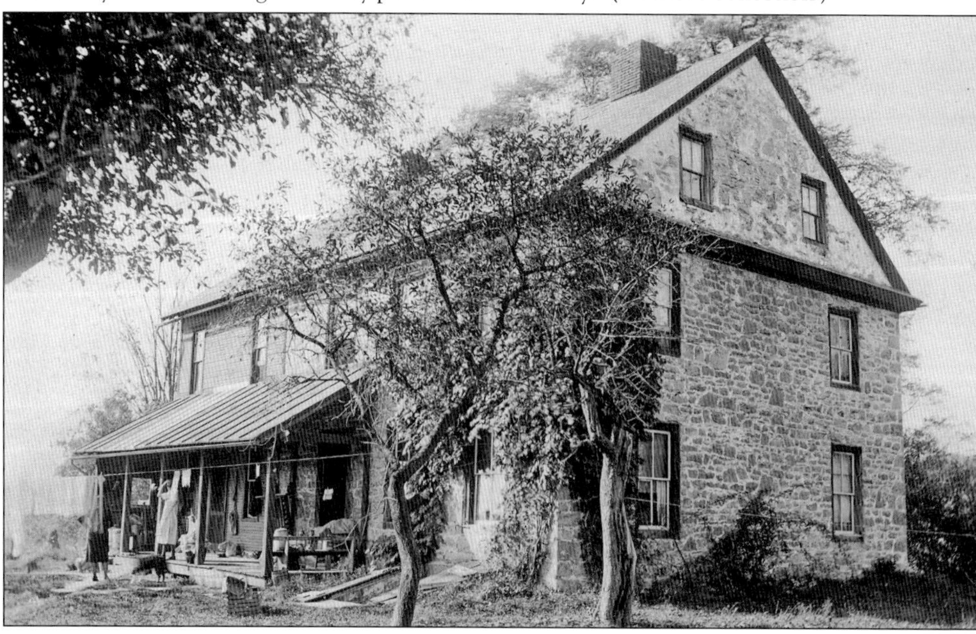

Pictured here is Adlum Farm, the home of John Adlum. Though Adlum was not a documented abolitionist, there has been speculation as to whether his home could have been part of the Underground Railroad, as his two sisters were close friends with the nearby Ellis family, identified as abolitionists. The architecture of the home may also point towards operative ties, with the attic containing a secret crawl space and the basement housing a tunnel. (Courtesy of the Muncy Historical Society.)

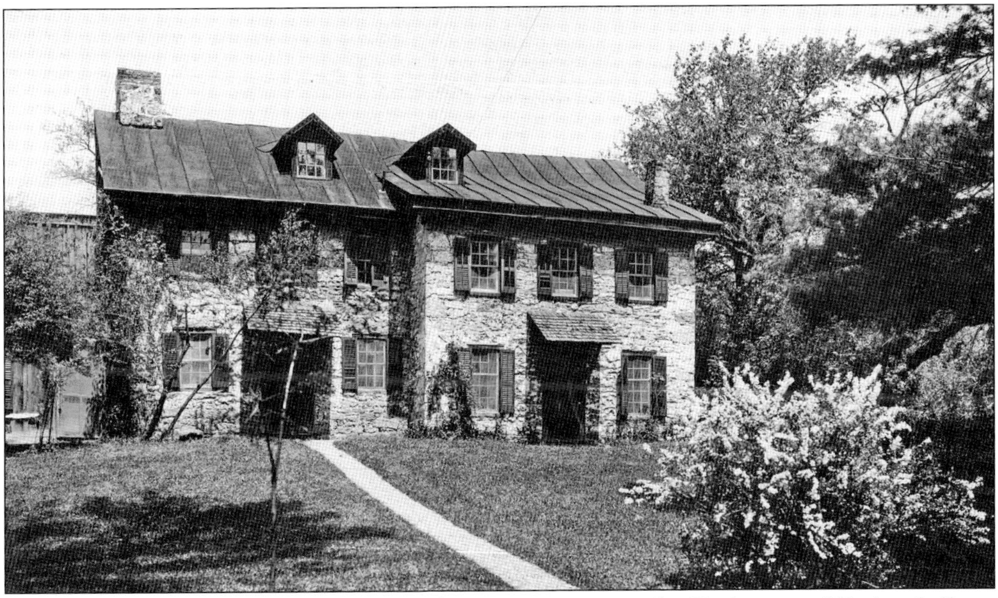

Known as the House of Many Stairs, this home was a stop on the Underground Railroad. Once occupied by Edward Morris and known as Bull's Tavern, this safe house gained its nickname because of almost a dozen staircases. Its architecture proved useful in protecting runaway slaves, as the attic, equipped with a lookout window, and nooks under the numerous stairways were utilized as hideaways. In 1936, the home was purchased from the Morrises by the Brant family, and it now serves as a private residence. (Courtesy of the Muncy Historical Society.)

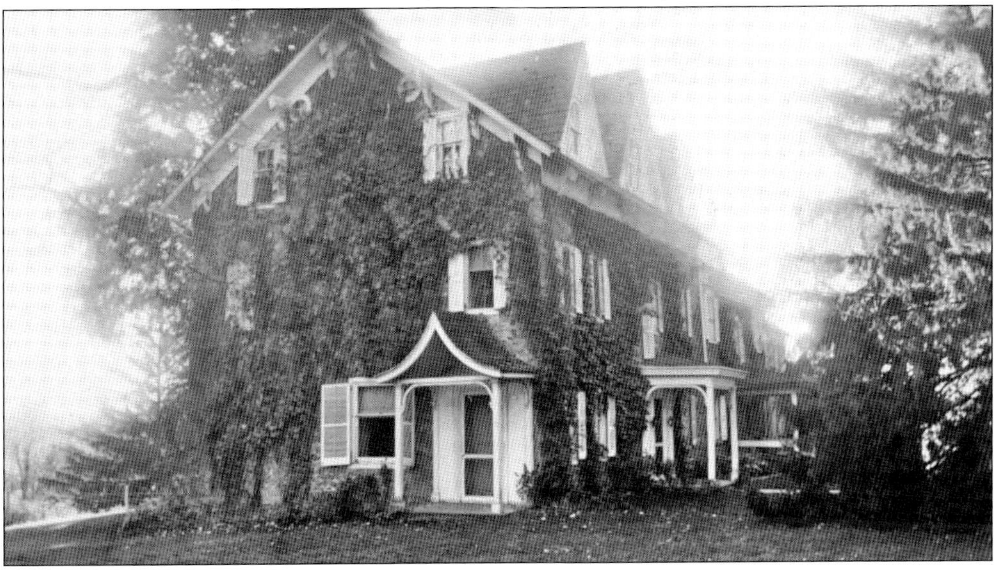

This home in Wolf Run began its identity as a stop on the Underground Railroad with its purchase by William and Mercy Cox Ellis. The Quaker family turned it into a legacy, as the property was inherited through multiple generations. Transporting runaways across Pennsylvania, Jacob Haines often signed his letters of introduction with the code word "humanity." The Wolf Run House was a part of the New York–Canada route—passengers then traveled towards Williamsport to the Updegraff home and then on to the Susquehanna River for transport to New York. (Courtesy of the Muncy Historical Society.)

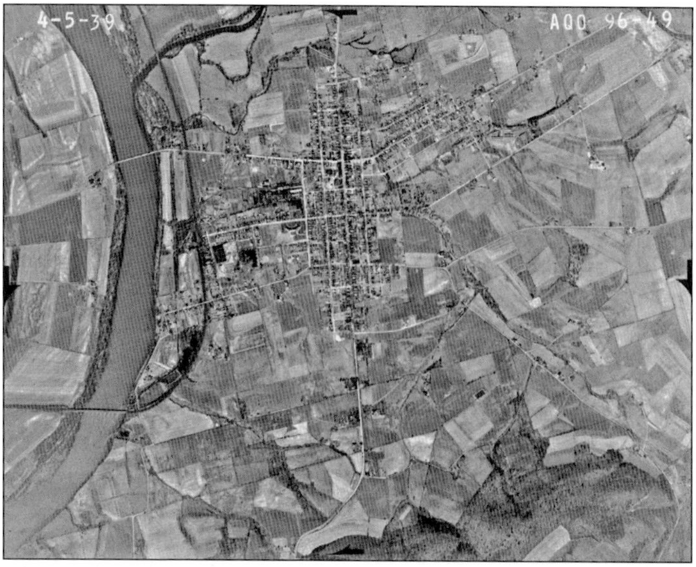

This aerial image, taken on April 5, 1939, shows Muncy at the brink of World War II. On the same day, Albert François Lebrun was re-elected by the French National Assembly to a second seven-year term as president of France; Britain's largest aircraft carrier, HMS *Illustrious*, was launched at Barrow-in-Furness; and Leka I, the Crown Prince of Albania, was born. He would die in 2011. (Courtesy of the Library of Congress.)

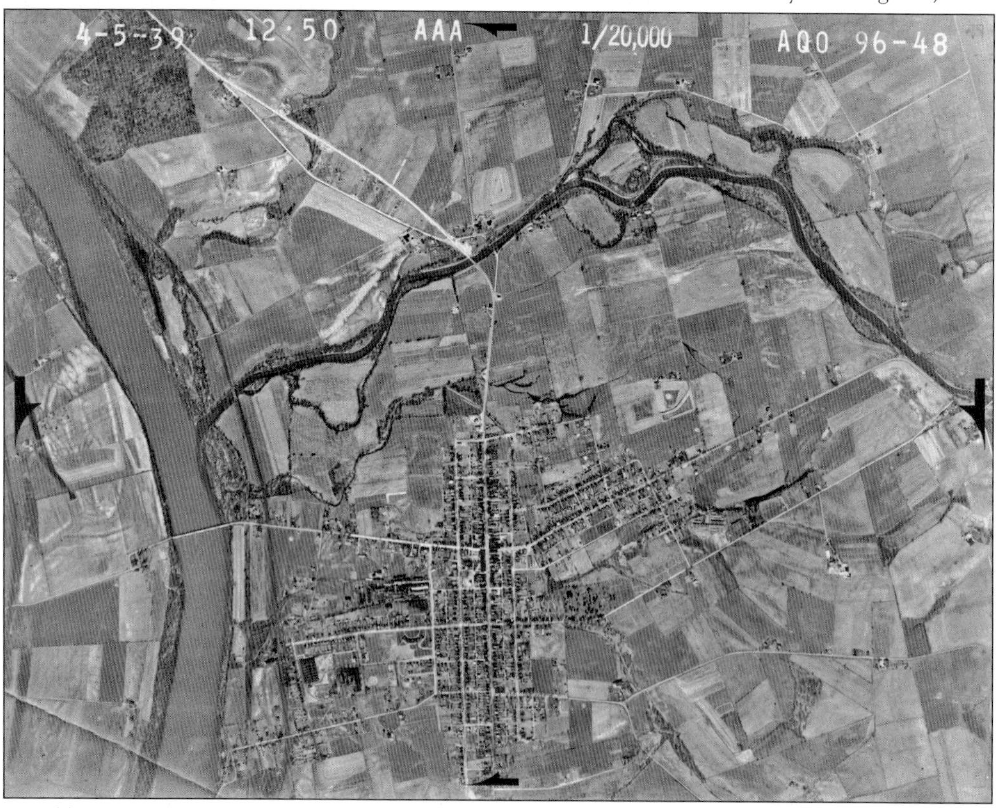

Local history also lists several important events on April 5. A skirmish after the end of the French and Indian War took place near Muncy on April 5, 1764, in which homes were burned and men, women, and children were killed. Joseph Shoemaker was named Muncy's justice of the peace on April 5, 1877. Simon Schuyler and W.P.I. Painter were elected to share the same post on April 5, 1865. This photograph was taken by the Work Projects Administration (WPA) on April 5, 1939. (Courtesy of the Library of Congress.)

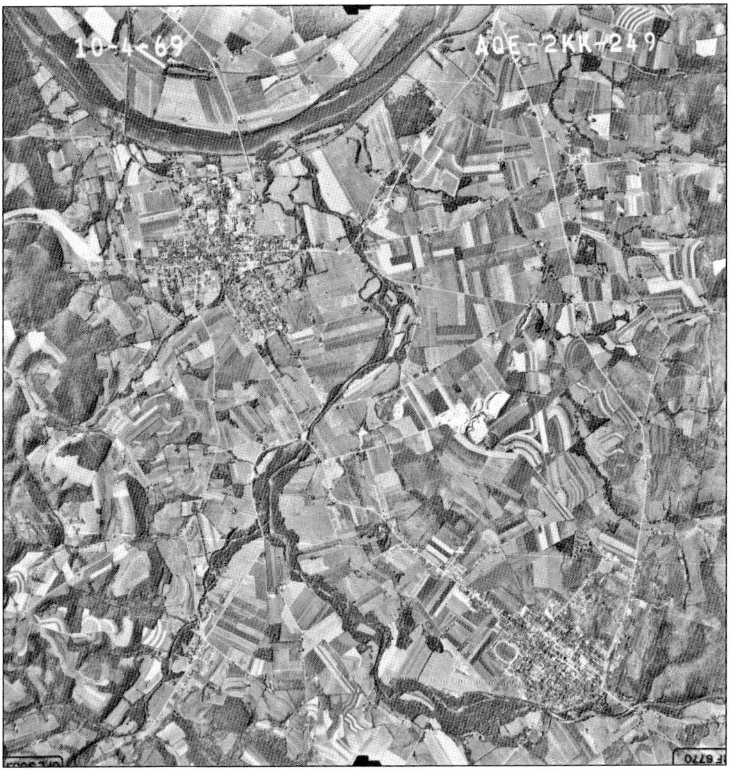

While things seemed to be quiet on this clear day in October for the denizens of Muncy, October 4 in years prior is loaded with world history. For example, in 1777, less than 100 miles away, American rebels under George Washington lost the Battle of Germantown to a vastly superior British force. Meanwhile, on this date in 1883, the first run of the Orient Express took place. Such an event would hold special interest for Muncy, as it was one of the largest rail stops in the area at the time. (Courtesy of the Library of Congress.)

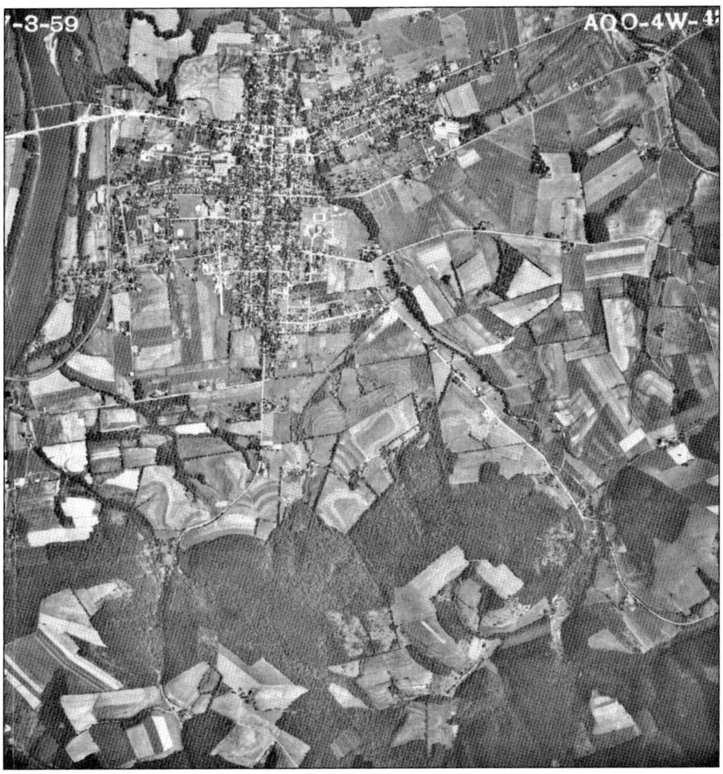

July 3, 1959, was a lazy day for the village of Muncy, with clear skies and ample opportunities for aerial views. However, on the same date in 1885, Rev. George Eichholtz, a titan of the early Lutheran church, passed away at the age of 71. On the same day, the Honorable Robert K. Reeder, formerly of the law offices of William E. Crawford, Esq., decided to open his own practice in Muncy. Finally, there was a fire on the roof of the Parker House in Muncy, although it was extinguished before damage occurred. (Courtesy of the Library of Congress.)

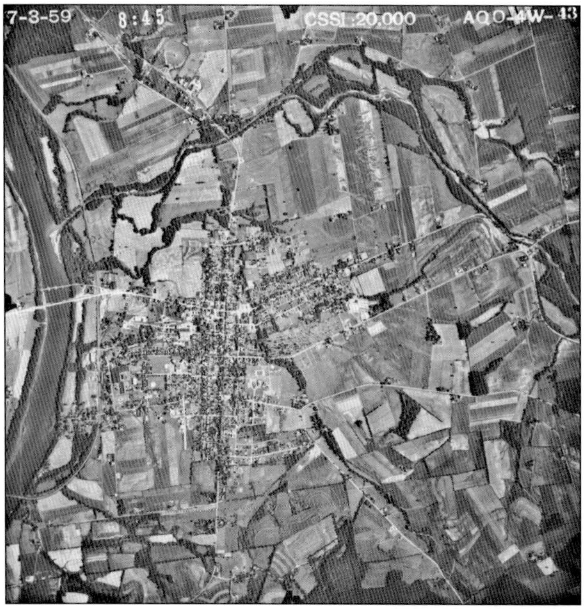

This aerial image of Muncy on July 5, 1959, was greeted with the same excitement as the one two days prior—that is to say, none. However, on the same date in 1917, there was a lot of excitement in the area. According to local media sources, grocer Homer J. Edwards encountered a bear, two deer, and a porcupine. On a more serious note, work was completed on the new foundry addition at the Sprout & Waldron plant, with interior renovations to follow. (Courtesy of the Library of Congress.)

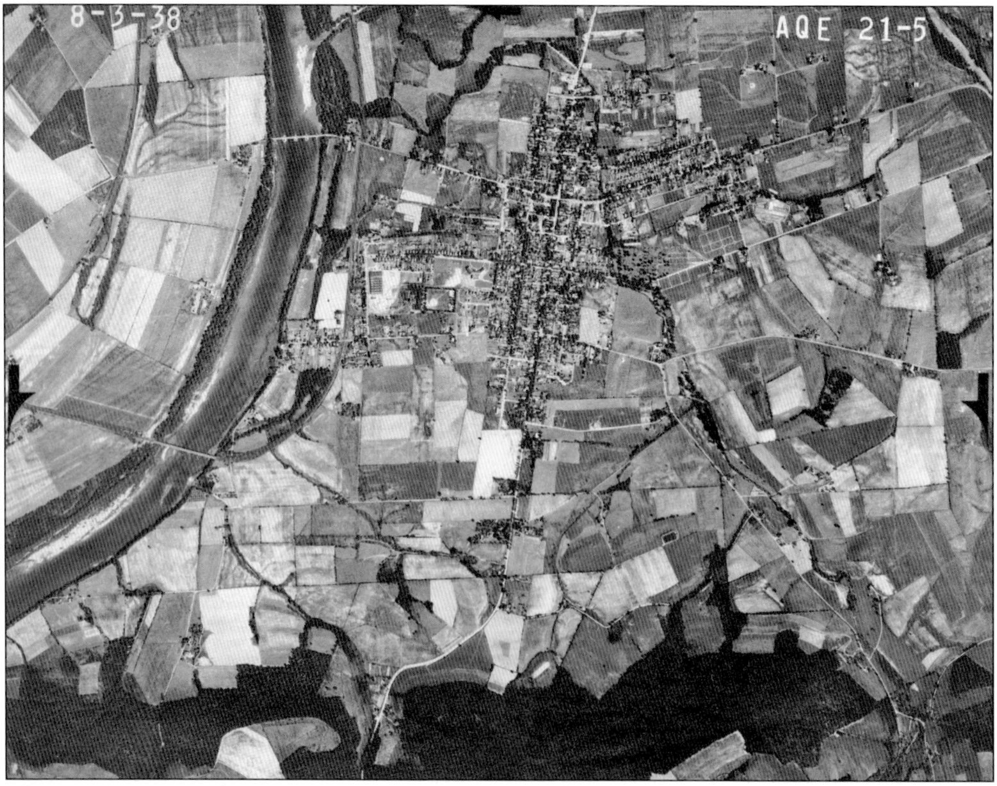

This WPA image, taken on August 3, 1938, shows a clear view of the Muncy Valley. Visible on the left is the Susquehanna River, which was vital for commerce in the timber and manufacturing sectors. At the bottom, one can see the beautiful Pocono Mountains, which are now divided from town by Interstate 80, part of President Eisenhower's Federal Highway Act of 1956. (Courtesy of the Library of Congress.)

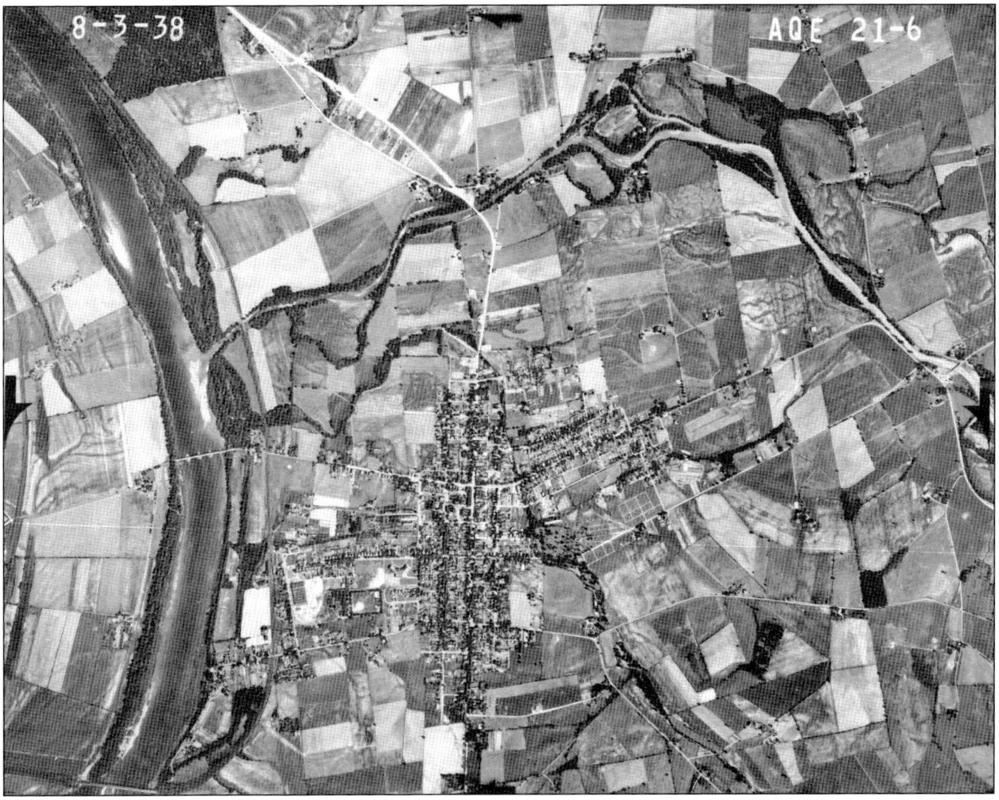

Although it was relatively quiet in Muncy on August 3, 1938, the same cannot be said for the same date in 1877. In keeping with the town's history of mild fires, the roof of J.D. Melick's barn was found ablaze, although the flames were extinguished before any serious damage could occur. Although the fire company was putting out fires left and right, it seems it still had time to open a couple of kegs of nails (beer) with the Muncy Cornet Band. (Courtesy of the Library of Congress.)

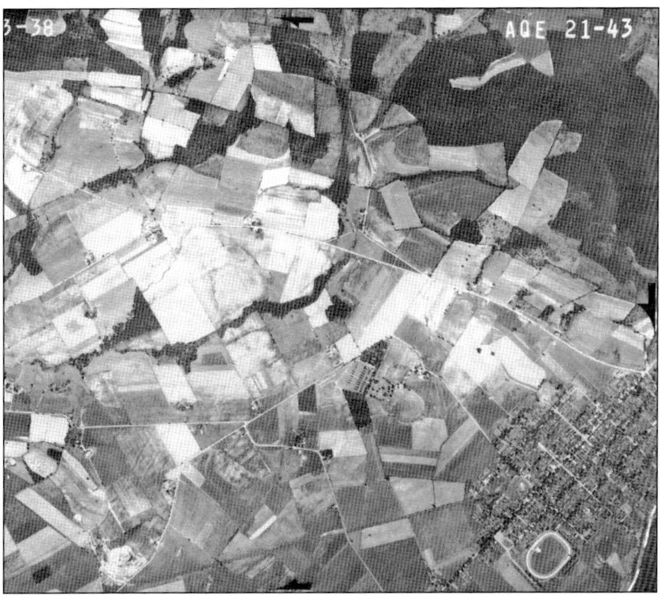

While things were peaceful in Muncy for this August 3, 1939, aerial, the same could not be said for a world on the brink of war. The British, under Neville Chamberlain, attempted to stem pending disaster with their policy of appeasement. On this date, they met with representatives of the German Sudetenland government, a breakaway faction in what is present-day Czechia that wished to join Hitler's Third Reich. Italy passed the first of many anti-Jewish laws under Benito Mussolini on the same day. (Courtesy of the Library of Congress.)

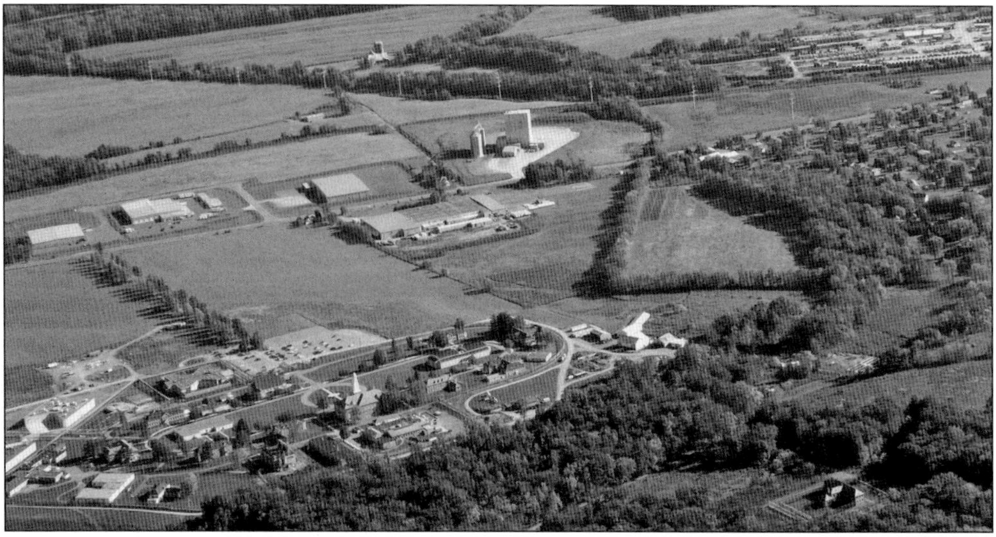

Shown here in a breathtaking aerial photograph is State Correctional Institution–Muncy (SCI Muncy), a prison for women. Built in 1953, it can trace its roots back to a prison work farm built on the same site in 1920. Today, SCI Muncy hosts death row for female inmates in the state of Pennsylvania. It is also home to the Canine Partners for Life program, which offers prisoners rehabilitation through the care and training of foster pets. As of 2017, the prison houses 1,400 inmates, including 170 on life sentences and three on death row. (Author's collection.)

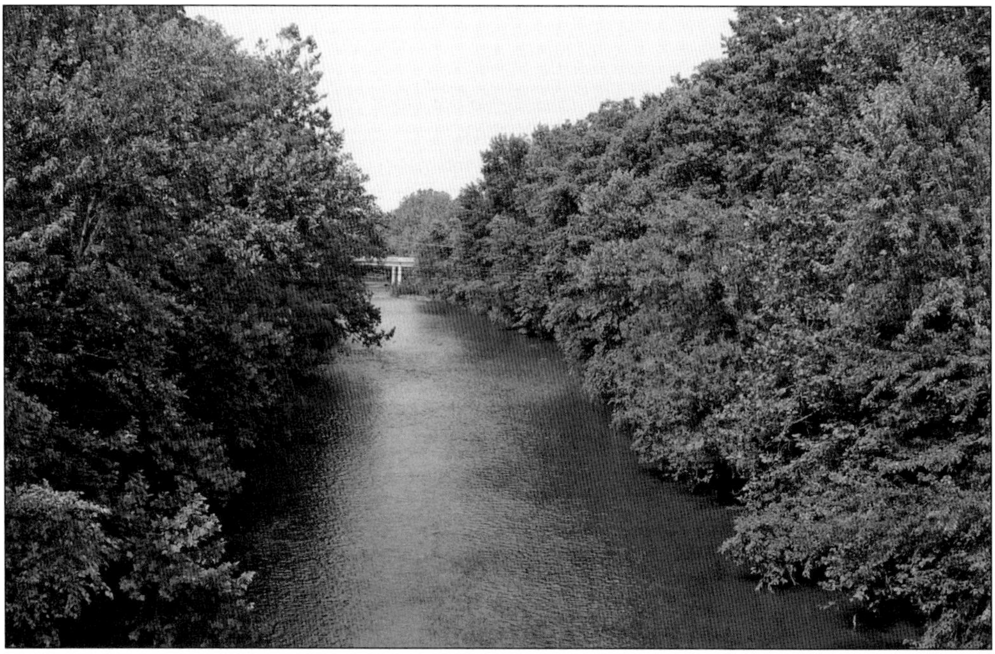

Muncy Creek is a big part of the Susquehanna River watershed in the area. Meandering 35.8 miles through the valley, it contains several lakes, including Eagles Mere, Highland, and Beaver. Known as Occohpocheny to the local native peoples, the river has two tributaries of its own: on the left is Little Muncy Creek and on the right is Wolf Run, both of which flood when the river does. Muncy Creek is one of the few in northern Pennsylvania to naturally contain trout, as both brook and brown trout reproduce in its shallow waters. (Author's collection.)

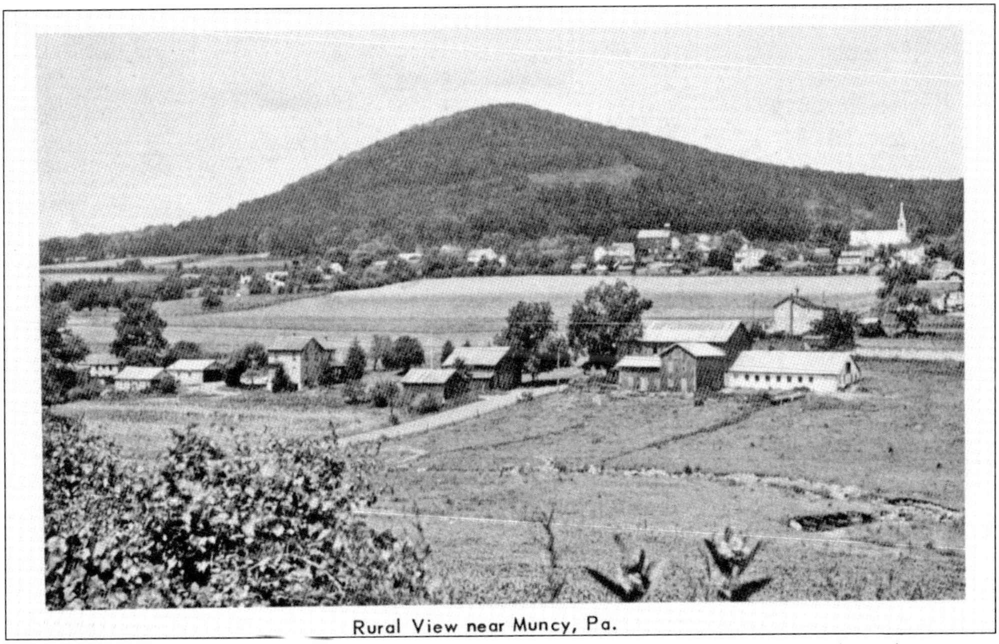

This image gives an elevated view of a rural, natural area in Muncy during the early 20th century. The Muncy area boasts several natural wonders, such as the West Branch of the Susquehanna River, floodplain forests that line Little Muncy Creek, several migratory bird nesting areas, the mouth of Lick Run (which feeds from Muncy Creek), and the still-developing nature trail off Muncy Heritage Park, an 11-acre development of trees, ponds, trails, and open space. (Author's collection.)

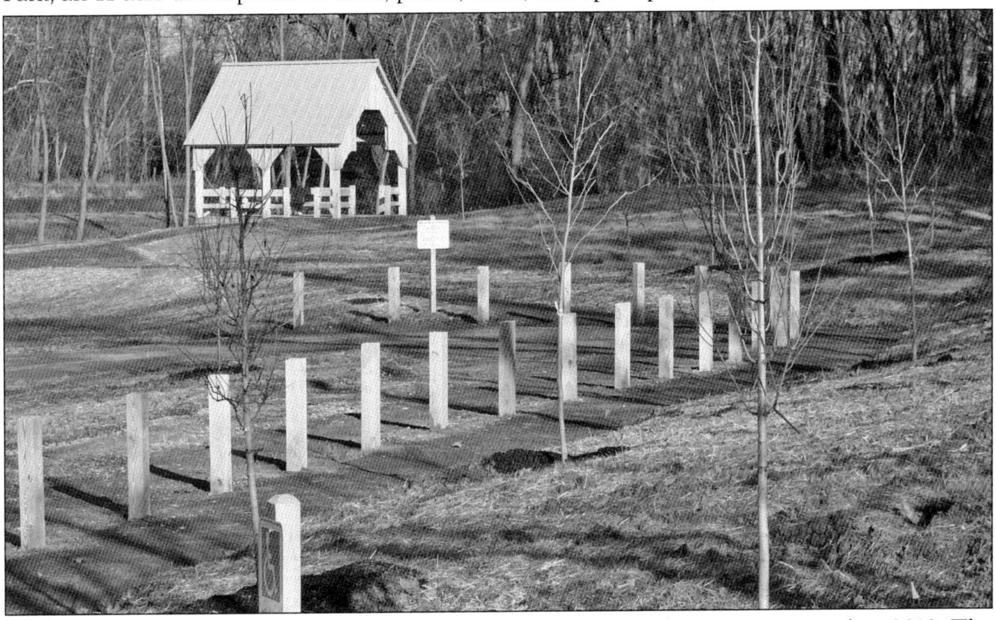

An educational and recreational resource, Muncy Heritage Park was constructed in 2013. The 11-acre preserve on the West Branch of the Susquehanna River houses flora and fauna local to the area and offers nature observation opportunities. Built in conjunction with the Muncy Historical Society, the park has pavilions with displays of Muncy's local history. Nearby are the remains of the West Branch Canal. The park was dedicated on May 19, 2013. (Author's collection.)

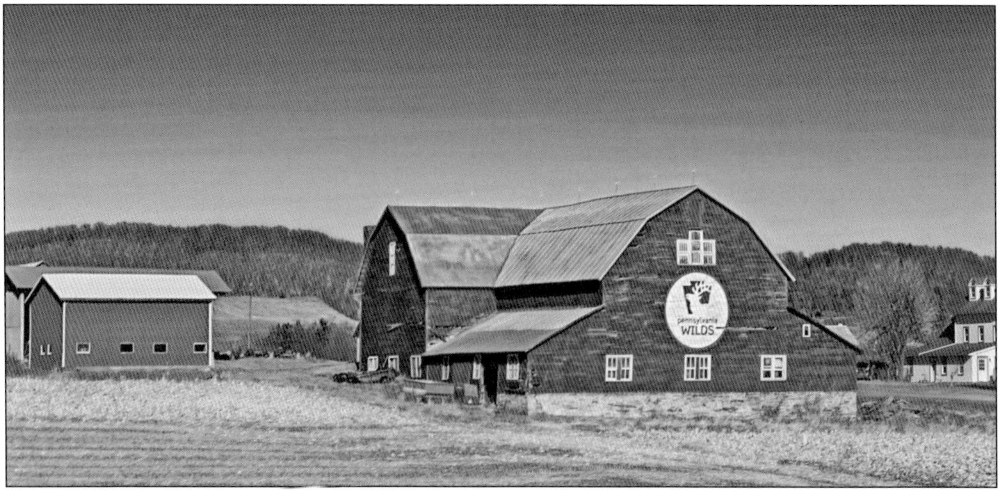

Nestled in the Muncy foothills, this barn bears the logo of PA Wilds, a project of the Wilds Cooperative of Pennsylvania. Serving as a sort of chamber of commerce for small businesses that cater to ecotourism across the Keystone State, the Wilds Cooperative of Pennsylvania currently boasts over 200 members. Business members include artisans, outfitters, and retail, recreational, cultural, and food establishments. Business members commit to stewardship and conservation of wildlands throughout the state. (Author's collection.)

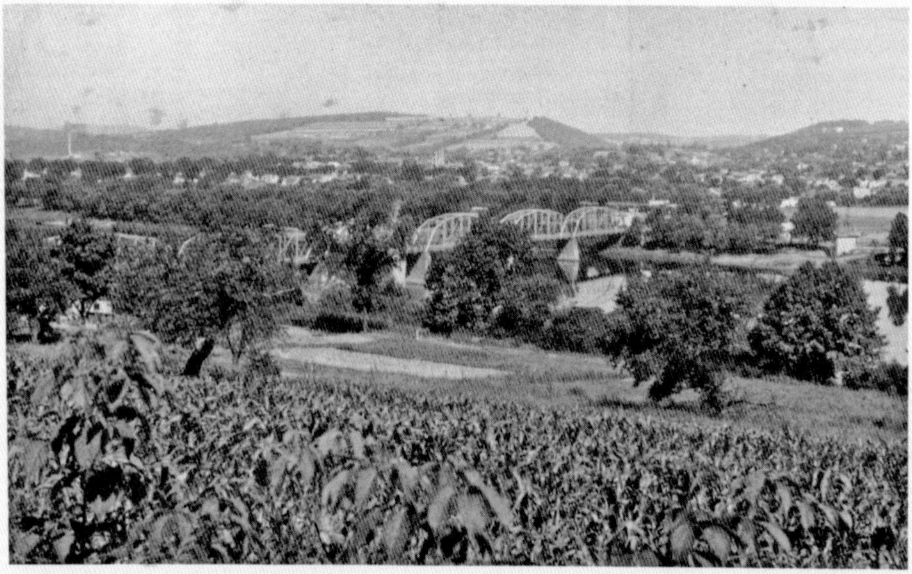

Bird's-eye View of Muncy, Pa.

This bird's-eye view of Muncy was taken sometime after 1915 from one of the hills of a nearby farm. Muncy is part of the Williamsport Metropolitan Statistical Area in the US Census and thus is considered a suburb of the home of the Little League World Series. Recent estimates place Muncy's population between 2,400 and 2,500. The town lies an almost equal distance between Pennsylvania's two biggest cities, Philadelphia (135 miles to the southeast) and Pittsburgh (160 miles west-southwest). (Author's collection.)

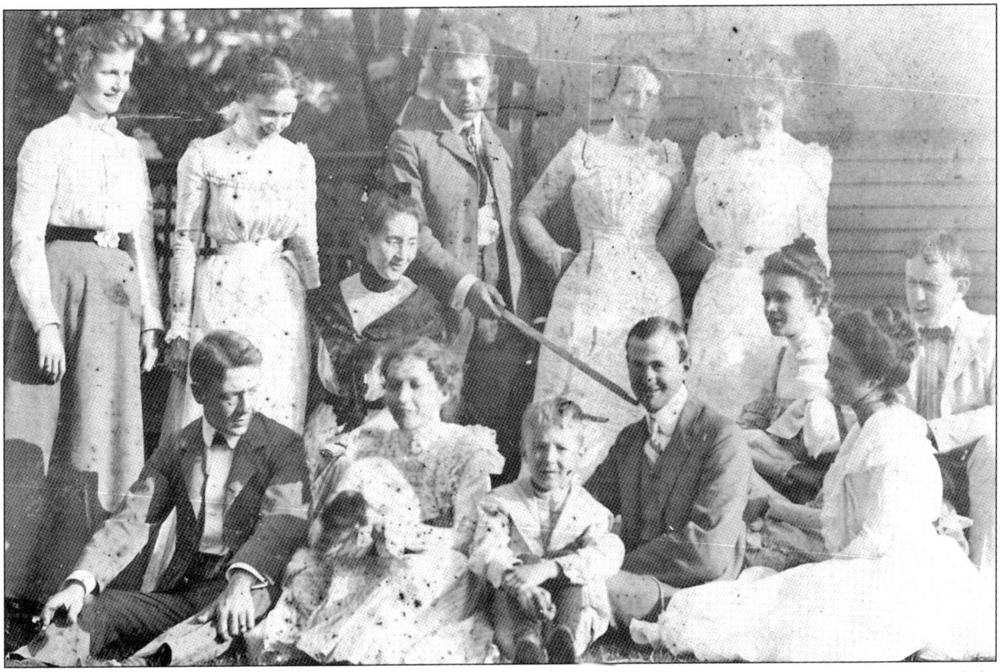

This turn-of-the-century photograph shows young people at a picnic at the former Ferndale Park along the banks of Muncy Creek. As identified on the back, they are (first row) Frank Rogers, Mabel Fargue, unidentified child, Noramay Thompson, and Emily Shoemaker; (second row) Jesse Shoemaker, Carrie Keller, and Lamont Magner; (third row) Lulu Magner, Ann Magner, Paul Shoemaker, Margaret Painter, and Blanche Coulter. (Courtesy of the Muncy Historical Society.)

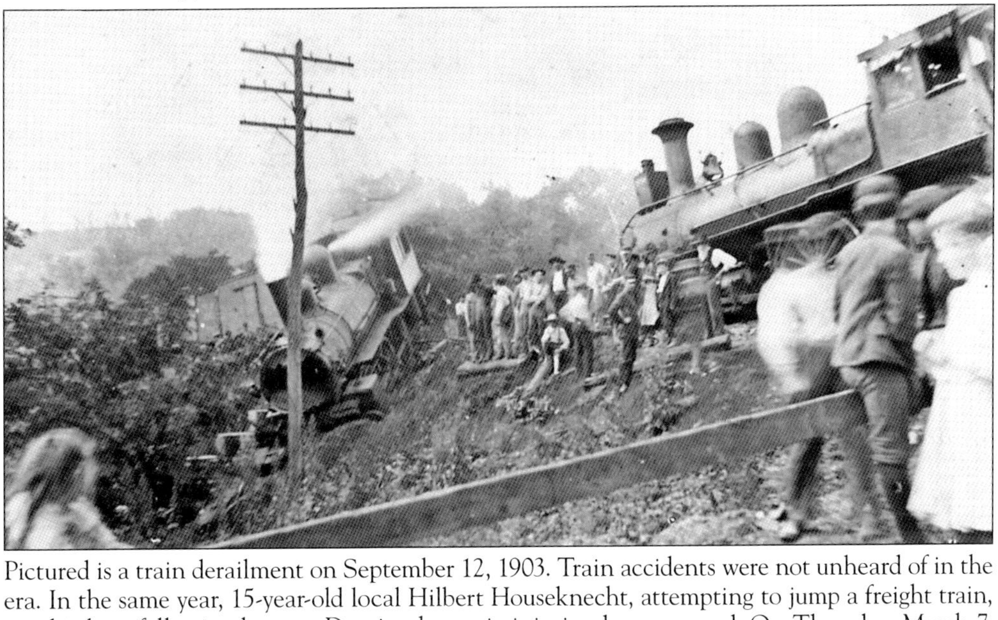

Pictured is a train derailment on September 12, 1903. Train accidents were not unheard of in the era. In the same year, 15-year-old local Hilbert Houseknecht, attempting to jump a freight train, was hit by a following boxcar. Despite dramatic injuries, he recovered. On Thursday, March 7, 1912, Philadelphia & Reading Railroad No. 699 blew up, killing four of the six crew members and injuring Clifford Warg, the local telegraph operator. (Courtesy of the Muncy Historical Society.)

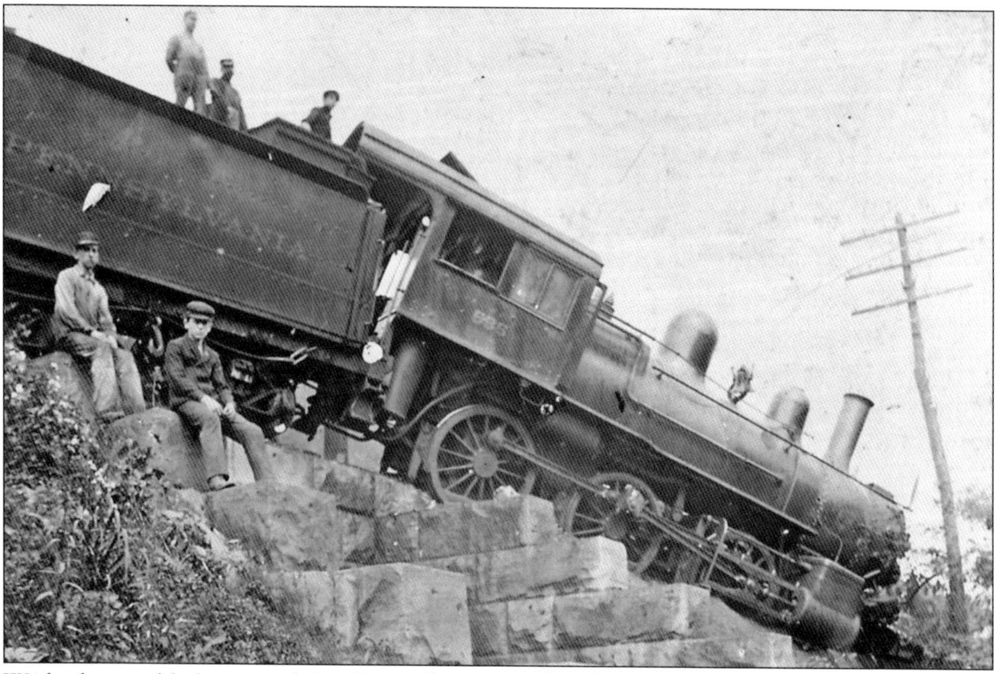

With the establishment of the Pennsylvania Railroad in 1846, Muncy, like towns across Pennsylvania, saw dramatic improvements in public and market transportation. However, this new transportation was quite unpredictable, and train derailments were not uncommon in the 19th century. Tensions increased in the early 20th century, when problems arose regarding passenger and freight transportation, heightened by the Connellsville train crash in 1903 in which a passenger train struck timber that had fallen from a freight train. (Courtesy of the Muncy Historical Society.)

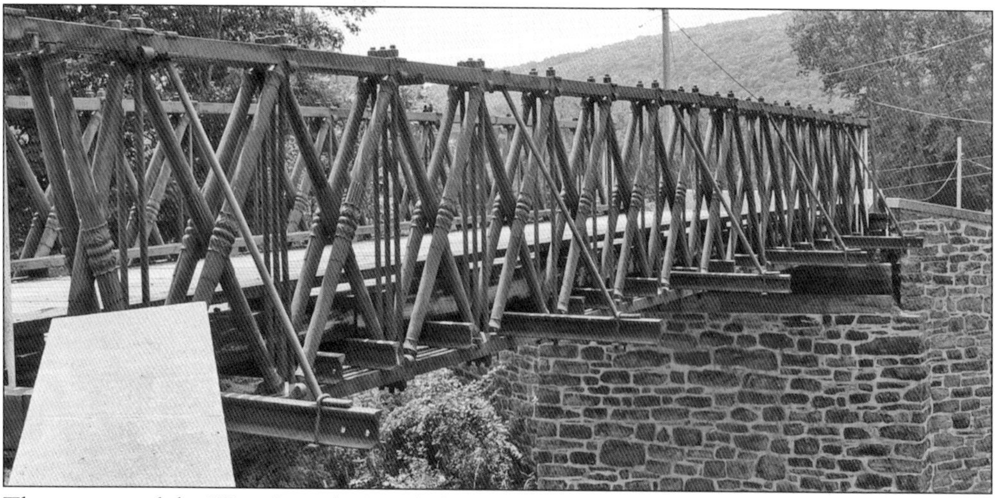

The cutting of the West Branch Canal through the heart of Muncy Farms necessitated the construction of the Muncy Farms Iron Bridge by Robert Coleman, a wealthy landowner, coal deposit pioneer, and state legislator. The bridge was built shortly after the canal bisected his land in 1834. The bridge stands today as the second-oldest iron bridge in the United States. At one point, it crossed directly in front of the mansion at Muncy Farms. (Courtesy of the Muncy Historical Society.)

Today, the Susquehanna River serves as a popular recreation location. A sort of precursor to the ever-popular river lot was the houseboat. Houseboats appeared in America soon after European settlement in order to transport goods. At the beginning of the 20th century, they reached their peak, with some cities containing over 1,000. In the latter half of the century, houseboats became popular for recreation, and today they continue to serve as another way to interact with the local landscape. (Courtesy of the Muncy Historical Society.)

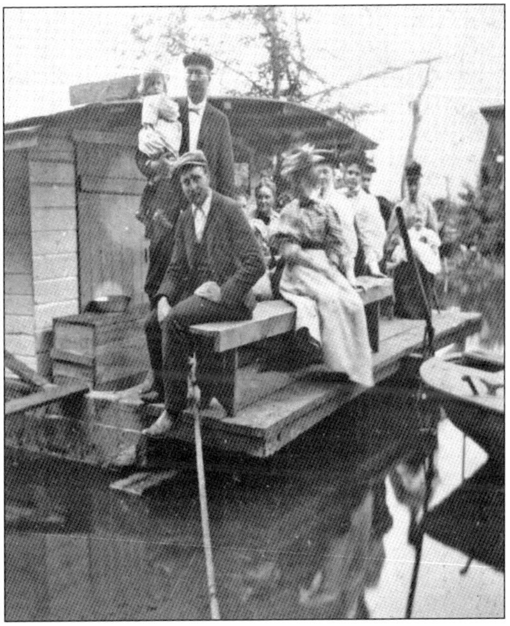

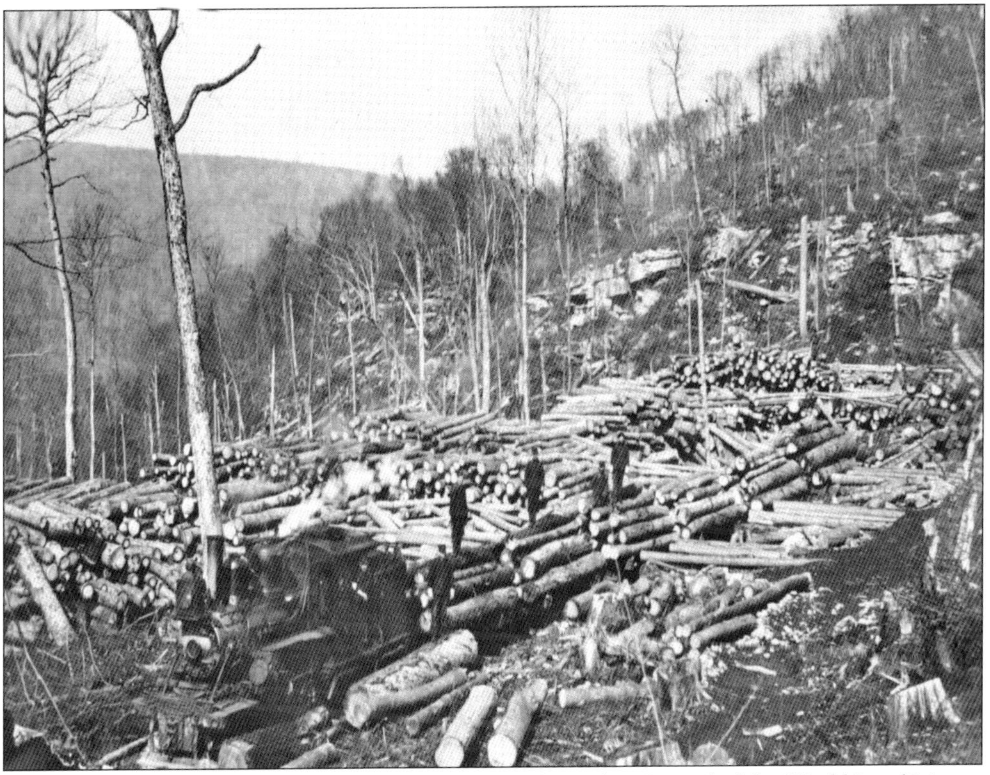

In the 19th century, Williamsport boasted the title of "Lumber Capital of the World," and Muncy was a contributor to and recipient of this fame. In its strategic position along the Susquehanna River, Muncy was situated on a primary mode of transportation. Muncy natives A.H. and John K. Heilman capitalized on the lumber industry in 1870 by establishing A.H. Heilman & Company, one of the oldest furniture manufacturers in Williamsport. (Courtesy of the Muncy Historical Society.)

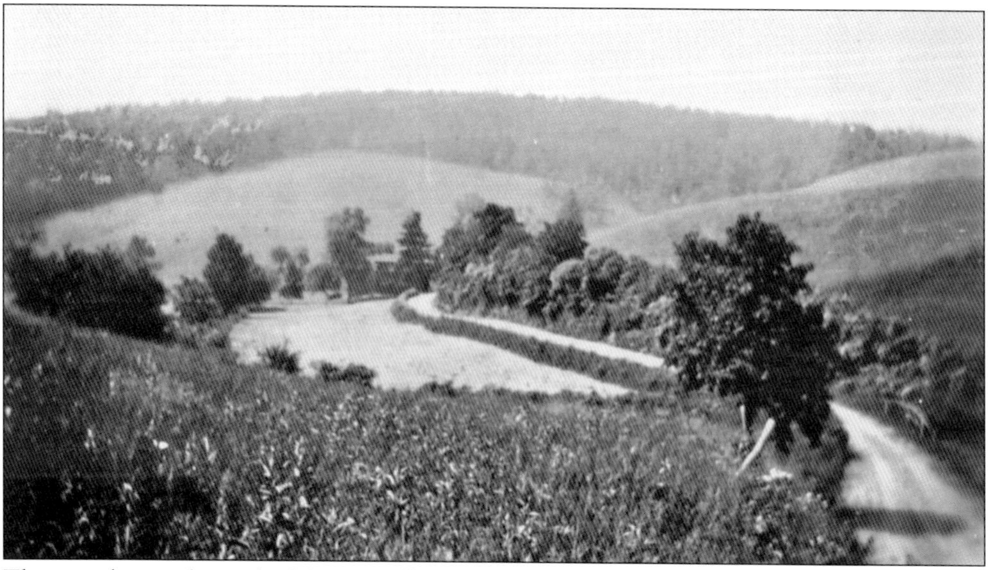

This aerial view shows the Muncy Valley around the turn of the century near the spot where the lookout tower stood. Farms dotted the area, and farming still plays a vital role in the Muncy economy. This is evidenced by the plethora of farms and farm-related business in the area, including the Green Berry Farm, Thomas C. Styer's Farm and Market, Brown's Tree Farm, Wentzler's Fruit Farm, and Floyd Fry Jr.'s used farm machinery market, which has equipment over several acres along Bush Hollow Road. (Courtesy of the Muncy Historical Society.)

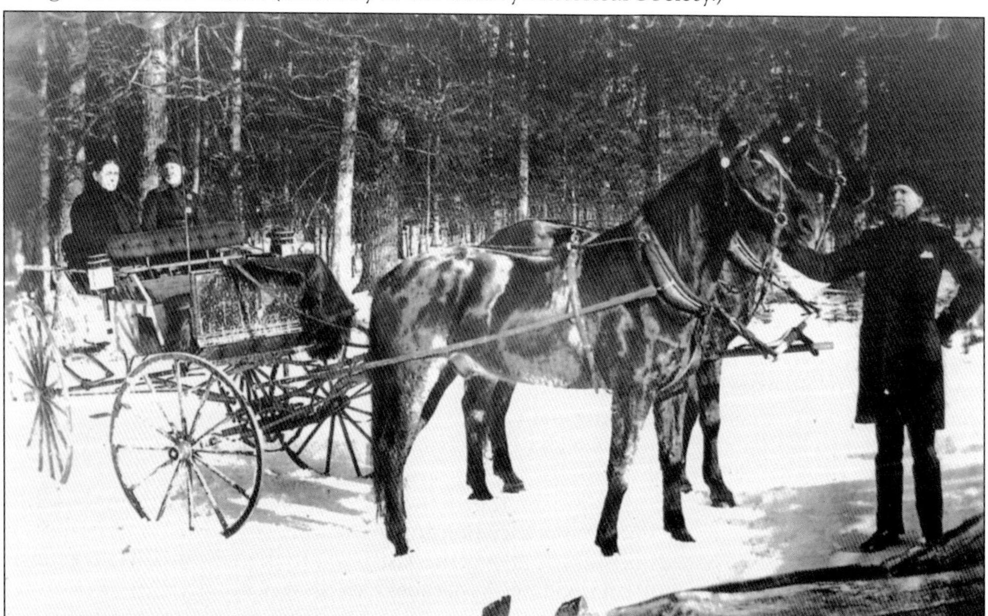

This photograph shows members of Muncy's Smith family as they are pulled down the snowy streets like Santa Claus during a turn-of-the-century winter day. The Muncy High School Parent, Teacher, Student Association hosts the Holiday Craft Show every November at the high school. Local vendors display and sell their wares, and the middle and high schools put on choral performances. Thankfully, the invention of snow tires precludes anyone from having to show up in a sleigh, leaving that to Santa himself. (Courtesy of the Muncy Historical Society.)

Four

When the Levee Breaks
Natural Disasters in Muncy

Sitting on the picturesque banks of the Susquehanna River, Muncy has been both blessed by its beautiful landscapes and cursed by the havoc of natural disasters. The town has been overwhelmed by decades of flooding, with each year seeming to outdo the last. Local flooding typically crests at well over 20 feet and reaches all the way to Main Street. Despite the damage, Muncy residents have continued to rally behind the common cause of protecting their homes and preserving the history and beauty of the town.

Reports of the Susquehanna flooding date back to 1792, but some of the most impactful and devastating incidents took place during the 20th century. One of the most destructive floods in Pennsylvania history, the St. Patrick's Day flood of 1936, brought enormous damage to towns across the state. Muncy was no exception: flooding crested at 35.9 feet, and the town remained without food or light for days. The flood made national headlines, with the *New York Times* featuring news of Williamsport flooding and reporting "Scene of Desolation; a City in Darkness and Damaged by Fire." Later decades saw similar destruction, with waters cresting at over 25 feet in the 1950s, 1960s, and 1970s.

Muncy residents have heroically conquered generations of flooding. Local churches, fire companies, and individuals supplied temporary housing, rescue missions, food, and optimism since the beginning of the 19th century. Though the last flood took place in 2011, the town continues to be concerned about local flooding. As decades have shown, however, Muncy's strong community ties have united residents and will continue to give them the ability and resilience to combat local natural disasters.

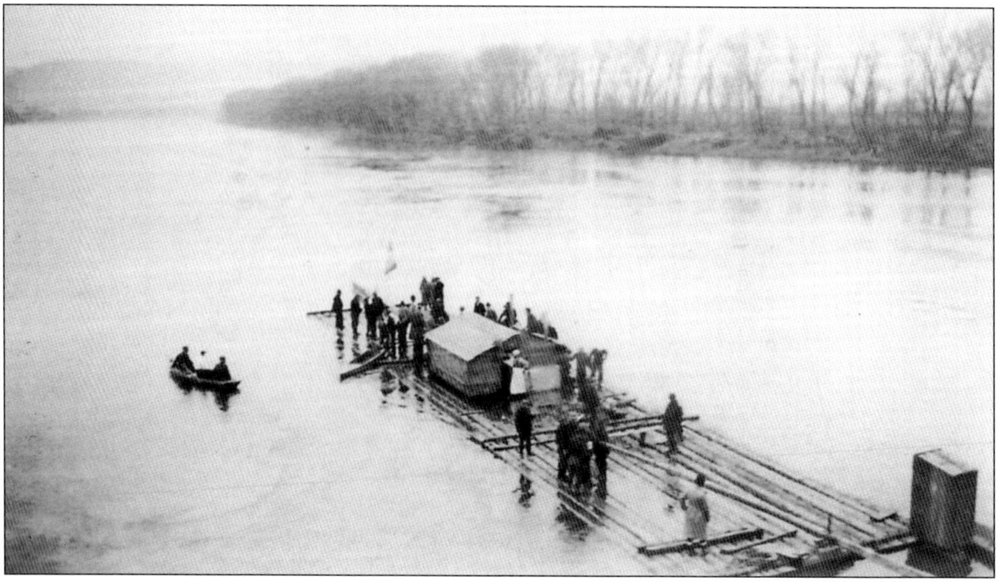

On March 14, 1938, a 112-foot-long timber raft was launched from Bell Township to commemorate the history of the logging industry in Pennsylvania. The "Last Raft," as it became known, had an intended destination of Harrisburg, but only hours after the raft began its journey, it crashed into the Reading Railroad Bridge in Muncy. With the event highly publicized and anticipated, there were throngs of onlookers to quickly rescue most of the 48 people submerged in the Susquehanna as the commemoration came to a frightening halt. (Courtesy of Janet Woodside Shoemaker.)

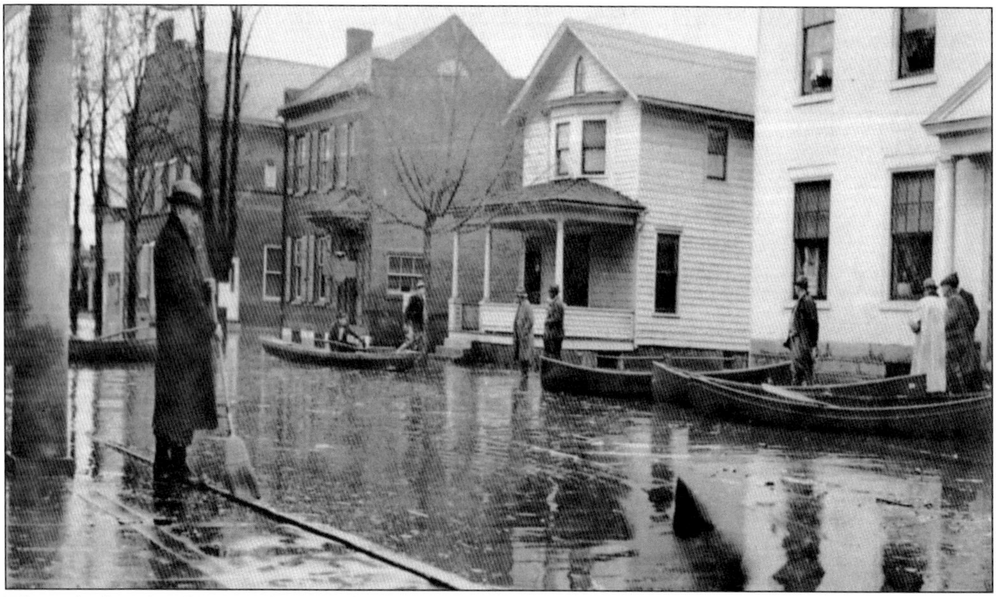

Though details of Susquehanna flooding date back to 1792, the flood of 1936 would shatter all previous records. The Susquehanna flooded twice that year, devastating numerous towns along the river. The St. Patrick's Day flood crested at 35.9 feet—almost the height of a telephone pole. More than 150 people died in Pennsylvania, and the state incurred over $300 million in damages ($5 billion today). This record remained intact until Hurricane Agnes swept through the town in 1972, when the river crested at 37.5 feet. (Courtesy of Bill Ritter.)

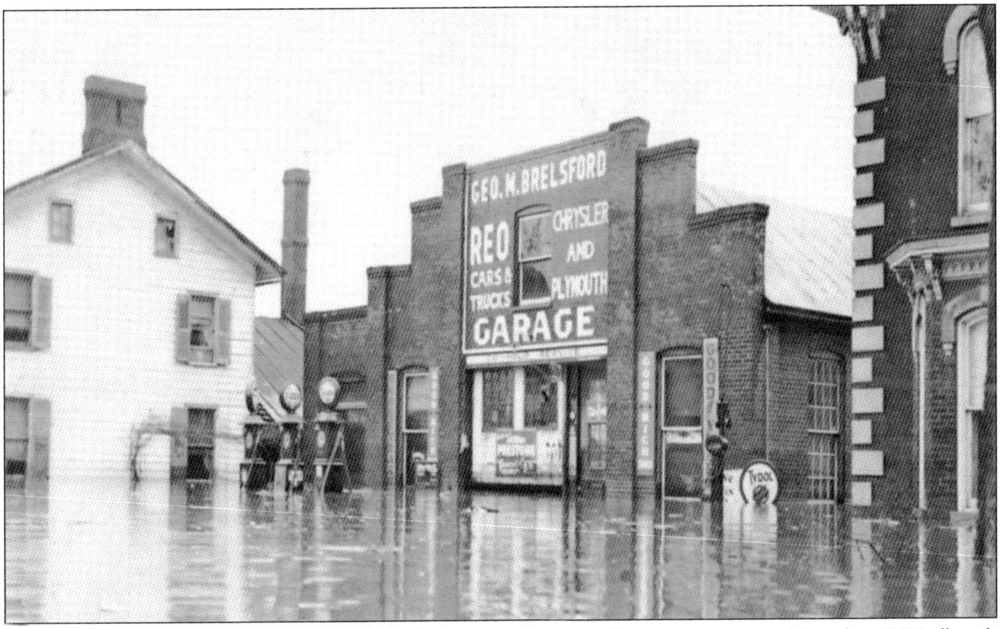

Numerous businesses, such as Brelsford Garage (pictured), were impacted by the 1936 flood. Businesses spent weeks recovering after the Susquehanna swept through the town. On March 21, locals set out to assess the damage and clear the debris. In a happy bit of news, and much to the delight of Muncy theatergoers, the March 26 *Luminary* announced the reopening of the Ritz movie theater after it was almost destroyed by the flood. (Courtesy of Bill Ritter.)

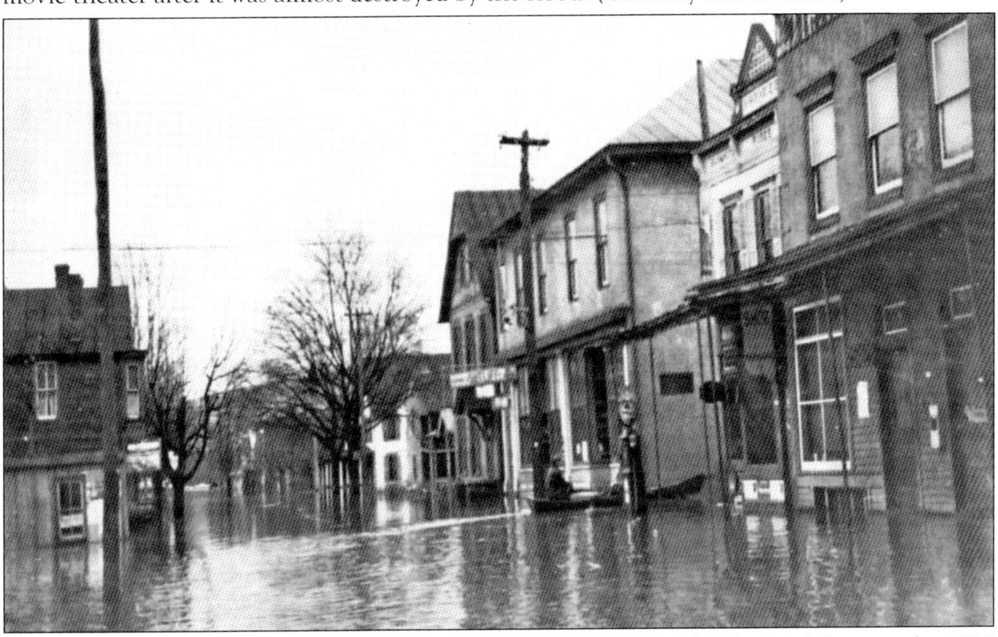

For days, Muncy remained without food or light. This image of desolation following the 1936 flood is representative of the bleakness of the area. Williamsport stores, characterized by broken windows, remained unprotected, and the town was under martial law. The 1936 flood made national headlines: the *New York Times* put Williamsport on the front page of its March 20 paper. (Courtesy of Bill Ritter.)

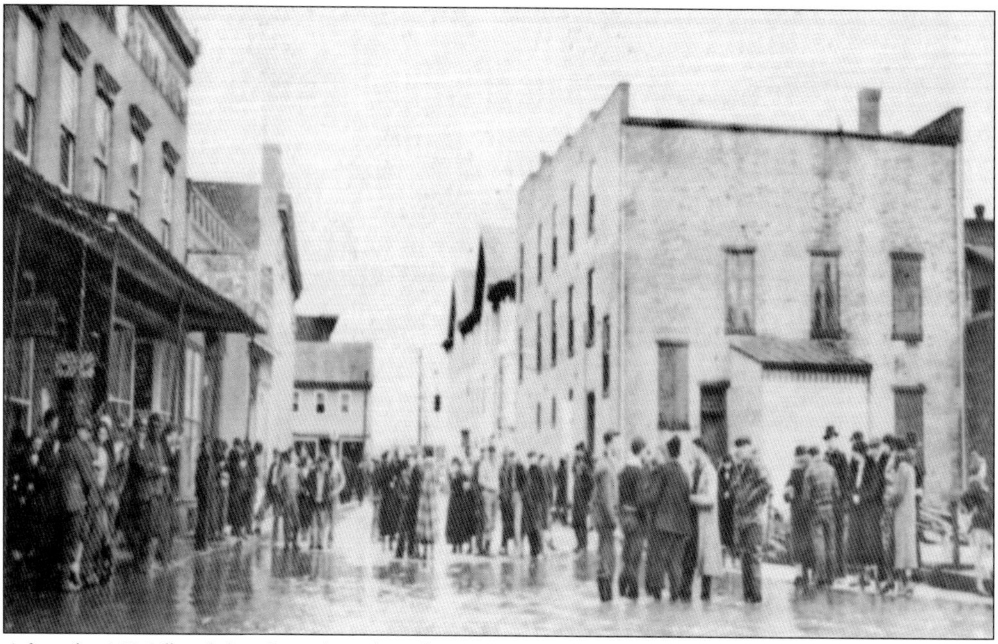

After the 1936 flood, locals gathered in downtown Muncy to assess the damage and make plans moving forward. Decades later, locals continue to worry about flood zones. Since 1978, there have been five million flood claims, and in 2016, the town underwent remapping eligibility reform for the National Flood Insurance Policy. Despite their breathtaking views along the Susquehanna, many homes remain susceptible to major flooding. The last flood in Muncy took place in 2011. (Courtesy of Bill Ritter.)

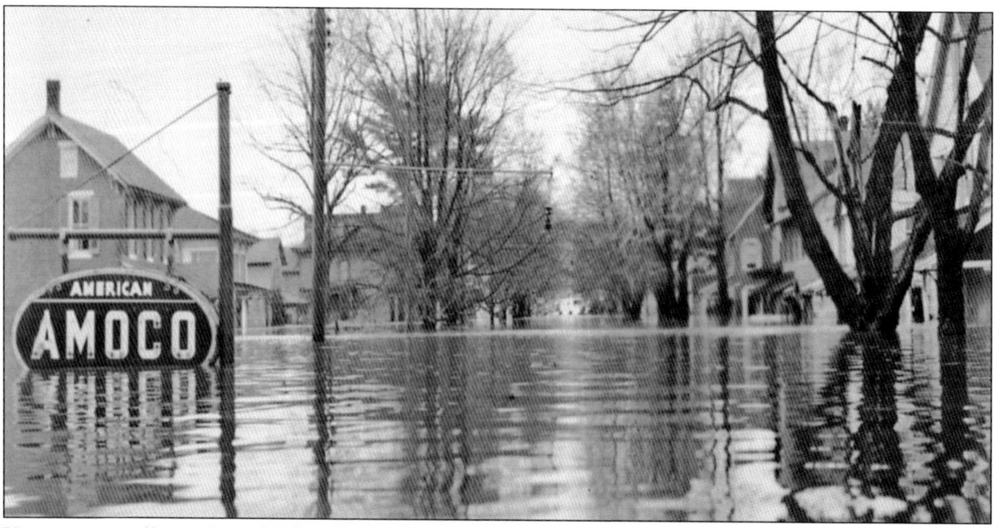

Known initially as Standard Oil of Indiana and now under the name BP, Amoco was backed by John D. Rockefeller, and by the 20th century, it became the leading provider of gasoline in the Midwest. By the end of the century, Amoco was the largest natural gas producer in North America. The 1936 St. Patrick's Day flood affected dozens of Amoco establishments across the state, including the one in Muncy (shown here). The Amoco storage plant near Pittsburgh experienced significant damage, as huge storage tanks were displaced by four days of torrential rain. (Courtesy of Bill Ritter.)

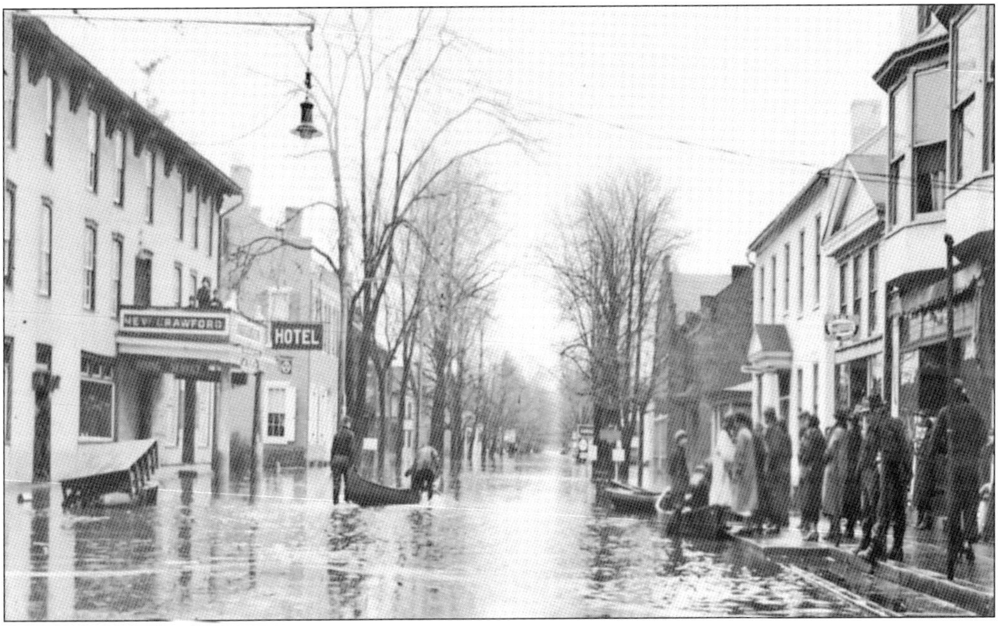

The 1936 flood brought devastating effects to the community, but the efforts of locals slowly normalized life in Muncy. The Red Cross and numerous churches in town united to provide housing and food to flood victims. Also playing a large role was the local fire station, the Keystone Hook and Ladder Company, which moved families and furniture from the flooded areas. (Courtesy of Bill Ritter.)

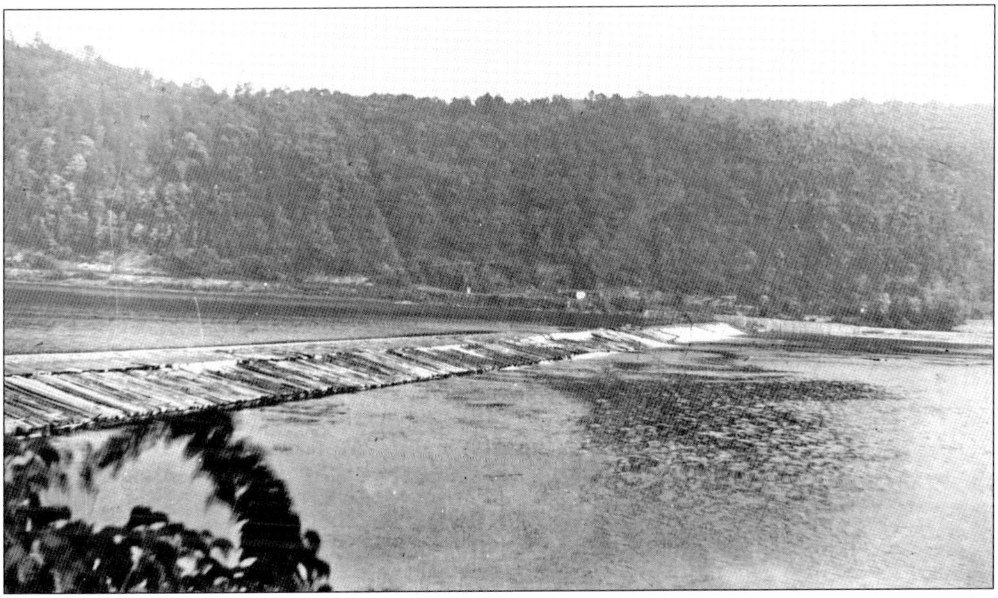

Muncy Dam once crossed the West Branch of the Susquehanna River. Shown in 1909, the dam and the area around it became known as Port Penn, which was known to house unsavory characters. Several floods washed the dam out, and rail became the preferred method of transport for raw materials. The back of the photograph reads, "Muncy Dam. View taken from north bank Susquehanna River. Fowler Farm, foreground - Penna. Canal background." (Courtesy of the Muncy Historical Society.)

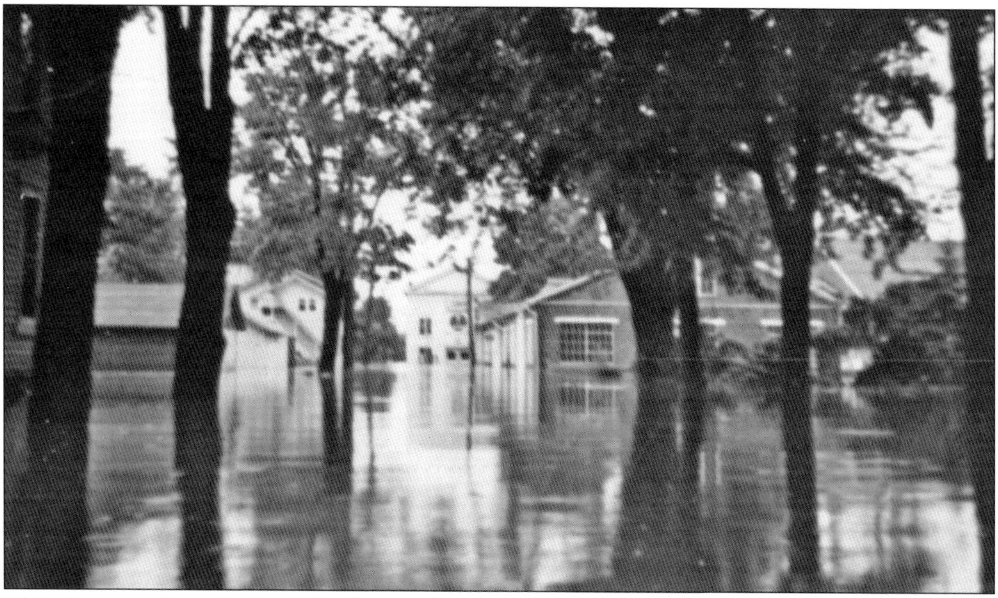

This photograph, with the old Lutheran church in the background, shows the rear of the Murray Motors Building after the flood of 1946. Although there is little doubt that the damage caused by this flood was extensive, Murray Motors still exists as a Ford dealer. The dealership has deep roots in the community, sponsoring Muncy Little League, the Muncy Valley Hospital Lawn Party, Muncy's Fourth Friday, the high school, and the North Central Mustang Club. (Courtesy of the Muncy Historical Society.)

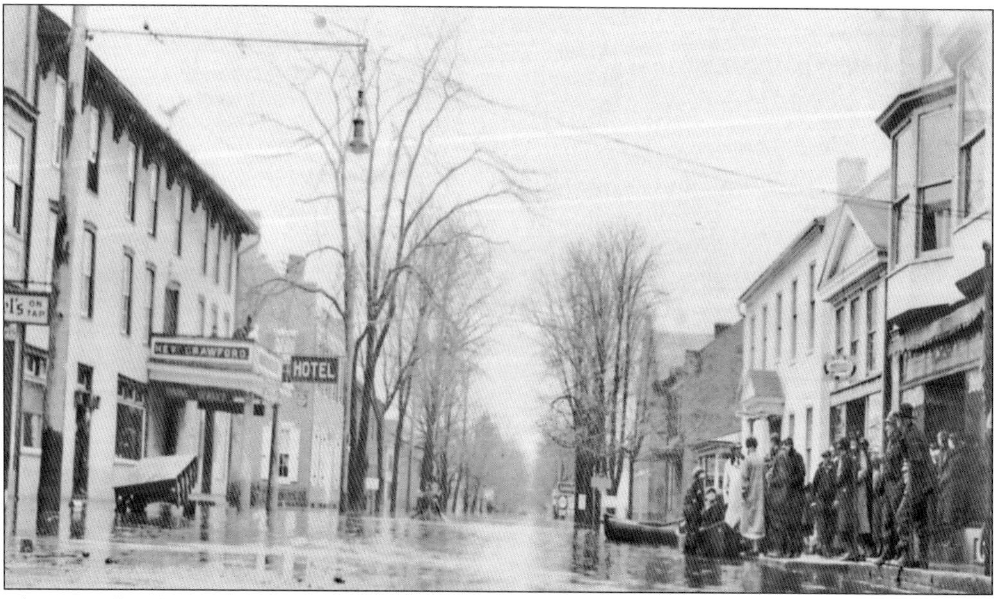

The 1936 flood caused significant damage to the businesses on Main Street, and the Crawford Hotel was no exception. Damage to the hotel affected not only travelers but also locals, as the hotel was used as a common meeting place in town. In May 1885, local tobacco growers met and created a tobacco exchange, and in 1936, a few months after the flood, the Crawford continued its presence as a meetinghouse by entertaining the Rotary Club in honor of two local newlyweds, the Finklers. (Courtesy of Bill Ritter.)

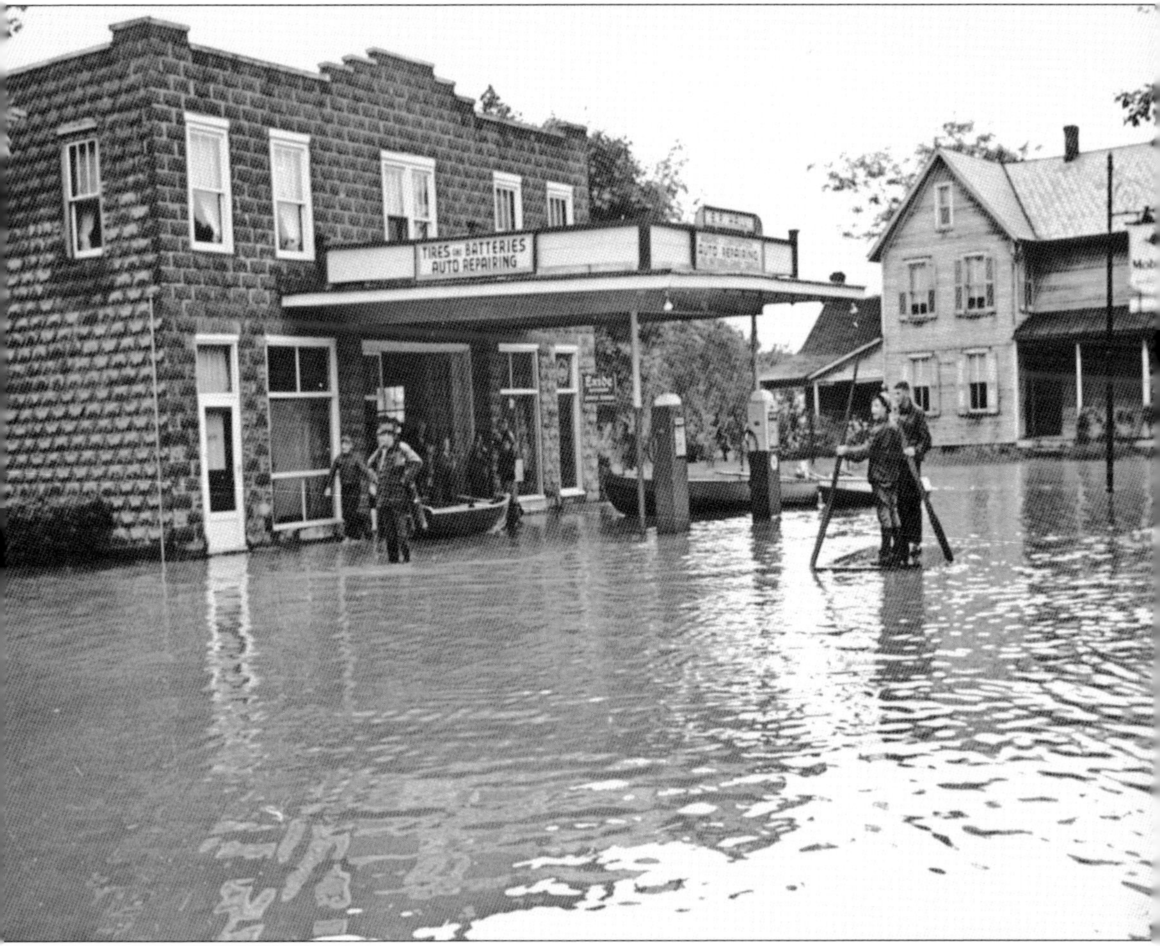

Here is the garage of Egbert "E.P." Hall during the flood of 1946. Although Hall was no longer alive to see his business flooded (he passed away on July 20, 1921, after a life of 78 years that saw him serve the Union during the Civil War), his family stayed active in Muncy politics. His son William was called to testify in the contested election of John J. Metzger, who was elected presiding judge of Pennsylvania's 29th District in 1888 by a grand total of 40 votes. Metzger's win as a Democratic nominee in Muncy was an aberration, as the county has been a Republican stronghold since the Civil War. (Courtesy of the Muncy Historical Society.)

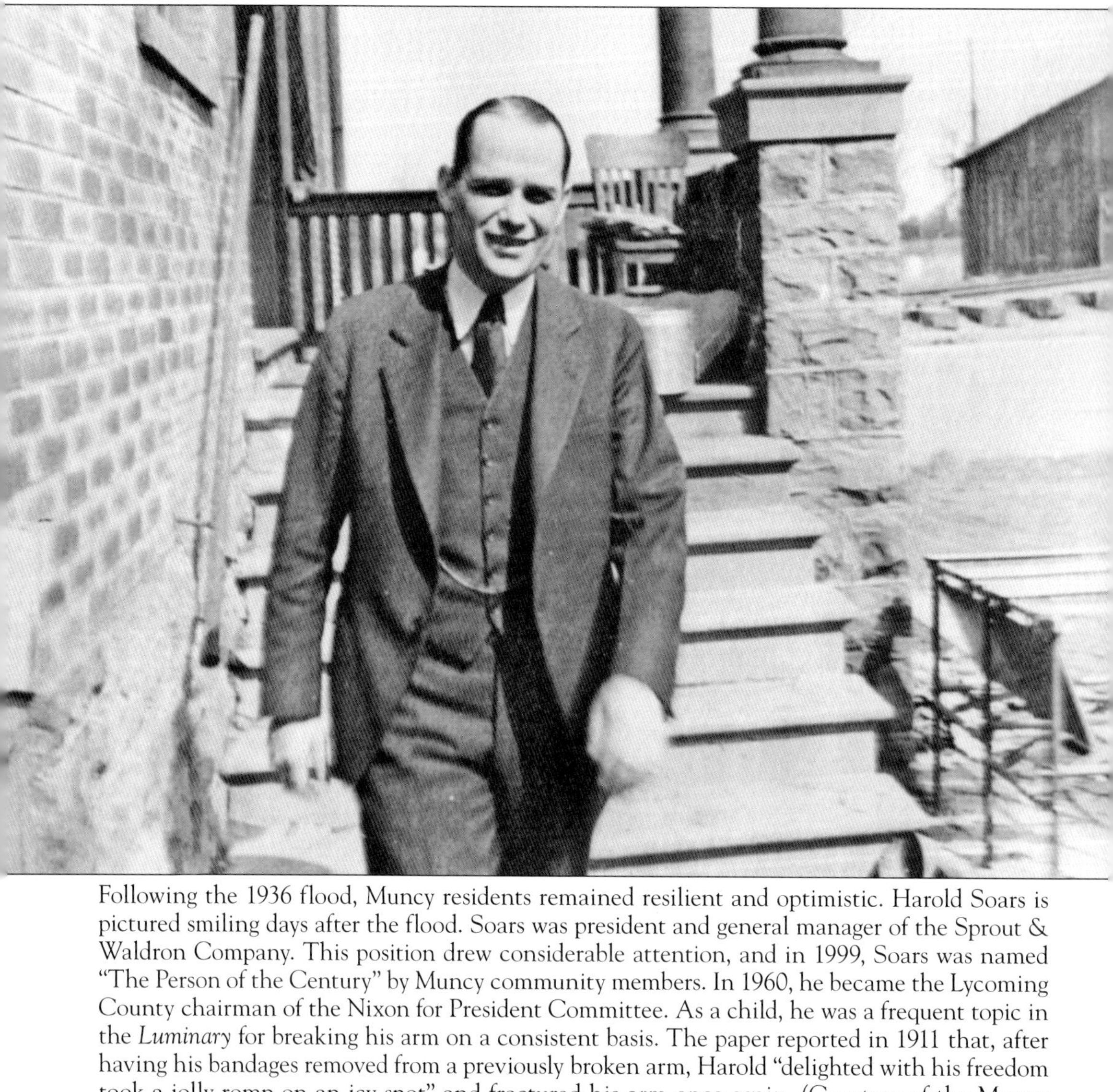

Following the 1936 flood, Muncy residents remained resilient and optimistic. Harold Soars is pictured smiling days after the flood. Soars was president and general manager of the Sprout & Waldron Company. This position drew considerable attention, and in 1999, Soars was named "The Person of the Century" by Muncy community members. In 1960, he became the Lycoming County chairman of the Nixon for President Committee. As a child, he was a frequent topic in the *Luminary* for breaking his arm on a consistent basis. The paper reported in 1911 that, after having his bandages removed from a previously broken arm, Harold "delighted with his freedom took a jolly romp on an icy spot" and fractured his arm once again. (Courtesy of the Muncy Historical Society.)

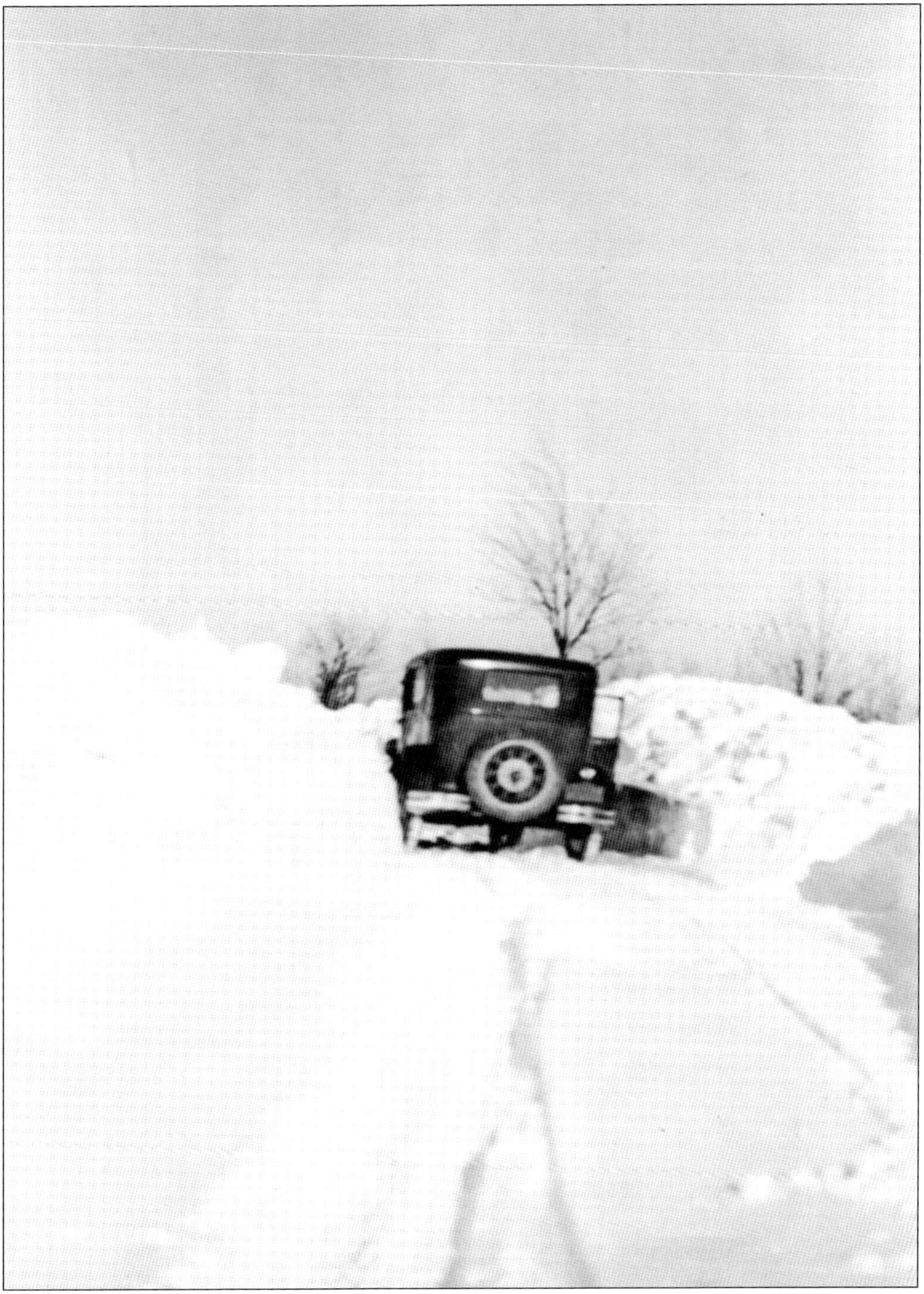

Pictured on February 10, 1936, is an old Ford automobile trying to make it up Muncy Hill after a deep snowfall. This photograph was taken a scant month before the St. Patrick's Day flood of 1936, and there is little doubt that such a huge accumulation of snow contributed to the flooding. The flood killed more than 150 and led to $300 million in damages. (Courtesy of the Muncy Historical Society.)

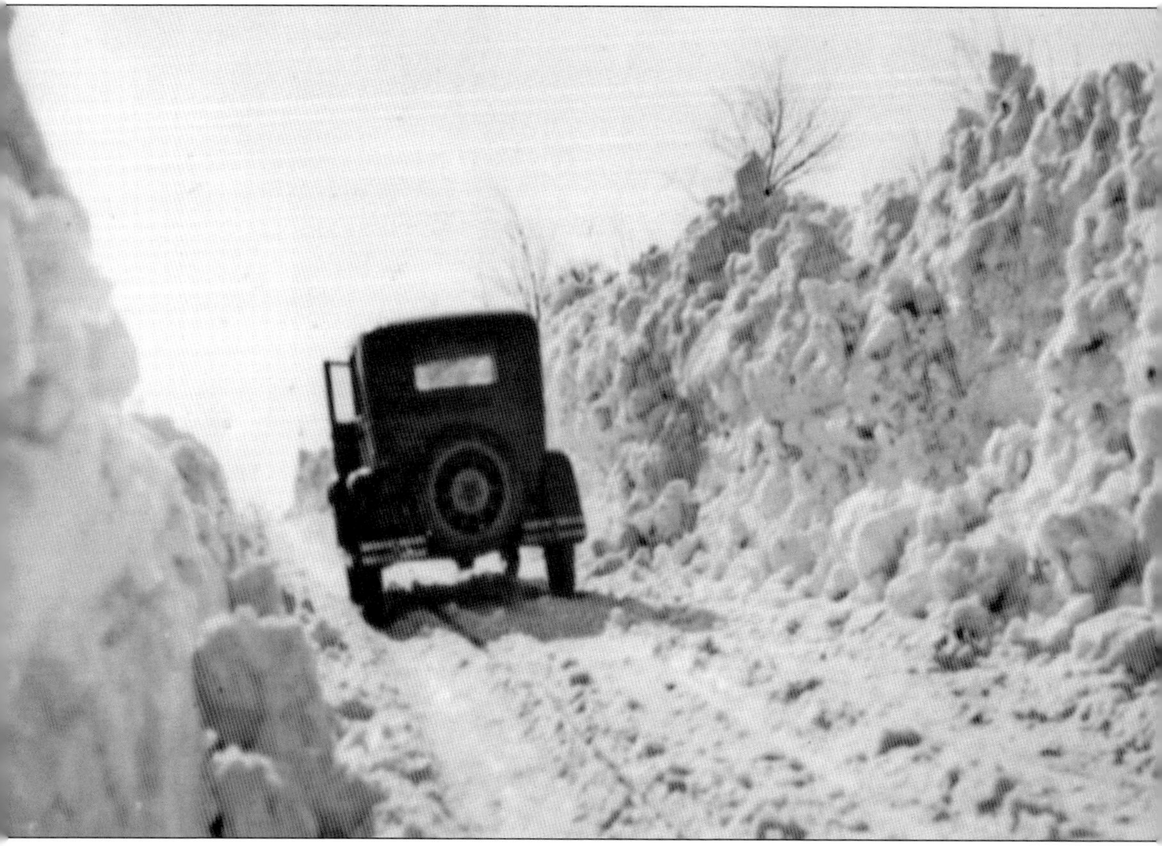

Another, more recent storm was Stella, a superstorm formed by a nor'easter in March 2017. The storm dumped close to 30 inches of snow on the area in a span of a few hours, with snowfall between three and four inches per hour at times. Technology was of great aid to the citizens of Muncy during this time, as social media shares and updates from the National Weather Service helped locals prepare for a record snowfall. There were no recorded deaths in the area. (Courtesy of the Muncy Historical Society.)

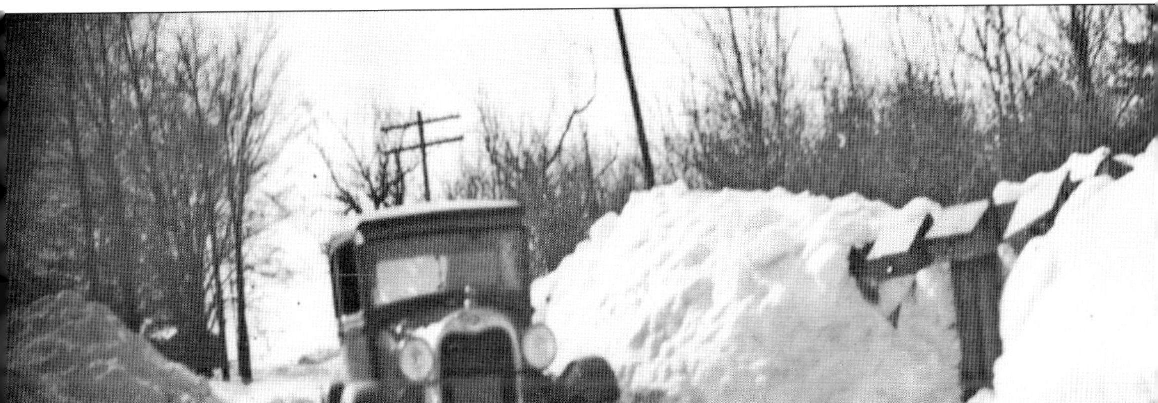

While records are sparse, a snowstorm in 1881 left its mark on the area. According to the *Muncy Luminary*, on Friday, March 4, a foot of snow blanketed the area in what the paper called "an old fashioned snow storm." Although the paper makes no mention of deaths related directly to the storm, it does note that H.G. Lichtenthler and Gussie Sprout were married on the day of the storm and that the state hospital for the insane was destroyed by fire caused by the efforts to heat the immense building. (Courtesy of the Muncy Historical Society.)

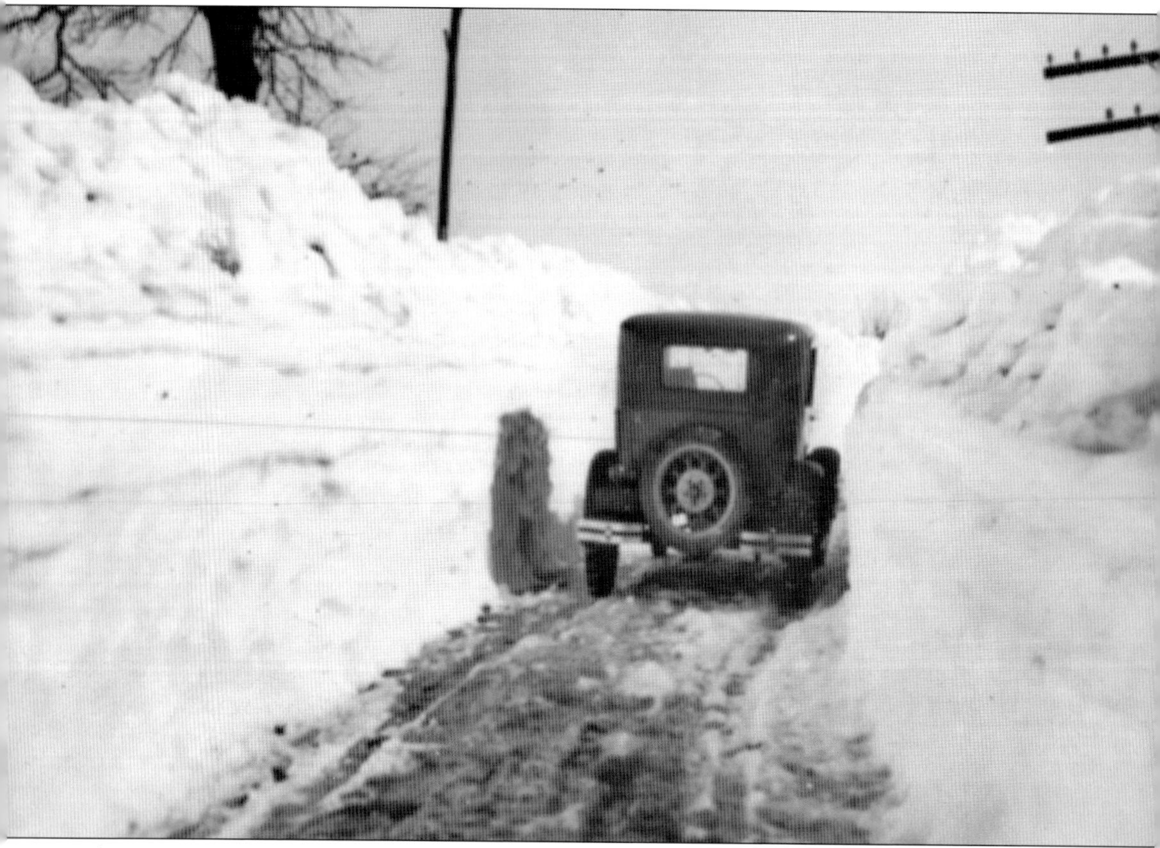

The automobile, as ill-equipped as it was for such conditions, was still leaps and bounds ahead of the archaic method of horses pulling a sleigh. This was never more evident than during a snowstorm in 1885. On February 20, Joseph Haberacker, his wife, Kate, and their three children—Mary, Henry, and Millie—were all killed in gruesome fashion when their sleigh overturned and the spooked horses dragged them close to 500 feet. Joseph died instantly due to a broken neck. Henry saw both of his legs severed, and he died shortly thereafter. While the news source postulates that Kate, Mary, and Millie died the same day, records cannot be confirmed, as the 1890 census records were destroyed by a fire. (Courtesy of the Muncy Historical Society.)

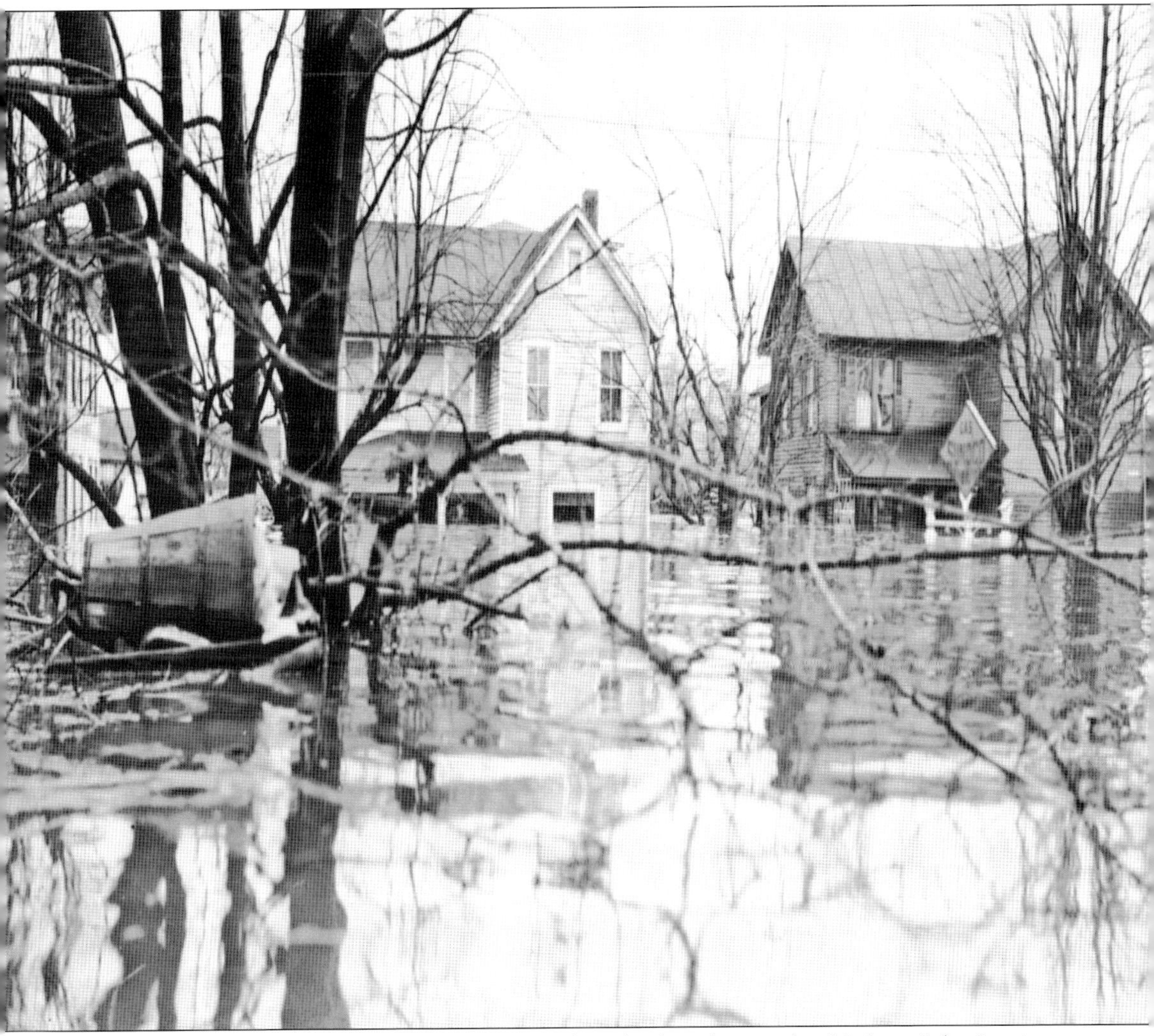

This image of the 1950 flood was taken by Bob Wilt, the editor and publisher of the *Luminary*. On November 11, waters reached a height of 28.8 feet. Following the flood, engineers warned residents to refrain from using water until the system could be cleared of the remaining muddy floodwater. This flood was not restricted to Muncy, as government records note record-breaking cold air that created a "coastal bomb" resulting in heavy rainfall across Lycoming County. Flooding continued into the 1960s, with newspaper headlines in 1964 announcing the worst flood since the 1950s. The *Luminary* reported the Susquehanna River spewing "ugly water" all over the local homes of Muncy, with waters cresting at 28.78 feet on March 11. Towns along the Susquehanna and tributaries in New York and Pennsylvania experienced dramatic flooding. Warm temperatures caused snow to rapidly melt, and the Report of the Chief of Engineers of the US Army notes Muncy, along with Milton and Lock Haven, receiving the greatest damage. (Courtesy of the Muncy Historical Society.)

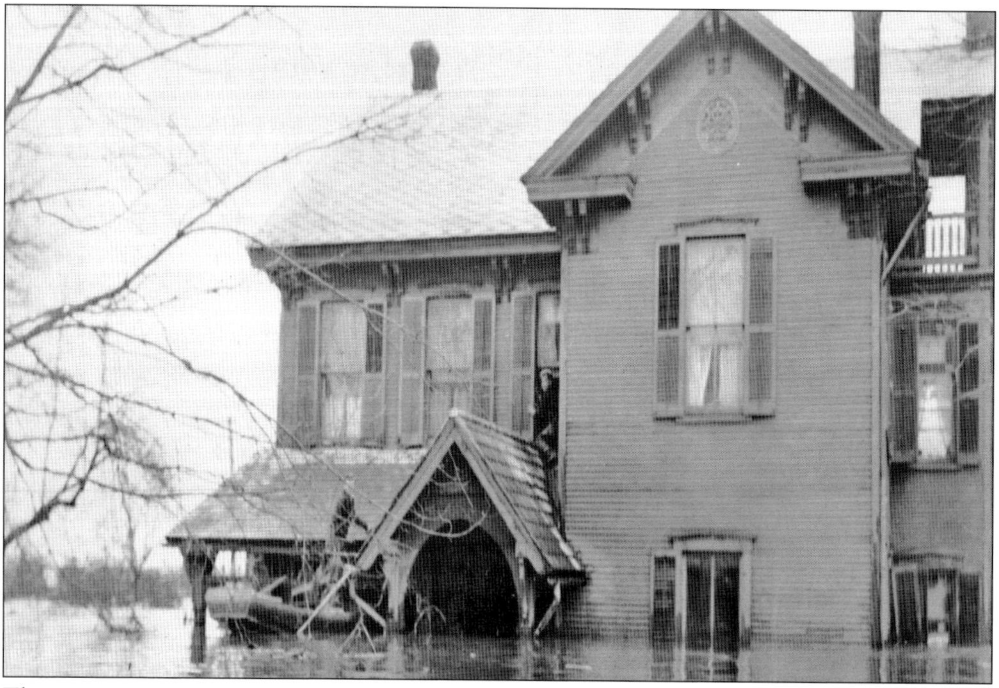

The 1970s were no exception to flooding in Muncy, as 1972, 1975, and 1979 saw four massive floods. In June 1972, Hurricane Agnes swept across the county and brought the greatest flood in Muncy history, with records topping 37 feet. Thousands of people across Pennsylvania were forced to evacuate their homes. Those who lived during the flooding continue to recount the devastating effects in their communities. (Courtesy of Bill Ritter.)

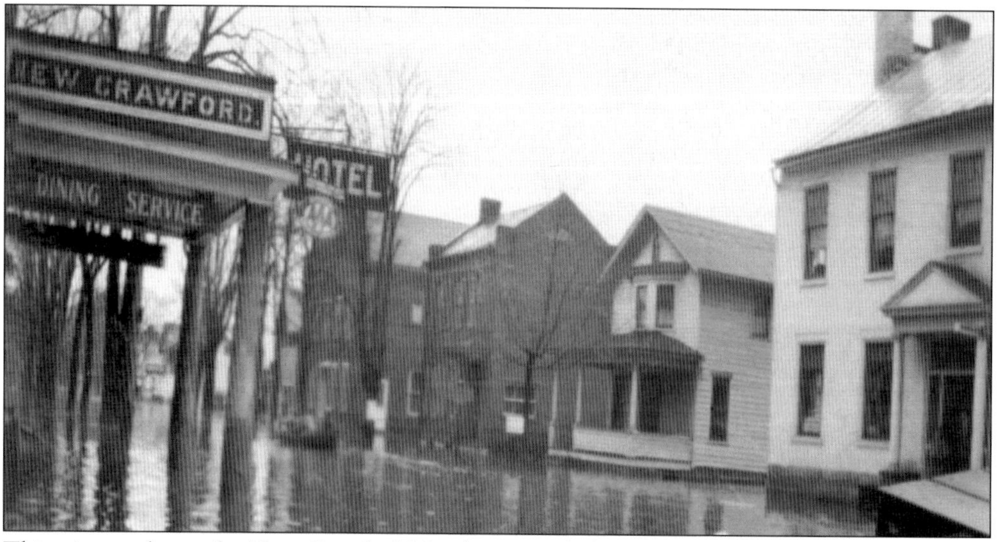

This picture shows the New Crawford Hotel surrounded by floodwaters during the March 17, 1936, flood that struck Muncy with a sound and a fury hard to imagine over 80 years later. According to the National Weather Service, the West Branch of the Susquehanna River has flooded Muncy an astounding 22 times since 1936, with six of those floods receiving a "major" classification, seven a "moderate" classification, and nine a "minor" classification. (Courtesy of the Muncy Historical Society.)

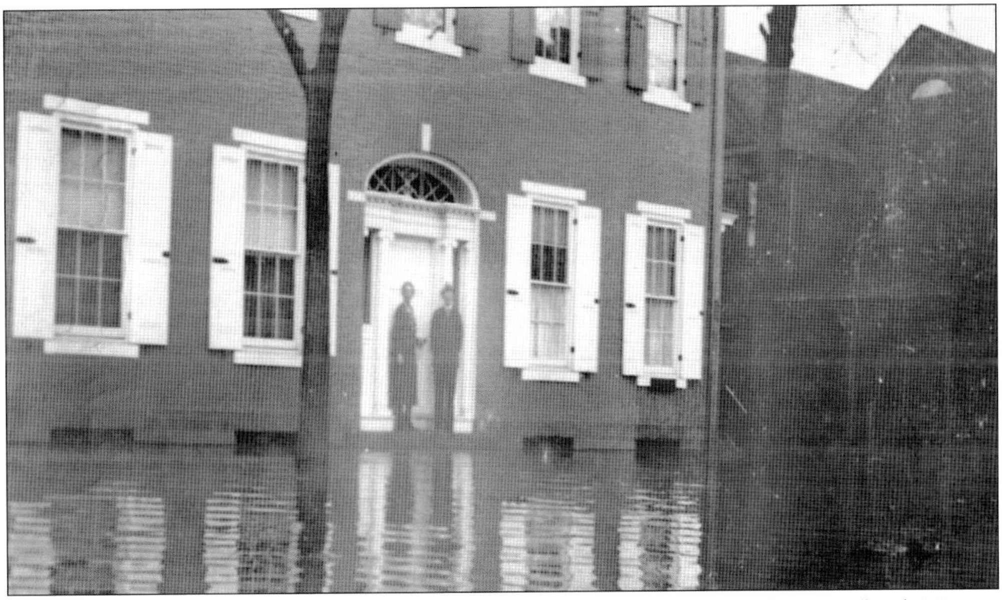

Two figures stand like ethereal apparitions in a Muncy doorway during the 1936 flood. Muncy, while a little off the beaten path, has its fair share of paranormal activity, so much so that the Heart of Pennsylvania Paranormal Society has a member, Laura Waltz, who resides in Muncy. Muncy's ghost history is tied into the nearby ghost town of Alvira, which sports the remains of three cemeteries, two churches, and the foundations of several homes. Most of the areas now lie on private property. (Courtesy of the Muncy Historical Society.)

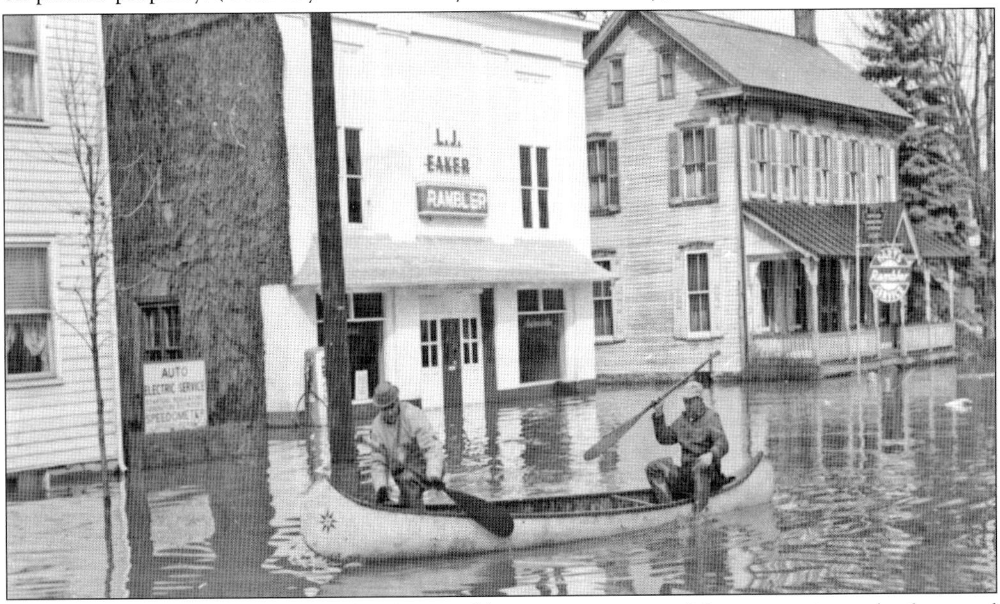

Shown here during the 1964 flood is the Rambler repair station in Muncy, serving as background to a couple of canoers who wish to escape the murky waters. The Rambler brand was first owned between 1900 and 1915 by the Thomas B. Jeffery Company. The brand disappeared for nearly 40 years before returning under the stewardship of Nash Motors from 1950 to 1954 and then under the American Motors Corporation from 1954 to its final death in 1969. The 1964 flood was a major one, with the river cresting at nearly 30 feet. (Courtesy of Bill Ritter.)

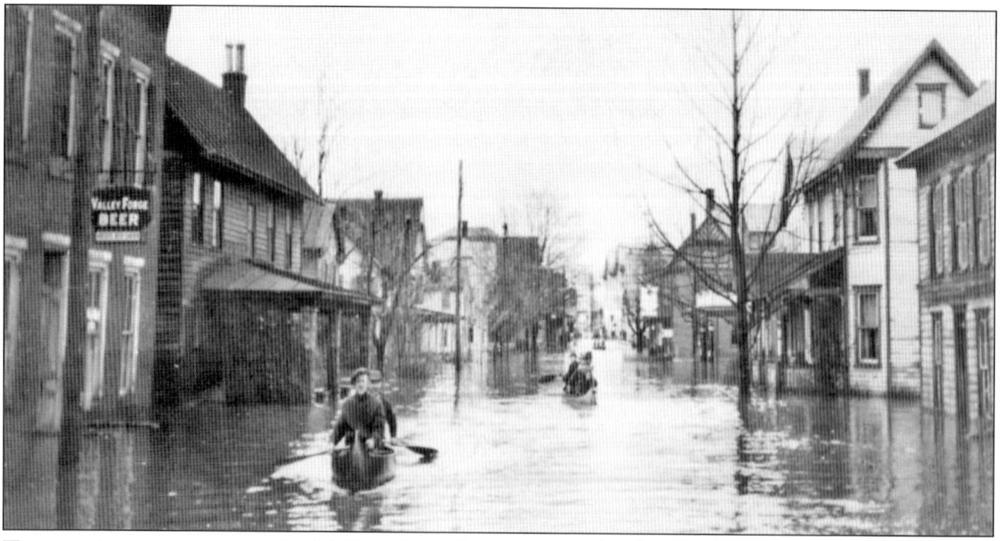

Two survivors canoe past the Valley Forge Beer sign in the flood of 1936. Although no longer brewed today, Valley Forge Beer was one of many brews made by the Adam Schedit Brewing Company, a company that made beer and other fine spirits from 1870 to 1954 with a small break for Prohibition. Based in Norristown, the seat of Montgomery County (one of Philadelphia's bedroom communities), the brewer produced nearly 750,000 barrels of beer during its 1940s heyday. It shut down for good in 1974. (Courtesy of Bill Ritter.)

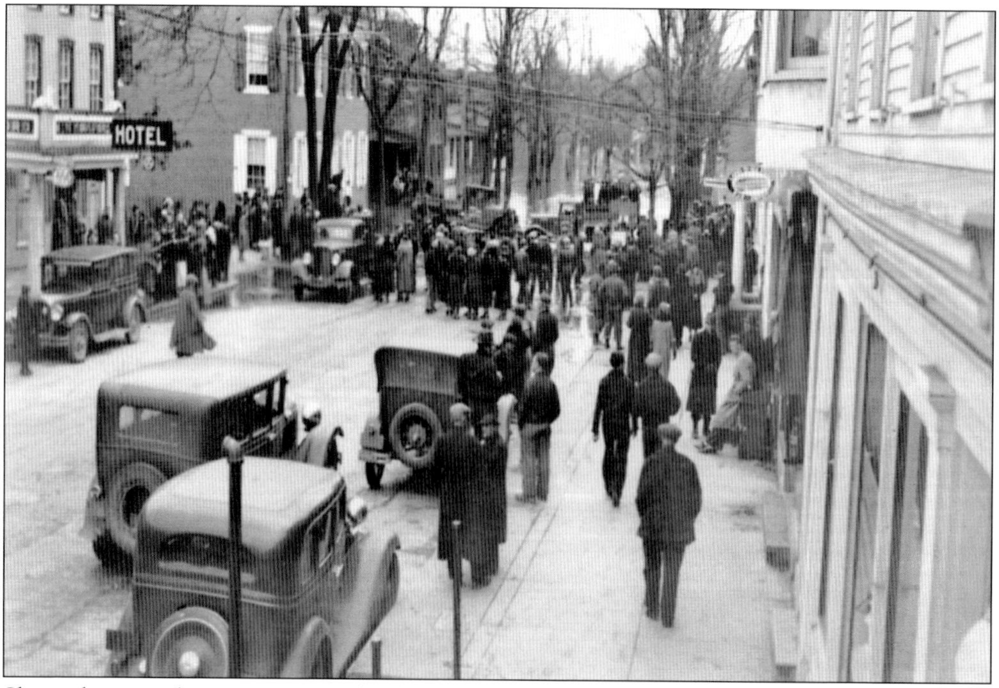

Shown here is a desperate attempt by the citizens of Muncy to save part of their town during the flood of 1936. A pair of trucks is parked at the edge of the water that is creeping up Main Street. One the left is the New Crawford Hotel, and to the right is the office of the Edwards Lakes to Sea bus station, founded in nearby Williamsport with Muncy serving as the first eastward stop on a route that stretched from Cleveland to New York. (Courtesy of Bill Ritter.)

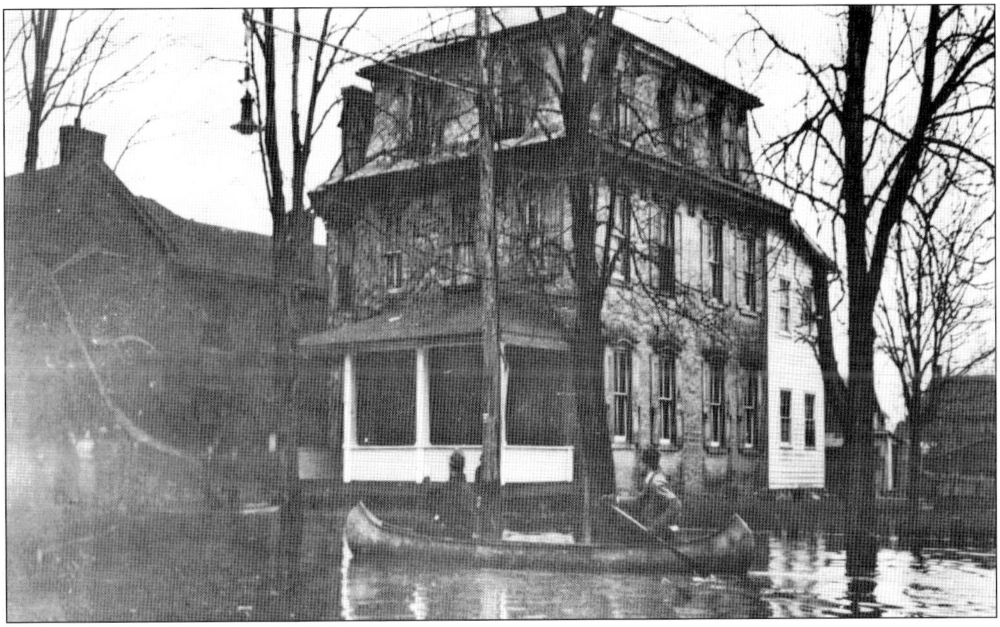

This photograph shows a home in the center of Muncy during the 1936 flood. The river crested at an unfathomable 35.9 feet, close to 16 feet above the 20-foot flood level. The drainage area was 209 square miles, and all of Lycoming County was affected by a flood that combined a massive March snowmelt with torrential rains. The canoe in the photograph could have been stood on end and it still would have been fully submerged. (Courtesy of the Muncy Historical Society.)

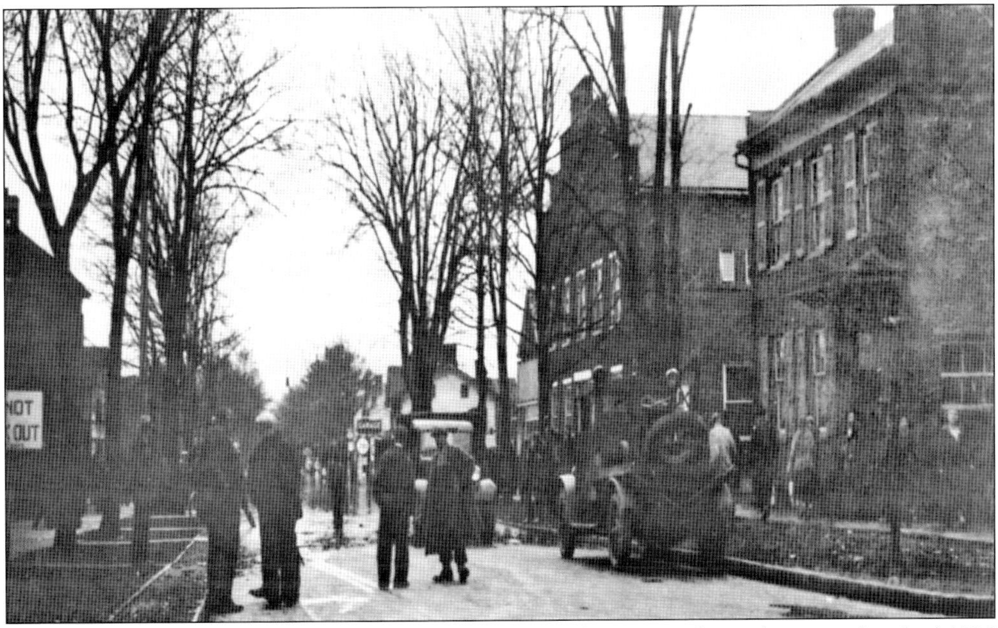

A group of concerned citizens watched helplessly as the waters from the great flood of 1936 consumed George M. Brelsford's garage. His garage focused on Reo cars. In 1897, Ransom Eli Olds founded the company that produced the curved-dash Oldsmobile, America's first mass-produced automobile. He sold Oldsmobile in 1905 to found Reo and owned more than half of the company stock. Reo manufactured vehicles until 1975. (Courtesy of the Muncy Historical Society.)

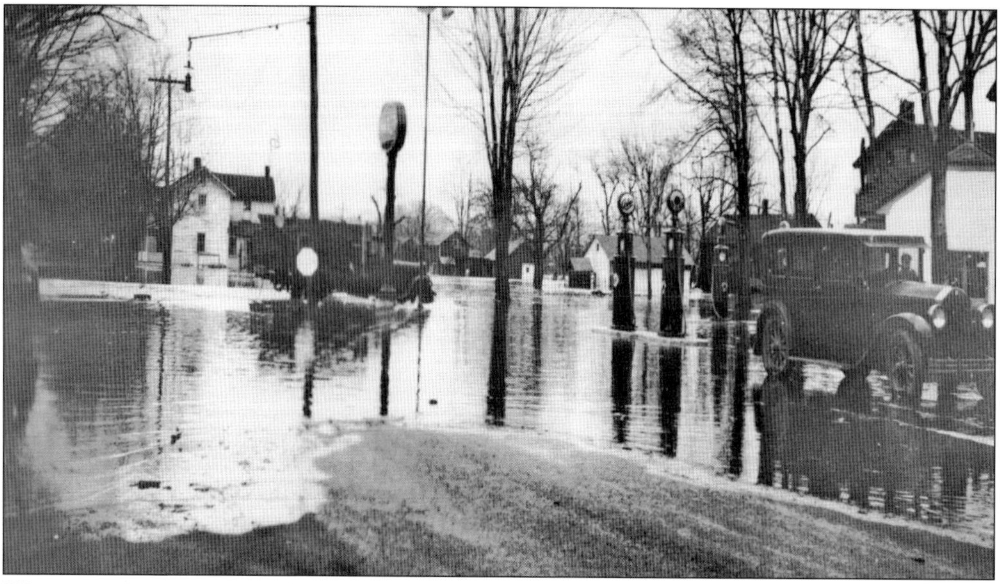

Wertman's Service Station had been on Water Street for less than a year when the great flood of 1936 struck. The business was opened in 1935 by Harry Wertman before being run by his widow from 1936 to 1968. After a four-year hiatus, the station was taken over by Larry and Linda Wertman in 1972. Standing now at 175 Water Street is Rothfuss Automotive, a full-service repair station. (Courtesy of the Muncy Historical Society.)

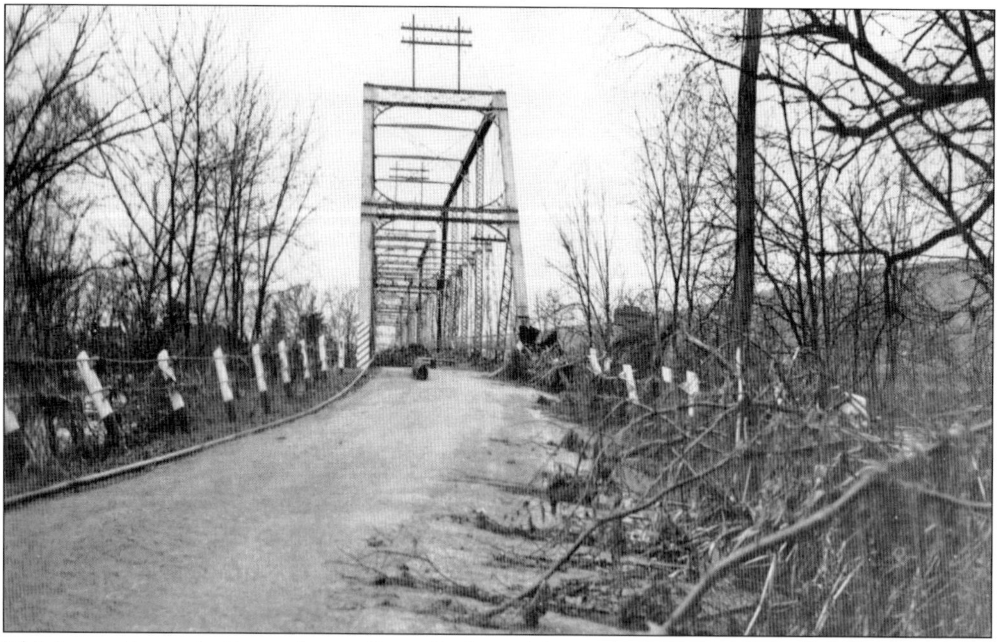

This image shows the Susquehanna River Bridge at Muncy shortly after the 1936 flood. Although the bridge was never in any danger, the road that it hosted was still littered with tree branches and debris, some of which came off in the storm and some of which was pushed up the banks of the river and along the shoreline. Aside from the floral damage, one can see a sign labeling the Susquehanna River standing proudly on the right side of the road. (Courtesy of the Muncy Historical Society.)

Five

Start Me Up
The Industry and Business of Muncy

Though rooted in a town that houses a little over 2,000 people, the businesses of Muncy influence communities across the state. Throughout the centuries, innovative residents have brought a wide array of industries to the Muncy area in an effort to better serve their community. Their outreach proved to extend much further.

Attracting students from all over the country, the Lycoming County Normal School prepared its students for careers in teaching. Local businesses showed their support for the school through numerous donations, raising money to finance a $30,000 building project. For years, Muncy High School has produced driven young residents to make an imprint on their community, with many going on to establish successful businesses in the area.

Harter's Drug Store, for example, last run by locals Mark and Theresa Tarquinio, served Muncy for over 100 years. The original owner, C.W. Harter, established the business as a franchise of Rexall Pharmacies, serving as the local pharmacist. In the later years of the 19th century, L.S. Smith and Son stood on North Main Street and faithfully served the community as both a brick-and-mortar store and a delivery service. Muncy was also connected to the greater Lycoming County community through its participation in the lumber boom. The Sprout & Waldron plant has had a large impact on the surrounding area, primarily manufacturing equipment for the pulp and paper industry.

Businesses such as the post office and the West Branch Bell Company attached Muncy to national institutions and employed numerous locals throughout the years. The post office building itself houses multiple historical tributes, such as the painting *Rachel Silverthorne's Ride* and a fallout shelter. The West Branch Bell Company was a part of the larger American Bell Company, an initiative by Alexander Graham Bell, and employed men and women of the Muncy community throughout the 20th century.

After decades of industrial success, Muncy residents continue to contribute on a national scale towards the development of new technology and the endurance of existing industries. Main Street remains important for local businesses such as Orlando's Restaurant, lawyers, accountants, and the Muncy Public Library.

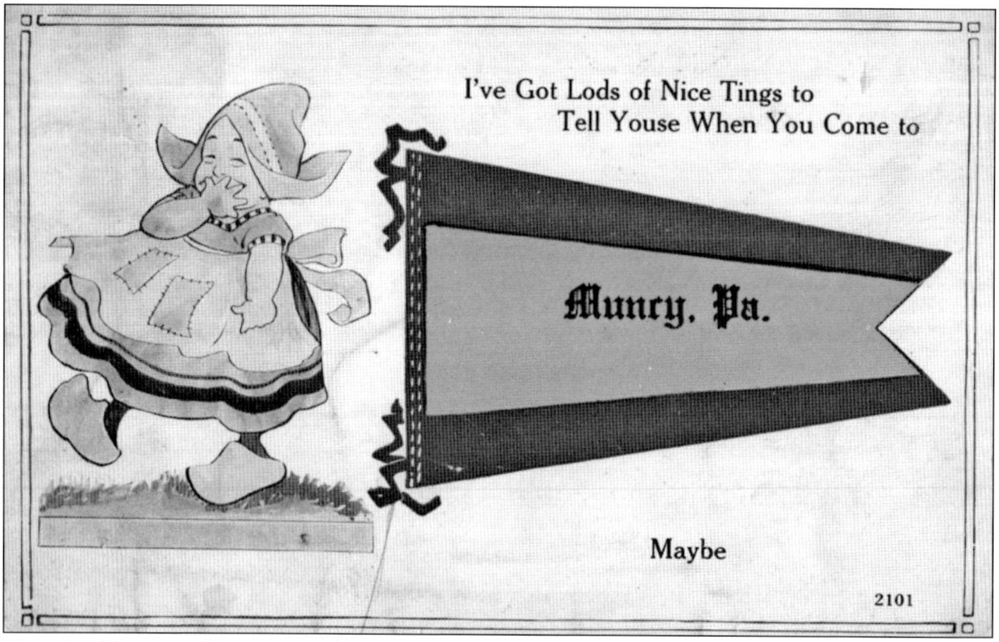

This playful postcard hints towards the influence of the Pennsylvania Dutch in Muncy. Descendants of German immigrants who settled in the area starting in 1683, the Pennsylvania Dutch established a religious presence in Pennsylvania. Muncy Mills, erected in 1772 by John Alwood, was purchased by the Shoemaker family, and a portion of the land was used for the establishment of the Old Dutch Church, now Old Immanuel Lutheran Church. First built with logs, the Old Dutch Church collapsed during a storm; it was rebuilt as a brick edifice in 1832. (Author's collection.)

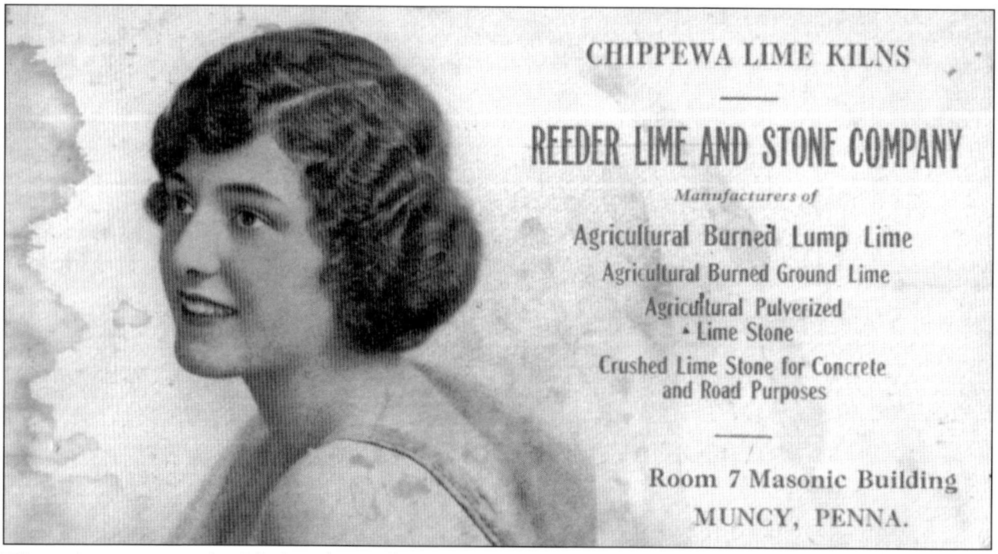

This advertisement highlights the influence of lime in Lycoming County, especially among the Pennsylvania German farmers. Many German settlers deemed farmland high quality by the presence of lime, an indication of good land in Germany. Eventually, a more profitable enterprise was fashioned around lime as a form of fertilizer. Advertisements such as this would have appealed to the high number of farmers in Muncy. Using commercial kilns such as these, farmers could obtain lime from a "lime burner." (Author's collection.)

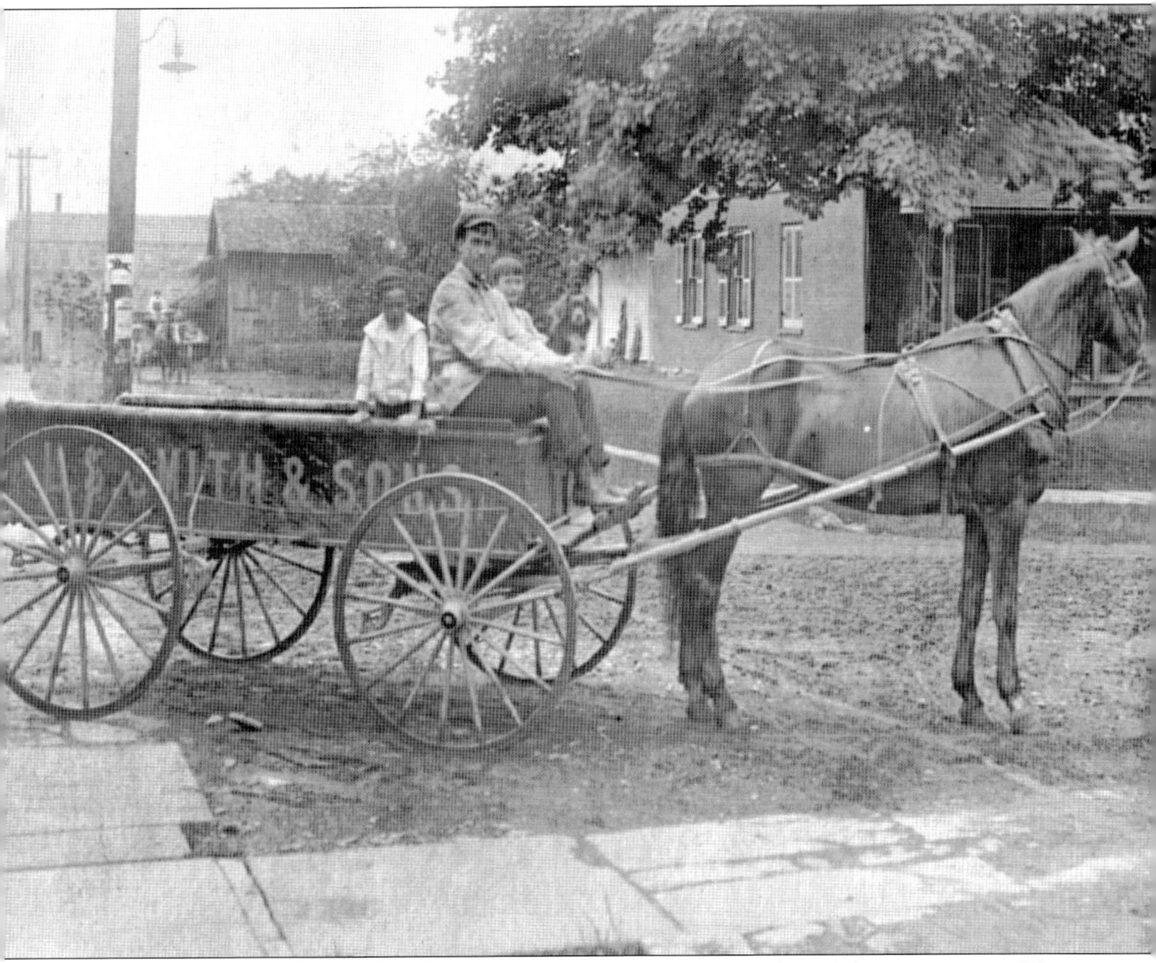

Located on North Main Street, L.S. Smith and Son was a large part of the community. The grand opening of the store took place on October 10, 1884. Throughout the store's lifetime, many Muncy residents would be given the title of store clerk. After serving in Company E, 137th Pennsylvania Volunteers during the Civil War, A.H. Gudykunst returned to Muncy and served as clerk of the store. Around this time, news about L.S. Smith and Son was an exciting topic in the *Muncy Luminary*. For example, on May 19, 1877, the store was broken into, and a ham, a box of candles, and a lot of potatoes were taken. (Courtesy of Bill Ritter.)

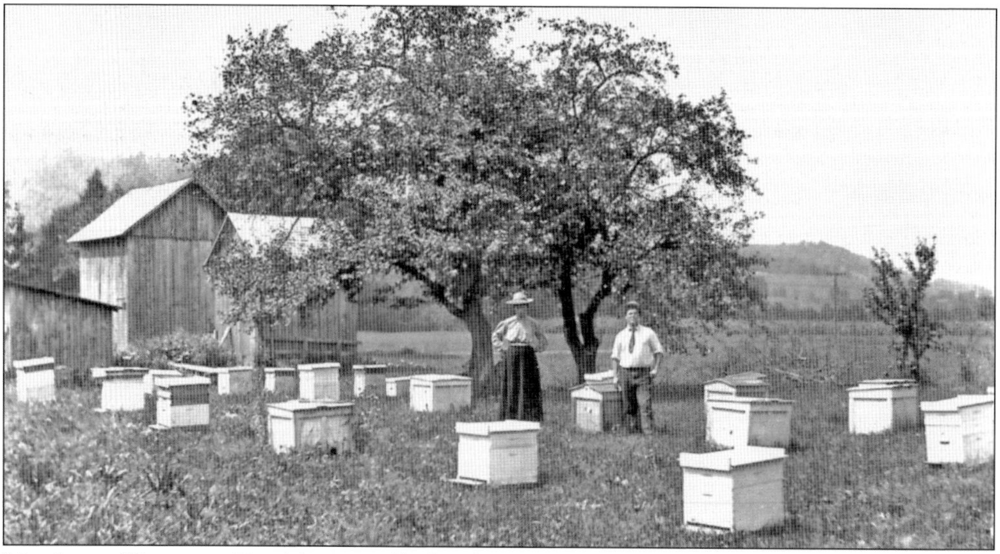

Members of Benjamin Franklin Merrill's family are pictured at work among their Depression-era beehives. The Merrill bee farm was at 18 Bruner Street. Despite the struggles of the era, beekeeping was still a somewhat lucrative job, as sweetener was still in demand and bees produced honey despite capitalist market forces. Frank Woodside, one of Merrill's descendants, occupied the property until it was torn down in the 2010s. The site now features part of a small set of condos that extend to 24 Bruner Street. (Courtesy of Janet Woodside Shoemaker.)

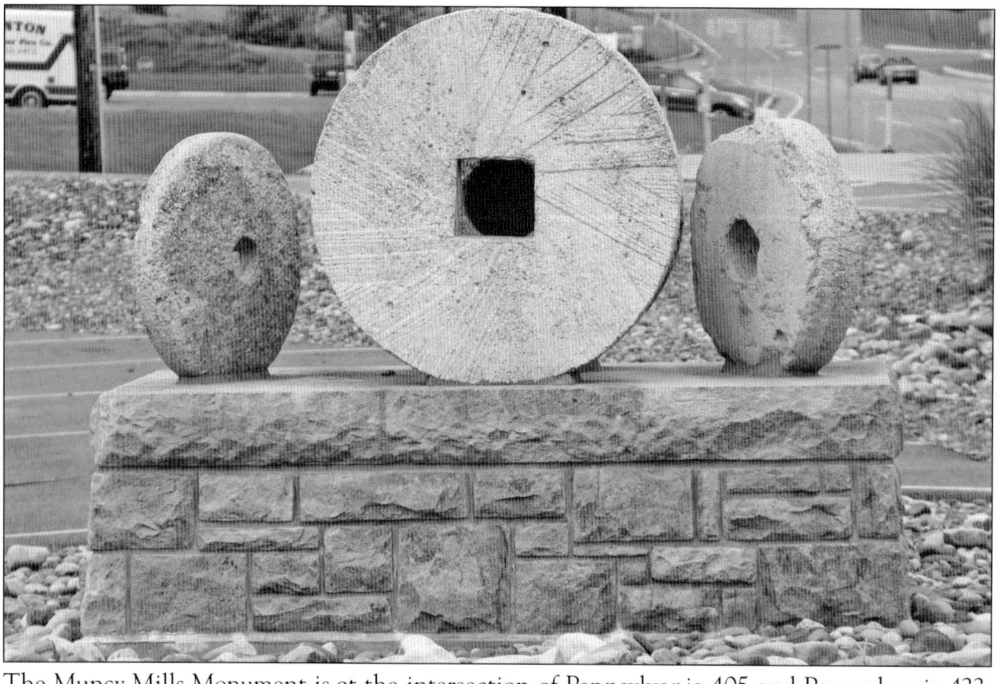

The Muncy Mills Monument is at the intersection of Pennsylvania 405 and Pennsylvania 422, just east of Muncy proper. This is the site where, in 1772, the first gristmill was built on Muncy Creek by John Alward. The mill would barely see the birth of a new nation before it was burned to the ground by Native Americans in 1779. Other mills were built on the same site in 1783 and 1800. The last mill remained in operation until 1872. (Author's collection.)

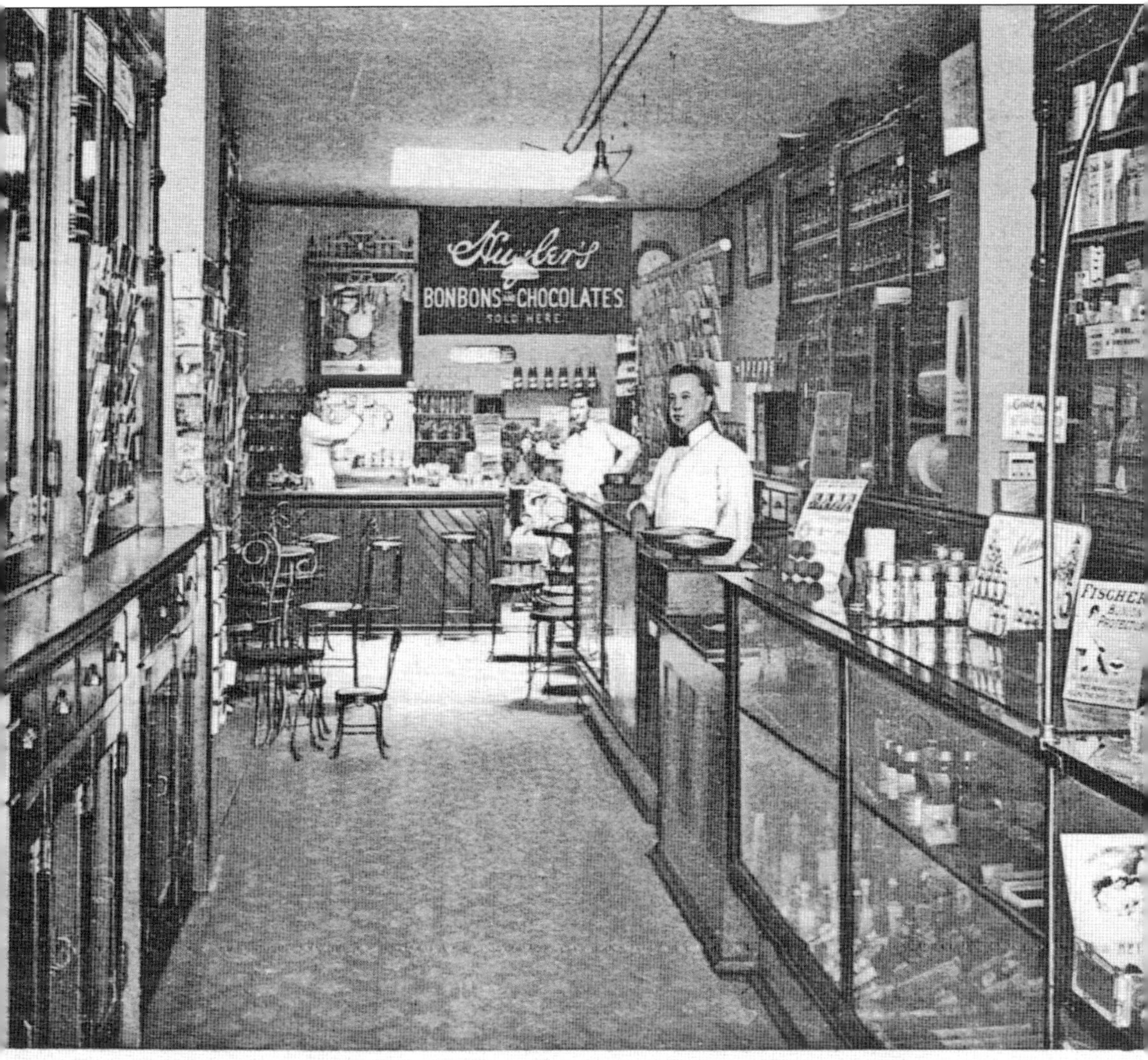

Interior C. W. Harters Drug Store, Muncy, Pa.

A business that evokes quintessential, small-town American charm, Harter's Drug Store served the community for over 100 years and claimed the title of the oldest continuous business in the borough of Muncy in 1960. The store was significant for its merchandise and for its playful participation in the local community. On December 14, 1911, the town received exciting news that the candle in the window of the store had burned out after 152 hours and seven minutes, apparently announcing the end of a contest in which three locals took home prizes consisting of a toilet set, an ivory clock, and a box of candy. In 2009, the doors to Harter's were closed. Mark and Theresa Tarquinio were the final owners of the business, serving the community with smiles and laughs for 28 years. (Courtesy of the Muncy Historical Society.)

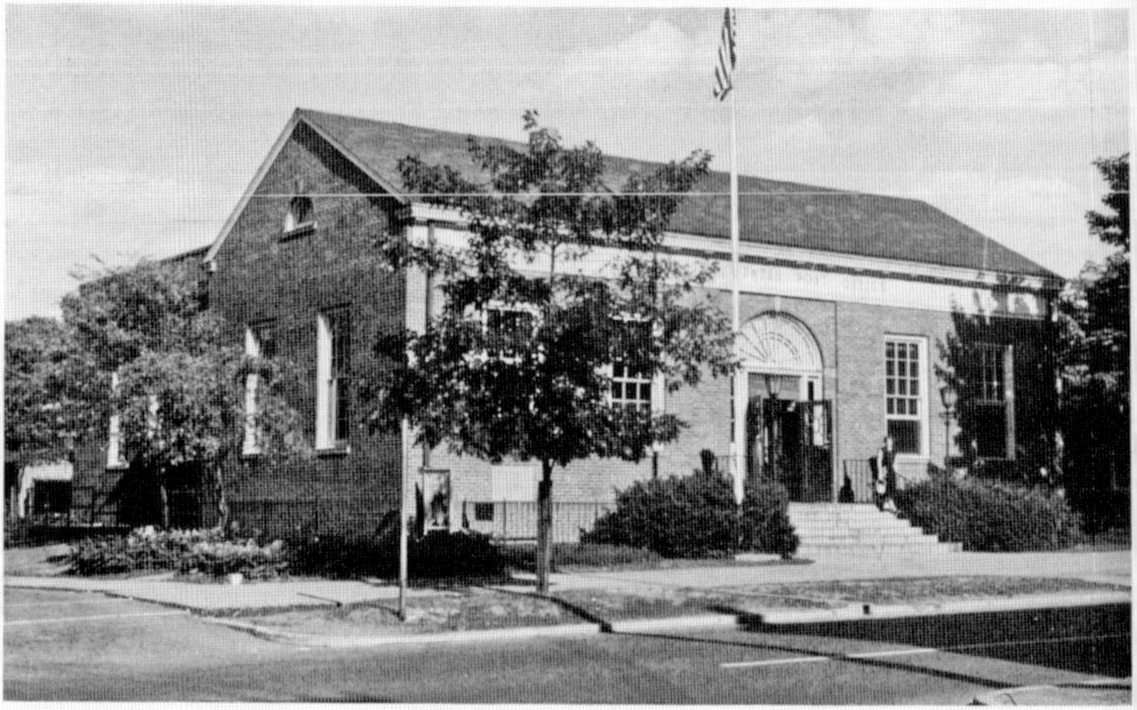

U. S. Post Office, Muncy, Pa.

The post office has a history that stretches over 200 years. The first post office in Muncy was established on April 1, 1800, with Henry Shoemaker as postmaster. Others to serve in that position include James Boal, appointed January 13, 1803; John Brindle, January 11, 1815; Abraham Taylor, December 28, 1816; William Pidcock, February 22, 1817; George Frederick Jr., December 4, 1819; William A. Petrikin, March 20, 1822; Cowden S. Wallis, December 22, 1840; John P. Schuyler, March 15, 1843; William Michael, December 14, 1844; John Whitlock, May 1, 1849; William Michael, July 11, 1857; and Enos Hawley, July 9, 1861. In 1869, the president of the United States assumed postmaster appointing duties. (Author's collection.)

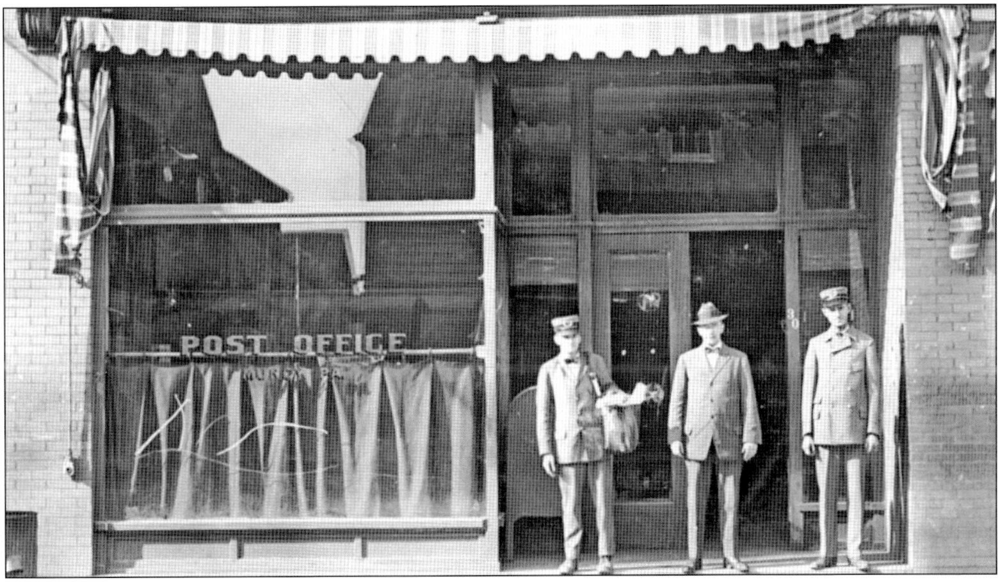

Three postal workers, including famous Muncy postmaster Brady Snyder (right), are pictured in front of the postal building. After the president assumed postmaster appointing duties, the postmasters were Enos Hawley, April 5, 1869; George E.T. Painter, March 12, 1873; James H. Fulmer, December 5, 1885; P.M. Trumbower, October 8, 1889; W.E. Mohr, February 29, 1890; and then Postmaster Snyder in 1916. In 1826, a mail route was established from Muncy to Meansville (Towanda, Bradford County), followed in 1832 by a route from Pottsville to Muncy to Cherry, Towanda, and Jersey Shore. (Courtesy of the Muncy Historical Society.)

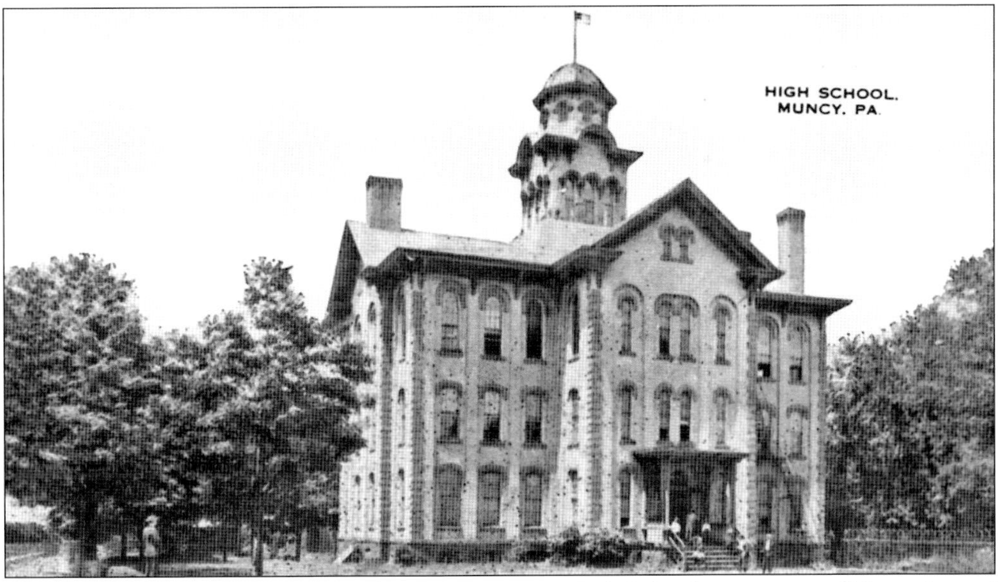

Pictured at the beginning of the 20th century, Muncy High School is now part of Muncy Junior/Senior High School. Today, the school stands as one of the few in the nation to have 100 percent "Highly Qualified" teachers under the No Child Left Behind Act. The school boasts an 11-to-1 student-teacher ratio and on average enrolls around 500 students. The school currently offers five advanced placement courses. Maggie Rymsza, the coauthor of this book, graduated from Muncy High School in 2015. (Author's collection.)

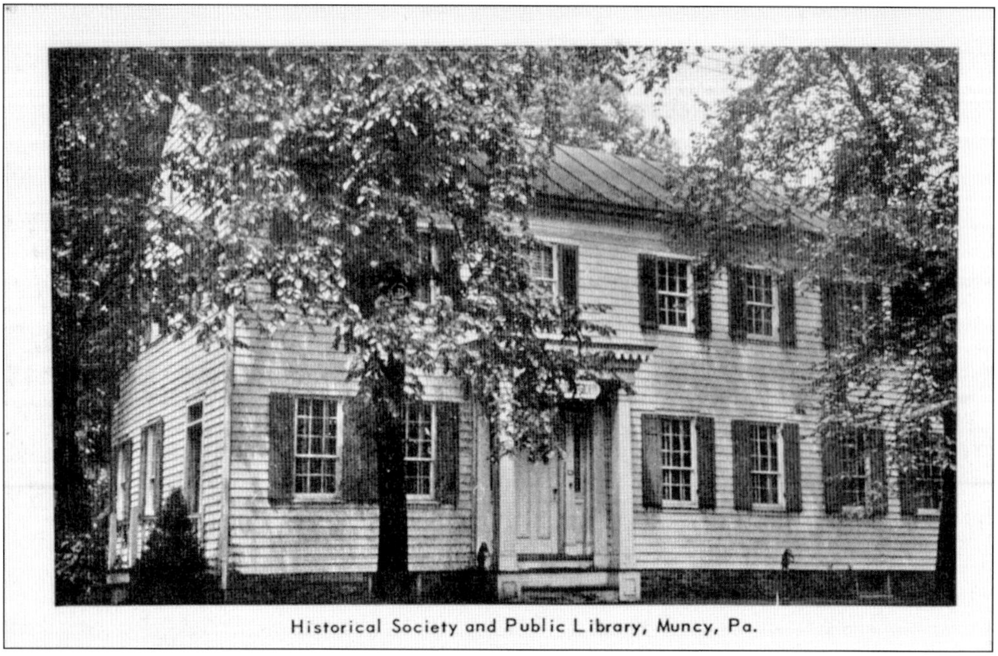

Founded in 1936, the Muncy Historical Society is, in coauthor M. Earl Smith's experience, one of the finest stewards of local history in the eastern United States of America. Consisting of period displays and document collections spanning a history older than America itself, the museum hosts several cultural and historical events throughout the year. The archives of documents and photographs contained at the historical society are vast, providing this volume with a clear majority of needed materials. It also at one time hosted Muncy's public library. (Author's collection.)

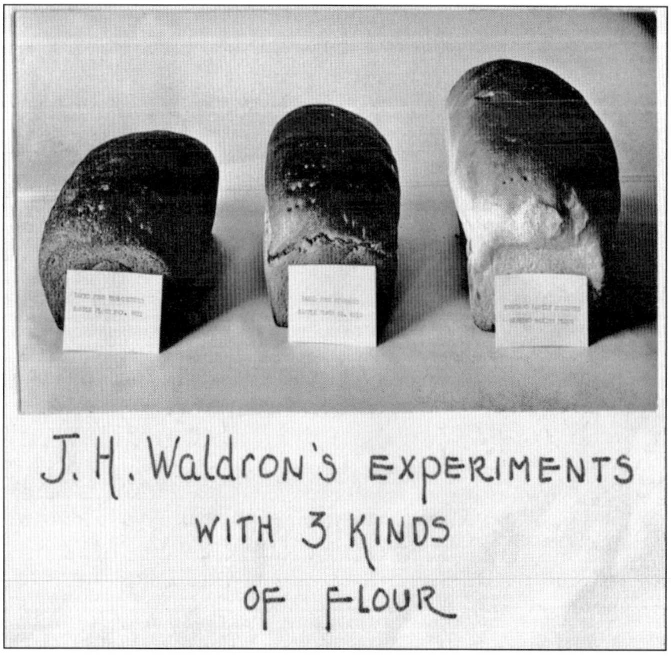

These three samples of bread were baked by J.H. Waldron (of Sprout & Waldron fame) sometime in the 1950s. The first was baked with unscreened flour, which is flour immediately after the meal (usually cereal) is ground into a powder. The second was made with screened flour, a process in which the flour is run through a sieve once to remove any impurities. The third sample contains basic store flour. Given Waldron's place in the mealing industry, such experiments were important. (Courtesy of the Muncy Historical Society.)

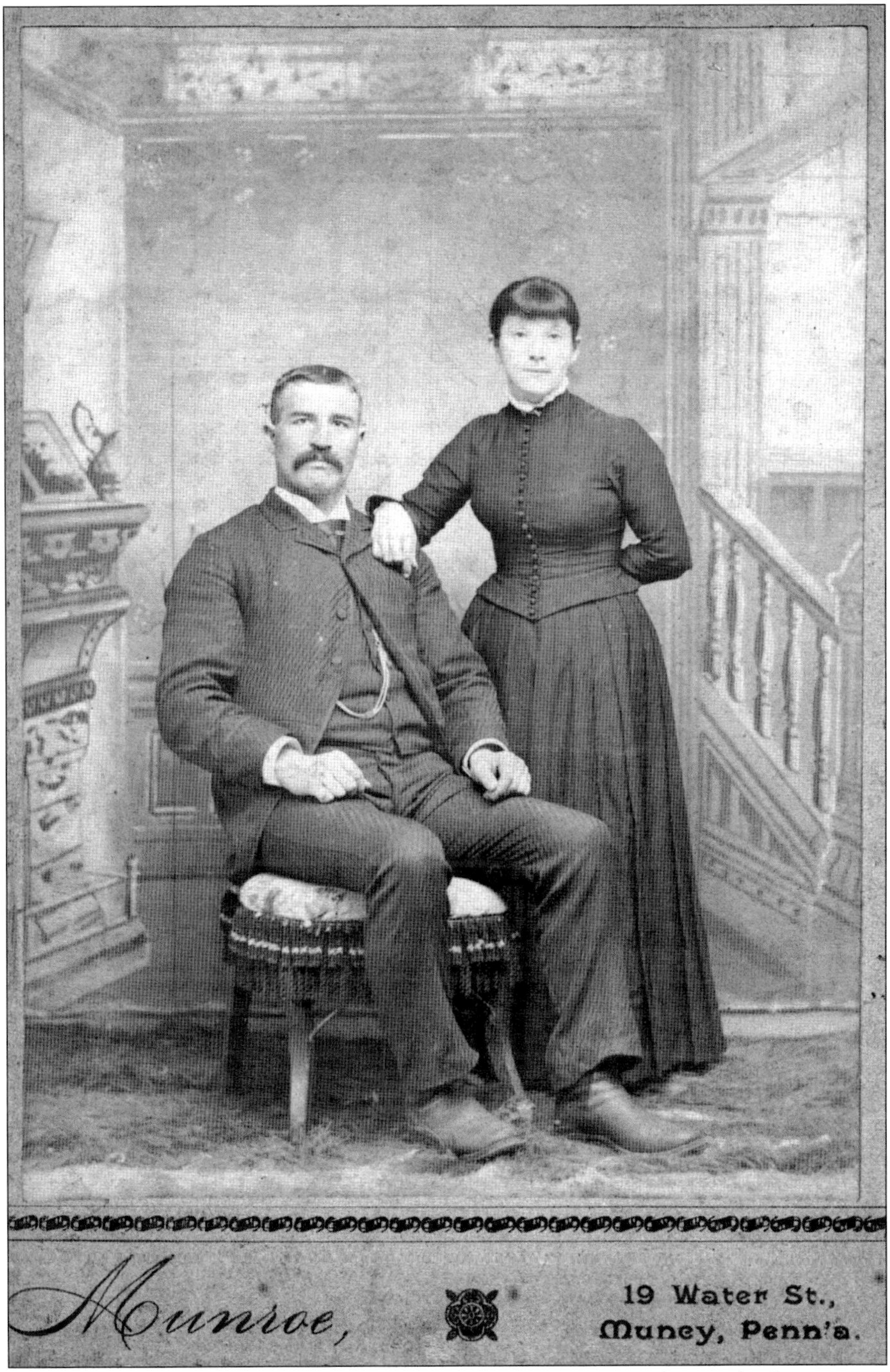

Although the building at 19 East Water Street now serves as a residence, the home was at the turn of the century the studio of photographer J.L. Munroe. No records of J.L. Munroe or of any variation thereof exist in the census data for the area from 1870 to 1910, so it is fair to assume that Munroe was a traveling photographer who would visit areas for a short period, take photographs, and come back on a recurring basis to offer both new images and reshoots. The identity of the couple in this photograph is unknown. (Courtesy of the Muncy Historical Society.)

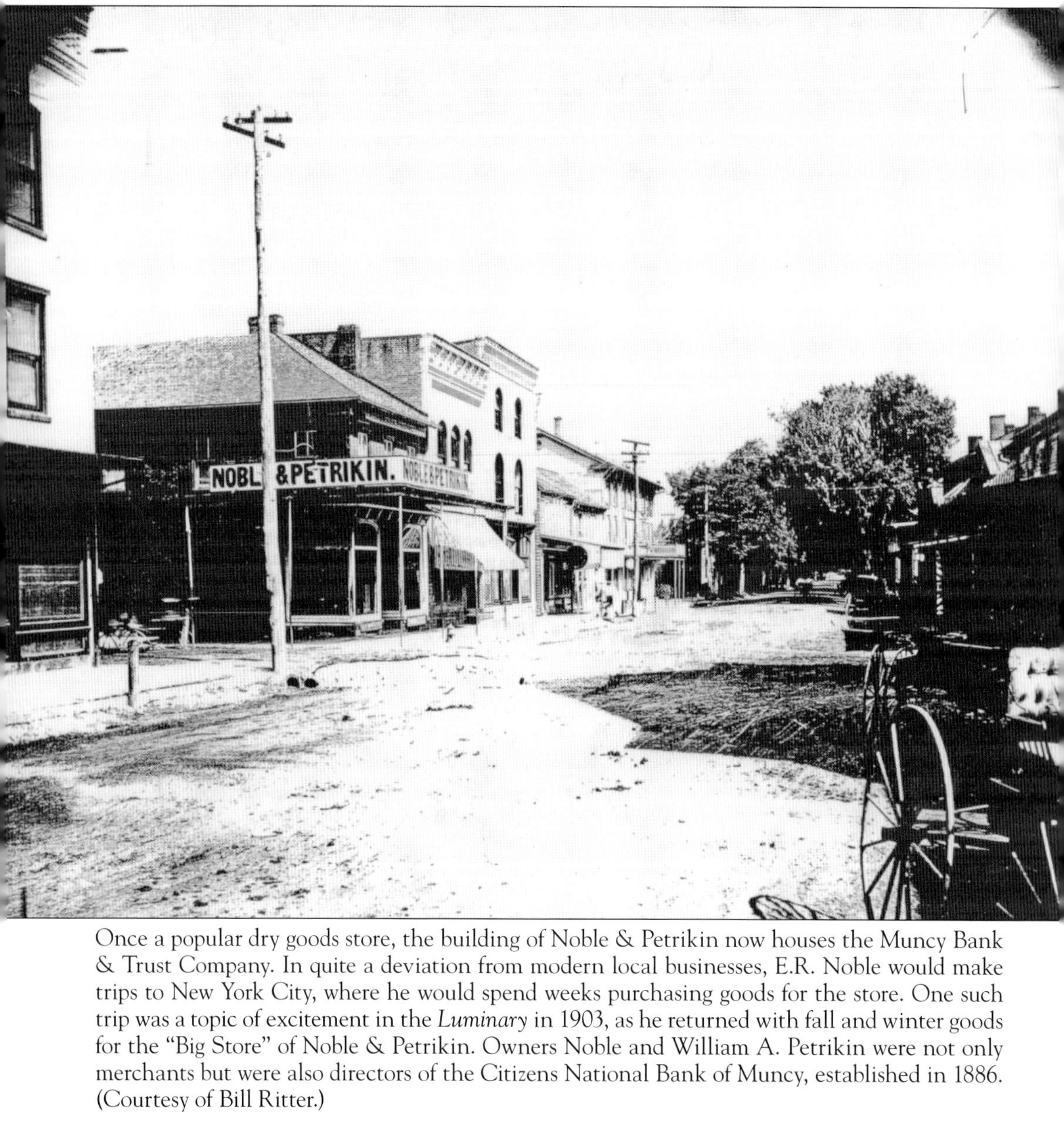

Once a popular dry goods store, the building of Noble & Petrikin now houses the Muncy Bank & Trust Company. In quite a deviation from modern local businesses, E.R. Noble would make trips to New York City, where he would spend weeks purchasing goods for the store. One such trip was a topic of excitement in the *Luminary* in 1903, as he returned with fall and winter goods for the "Big Store" of Noble & Petrikin. Owners Noble and William A. Petrikin were not only merchants but were also directors of the Citizens National Bank of Muncy, established in 1886. (Courtesy of Bill Ritter.)

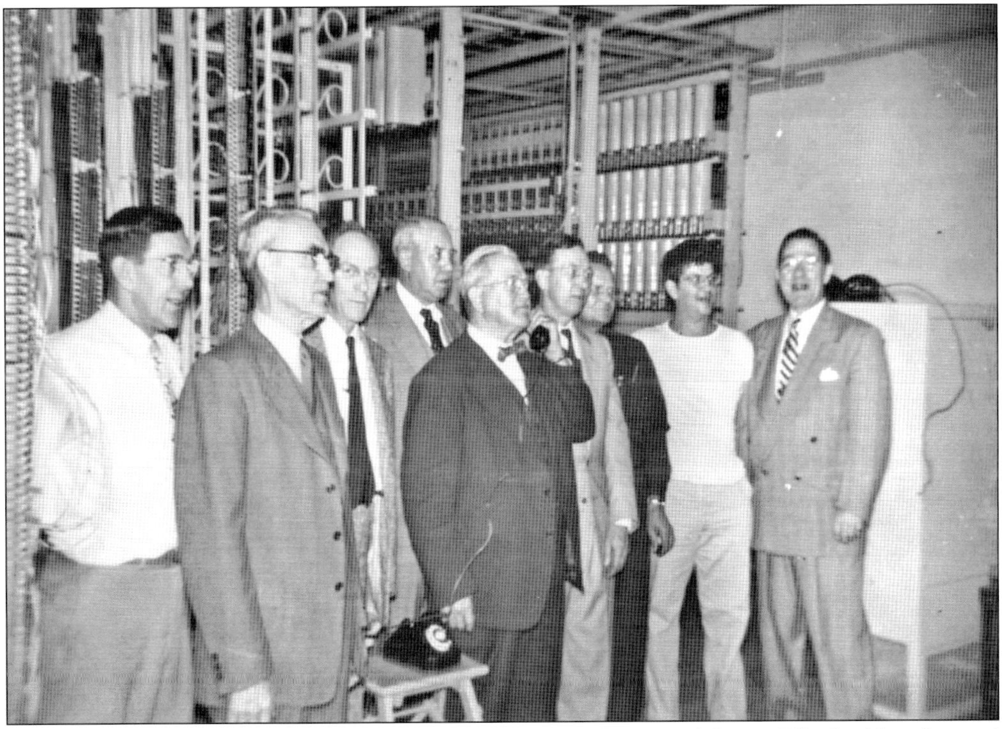

The West Branch Bell Company building was on Main Street in Muncy. The building housed both the company and Ruth's Dress Shop, which replaced the Muncy Candy Company in 1939. Pictured are, from left to right, Clyde Hofer, Dick Lowe, Ralph Decker, Bill Smith, and Mike Kilgus, local employees of the Bell Telephone Company. (Courtesy of the Muncy Historical Society.)

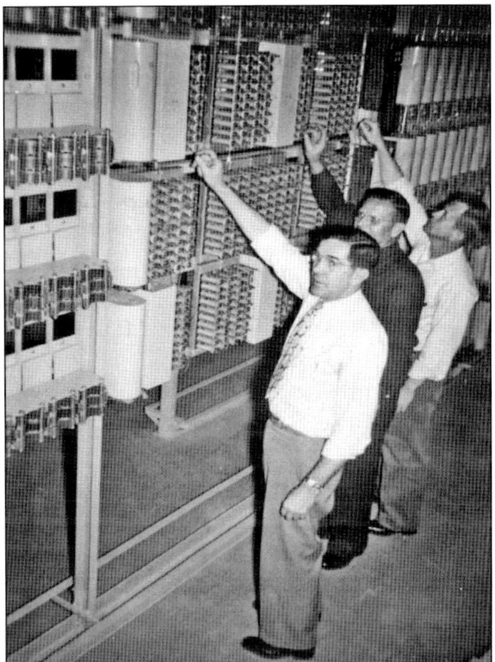

The West Branch Bell Telephone Company was part of the American Bell Company, which had its origins in the National Bell Telephone Company and eventually evolved into AT&T. Beginning with the famous words uttered by Alexander Graham Bell into the first practical telephone, the Bell system completed its first line between New York and Philadelphia in 1885. The American Bell Company became the world's largest corporation and, despite ongoing legal disputes during the 20th century, has supplied the United States with one of the most efficient communication systems in the world. (Courtesy of the Muncy Historical Society.)

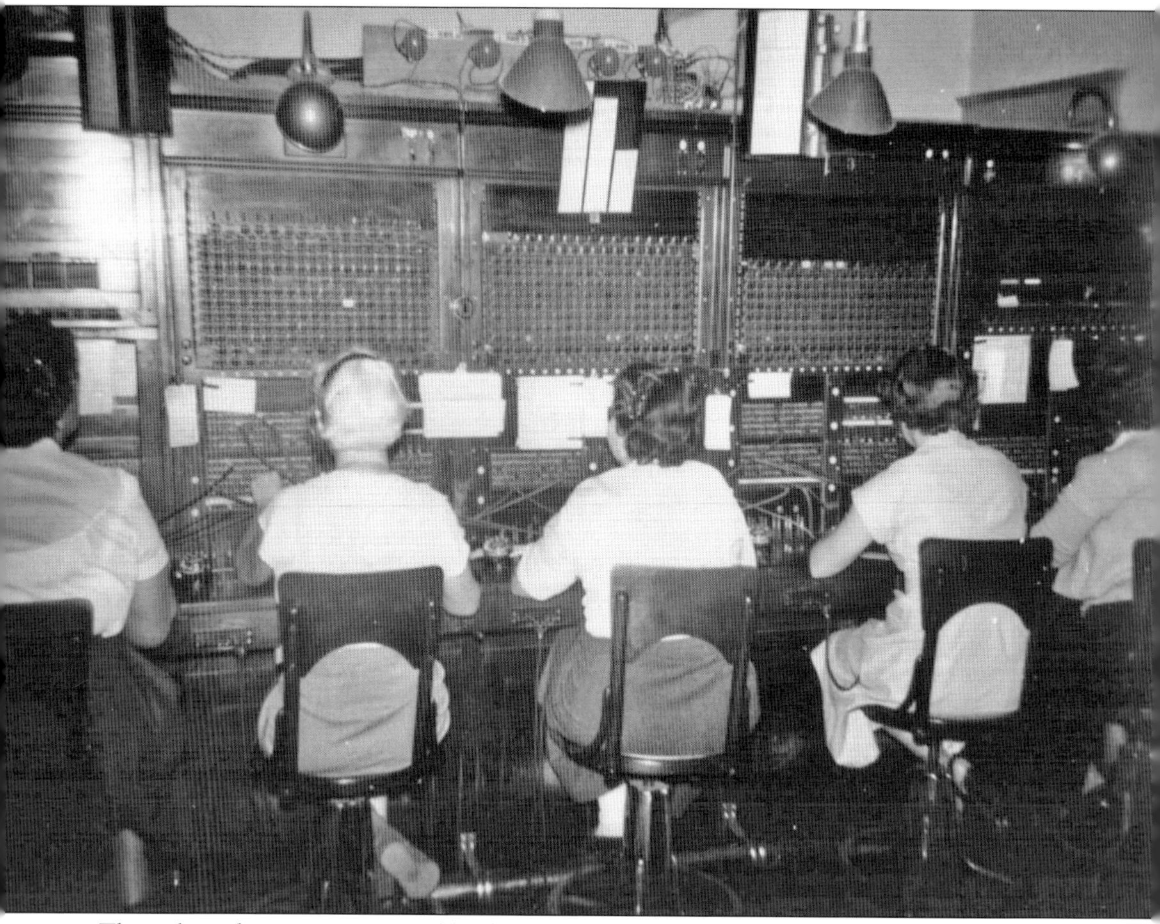

Throughout the country, women like the Muncy locals pictured here were employed as telephone operators for the Bell Telephone Company. In the early years, these switchboard operators served only a small number of people each day, but they often interacted with the same clients, creating an environment that required local knowledge of names, addresses, news, weather, and gossip. These jobs were not always as simple as flipping a switch—women were often required to do technical work such as testing trunk lines, splicing cables, or adjusting a lighter arrester. (Courtesy of the Muncy Historical Society.)

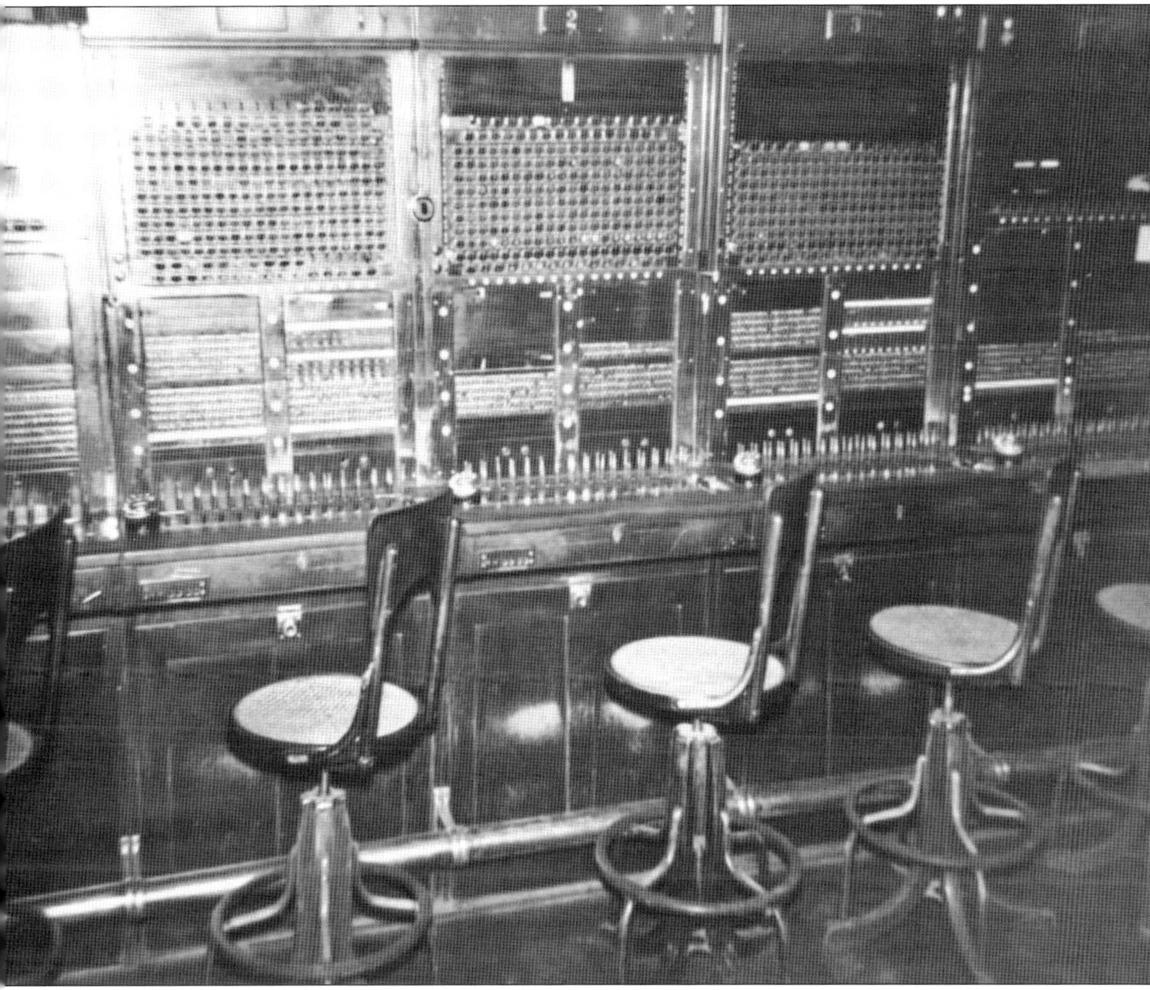

In 1965, Muncy resident Mildred Hall was sent as a guest of the Bell Telephone Company to the New York World's Fair. As a visitor to the fair, Hall would have experienced the new touch-tone push-button model, traveled through time on the history of communications ride, and played games in the Bell System exhibit hall. Among the new services of the company was "visible speech," where a device projected pictures of voices onto a television screen, showing that voices are "as distinctive as fingerprints." Younger visitors to the fair could call their favorite Disney characters and hear messages from them or have their ages guessed using the principles of telephone switching. (Courtesy of the Muncy Historical Society.)

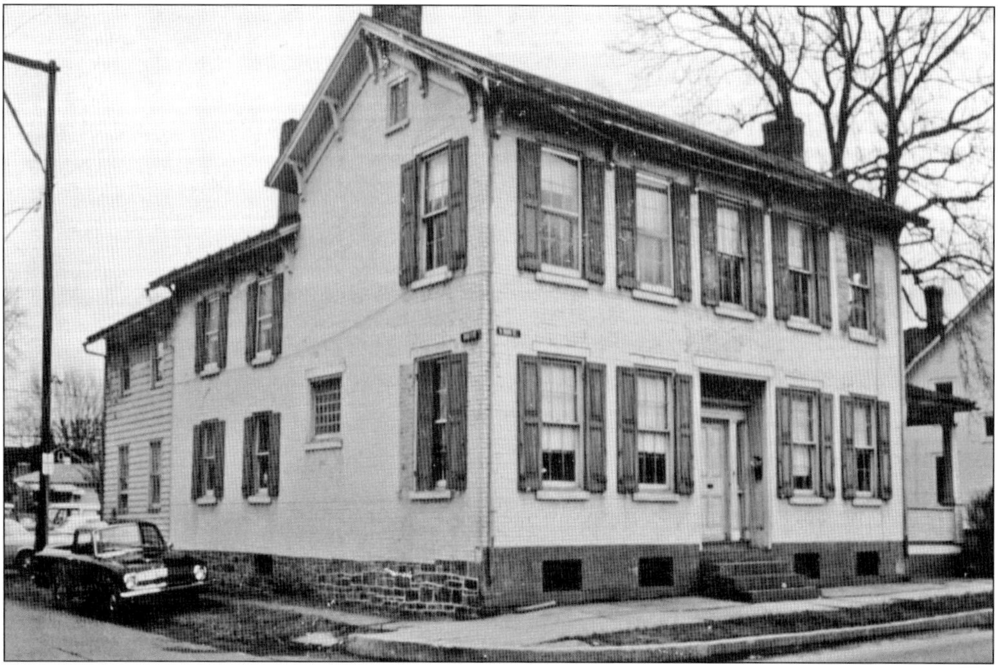

Torn down shortly after this February 1969 photograph, this house stood on the southeast corner of North Main and Mechanic Streets. In its place stands the Paul Geringer Social Hall, an outreach project of the Muncy Area Volunteer Fire Company. The hall is a vibrant part of the community, hosting everything from pancake breakfasts to antiques roadshows to town hall meetings to retirement ceremonies for civic and spiritual leaders. (Courtesy of the Muncy Historical Society.)

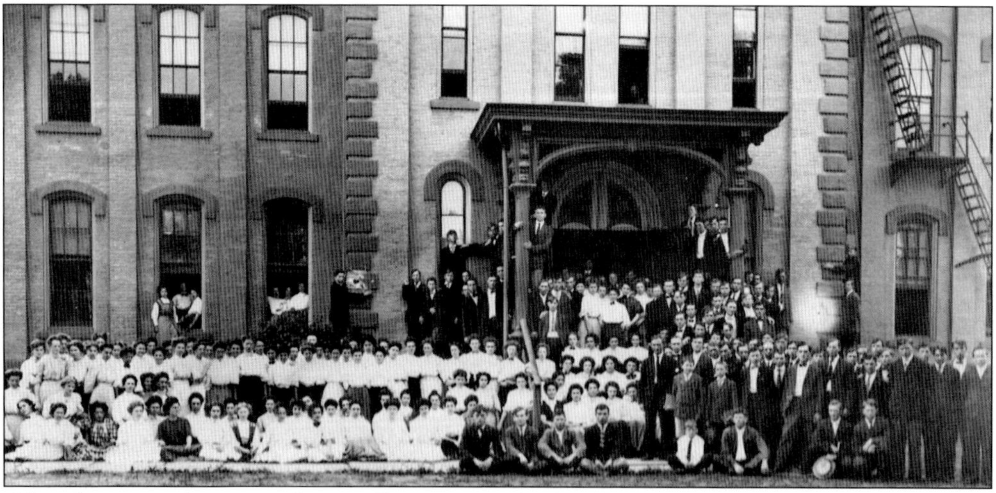

Often known today as teachers' colleges, normal schools were located across the country as institutions to train its students in teaching. The normal school opened in Muncy on April 10, 1870, and educated upwards of 100 scholars. Students included locals and even foreign residents, with two students from Mexico City and three from Cuba in 1905. The finalized building was a large project, costing $30,000, and community members were quick to support the school, with locals such as Augustus Foucart, a jeweler, donating $25 in 1880. (Courtesy of the Muncy Historical Society.)

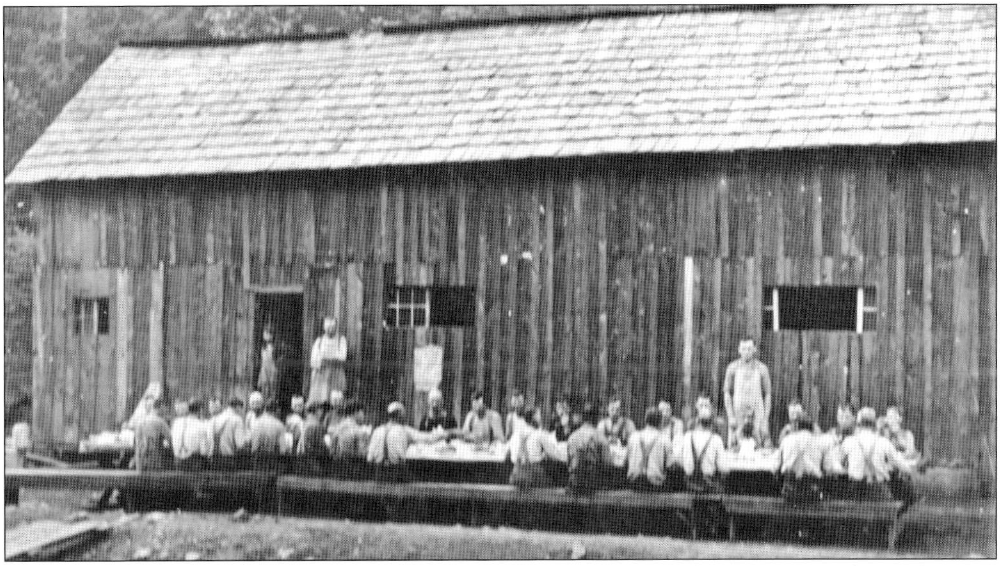

Muncy citizens Floyd More and Fred Lewis Cook traveled to Hillsgrove Township, a logging community about 35 miles north of Muncy, to join a logging camp in 1907. The back of this photograph reads, "C.W. Sones logging camp on Kettle Creek near Hillsgrove 1907. Floyd More Fred Lewis Cook near boy in the door." Logging was, is, and will be a profitable business in the area, as Pennsylvania's reputation as a forest state remains unrivaled. (Courtesy of the Muncy Historical Society.)

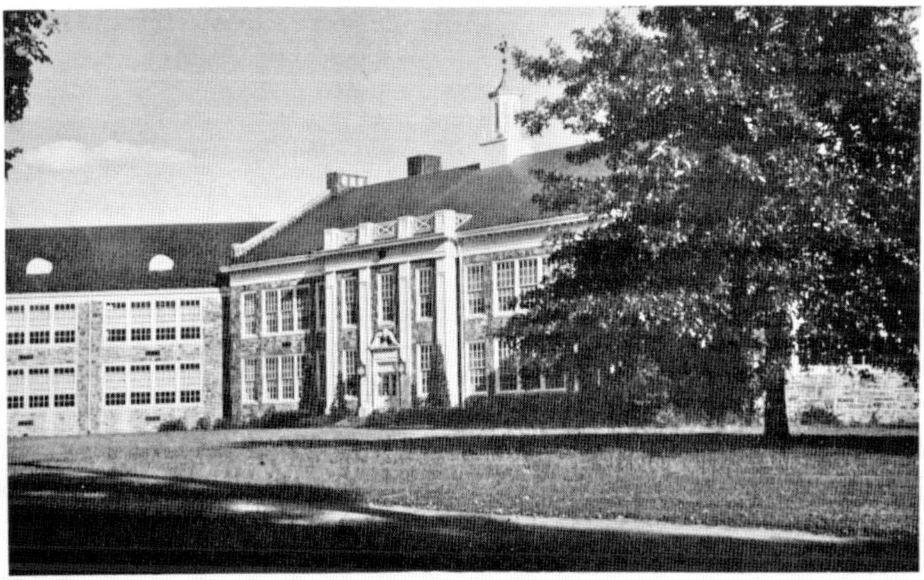

Muncy Joint School

This postcard shows what was known as the Muncy Joint School in the early 1900s. By 1834, there were over 20 schools in the area. The opening of Muncy Joint School in 1855 marked the first time that every student in the area had access to a high school education. The school would stand until 1932, when ground for the present school was broken. When it opened, it served a grand total of seven children, ranging from first grade to twelfth. (Author's collection.)

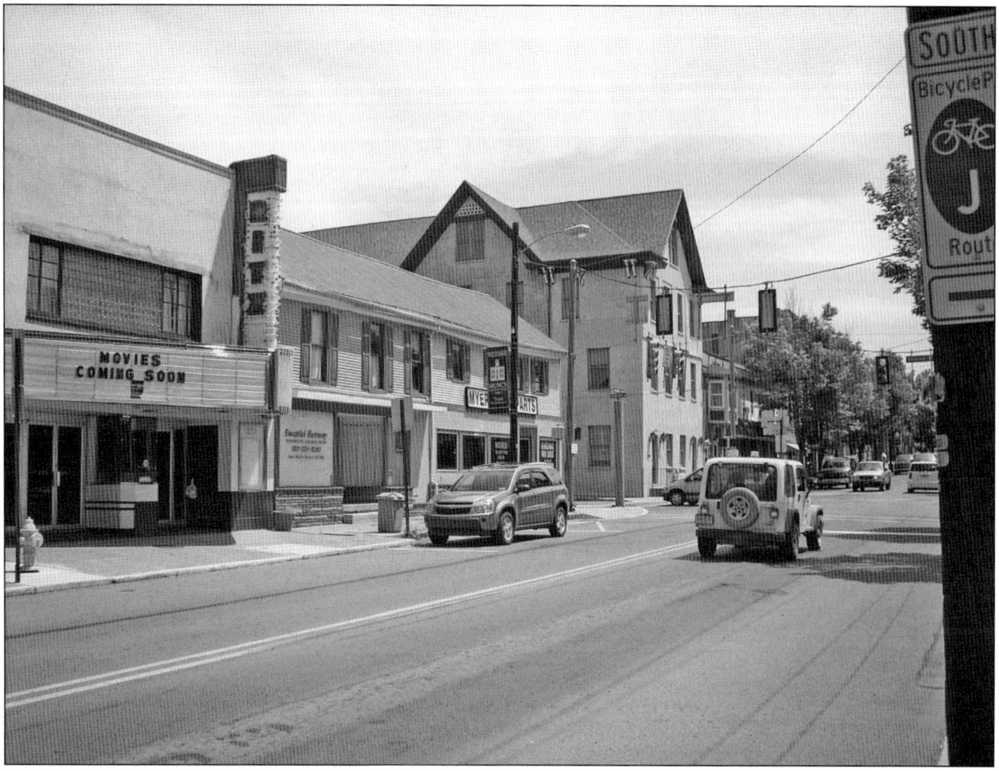

The Ritz Theatre opened in Muncy in the early 1920s with a showing of *The Queen of Sheba*, a film starring Betty Blythe (who was one of the first actresses to appear nude on camera) in the title role. After nearly a century of delighting Muncy audiences, the theater closed in 2014 with the failing health of present ownership. The building stands empty today, available for purchase to anyone who can meet the zoning requirements. The natives of Muncy still delight at the memories of decades of films, both silent and otherwise. (Author's collection.)

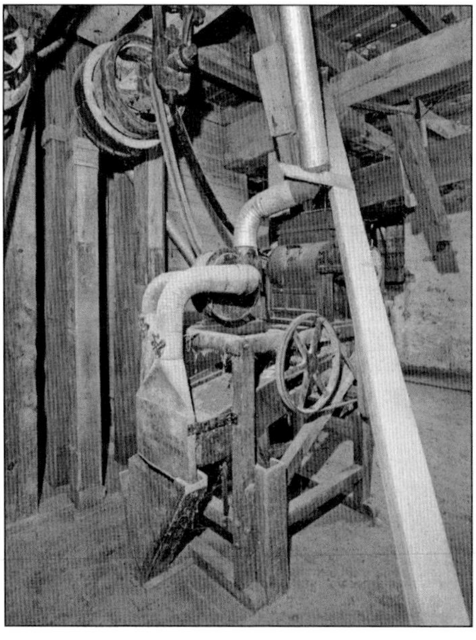

Among its many products, Sprout & Waldron sold mills for residential and commercial livestock use. In this photograph is a commercial corn-cracking mill. The mill was steam-powered, and corn kernels were fed through the top and between two heavy weights, which ground the kernels into a fine powder. The mill would be used to feed a variety of livestock, including cows, birds, and pigs. Today, most machines are mechanical, with metal blades. (Author's collection.)

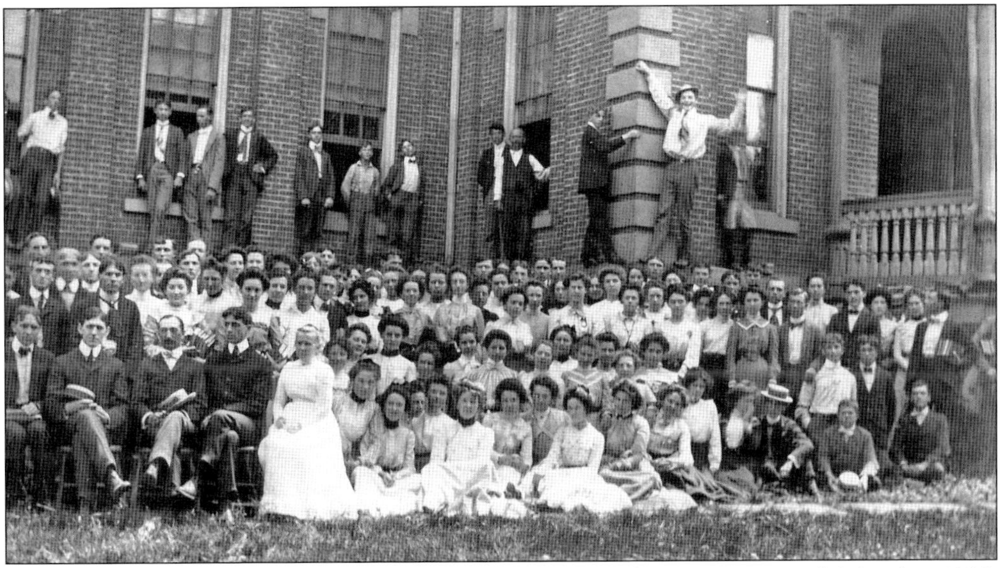

Smiling faces and serious students populate this picture of the Muncy Normal School in 1900. The school was first based in Montoursville, but due to its growth, it was moved to Muncy in 1877. The school also expanded past the typical teachers' course, offering both a college prep course and two scholarships to local high school students. Soon after this picture was taken, Prof. Harris A. Spotts was reelected as principal of the Muncy schools, with the school board giving him a salary of $10 a month, about $260 in today's money. (Courtesy of the Muncy Historical Society.)

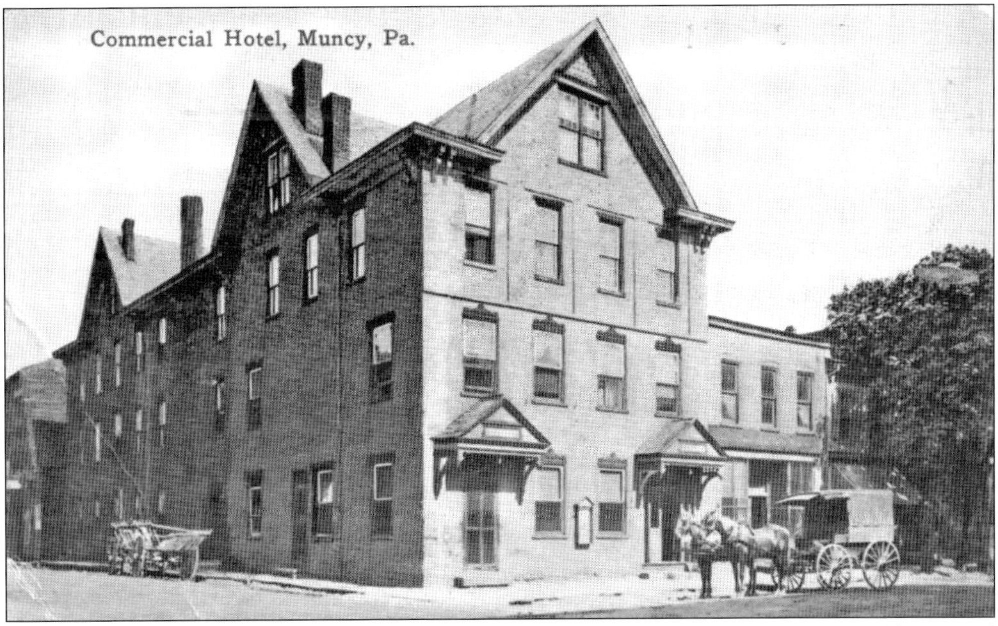

Shown here over 100 years ago is the Commercial Hotel in Muncy. It was once owned by Daniel Yothers, a former oilman who went belly-up three times, the worst of which occurred after oil was discovered in nearby Butler County. He fared better with the hotel; a book written in 1892 details the huge hit the hotel had become. Ads for the establishment can be found as late as 1917 in the *Muncy Luminary*. The success of the hotel led to Yothers being elected a councilman for the borough in 1886. (Author's collection.)

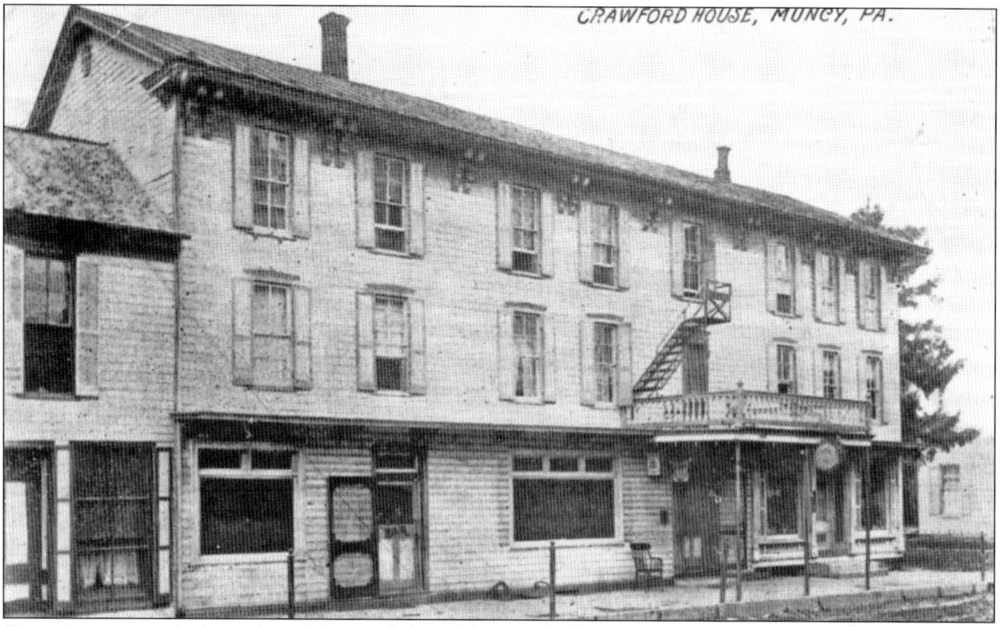

One theater guide lists the address of the old Crawford House Hotel at 19 North Main Street. Volume 13 of *Julius Cahn's Official Theatrical Guide*, published in 1908, also lists the Crawford House as an option for traveling theater fans. Before being known as the Crawford House Hotel, the inn was listed in 1841 as the Franklin Hotel. Initially owned by the Franklin family, it passed to John Shaffer and was an early popular hangout for temperance revivals. (Author's collection.)

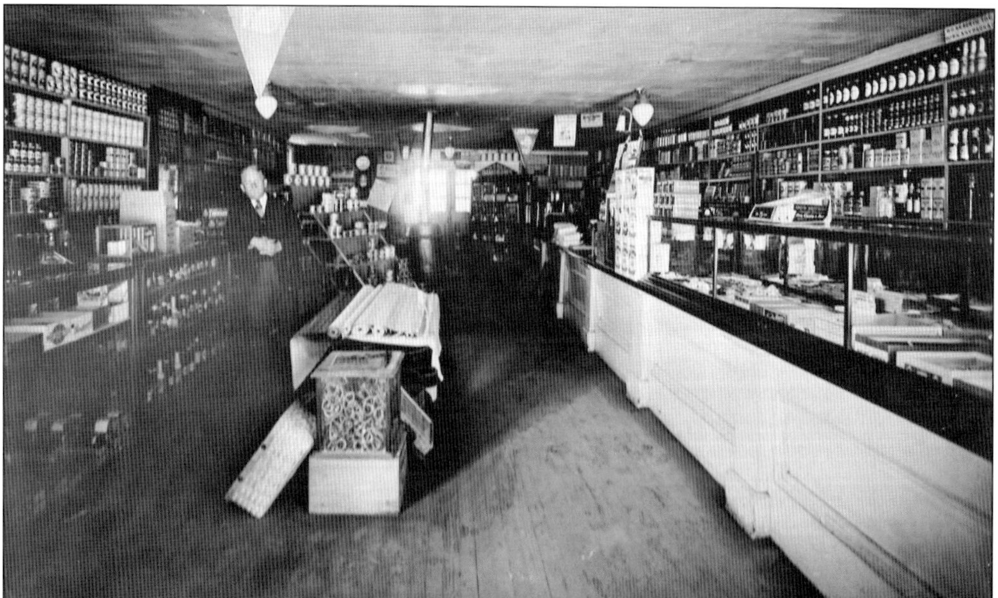

The interior of the Stolz grocery store in Muncy is shown here. The back of the photograph reads: "Old Stolz Grocery Store. Bruce Stolz (man on picture). Green trimmed churn with the words 'the gem' came out of this store." A grocery store served several purposes in this era, including foodstuffs, dry goods, and items needed for around the home, ranging from rat poison to gardening needs. (Courtesy of the Muncy Historical Society.)

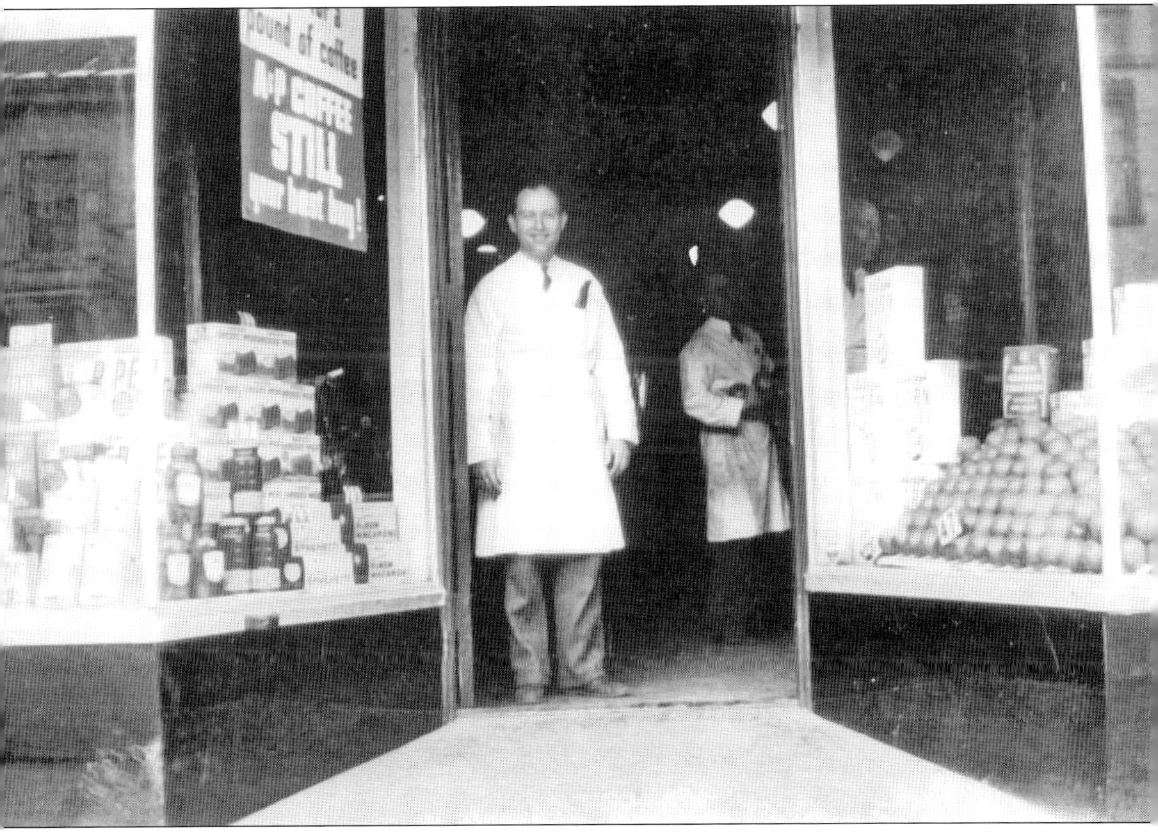

Shown here is an American grocery staple, the A&P. Although the chain is immortalized by John Updike in his eponymous short story (published in the *New Yorker* in 1961), each A&P has a history that goes well beyond Updike's story. The back of this photograph reads, "Donnie Balliet in front of Main St. A&P Store." Although the A&P was the largest grocery store chain in America from 1915 to 1975, the last corporate A&P store ceased operations in 2015. Lauded by many economists as a beacon of capitalism, today the chain stands as a stark warning against such excesses. (Courtesy of the Muncy Historical Society.)

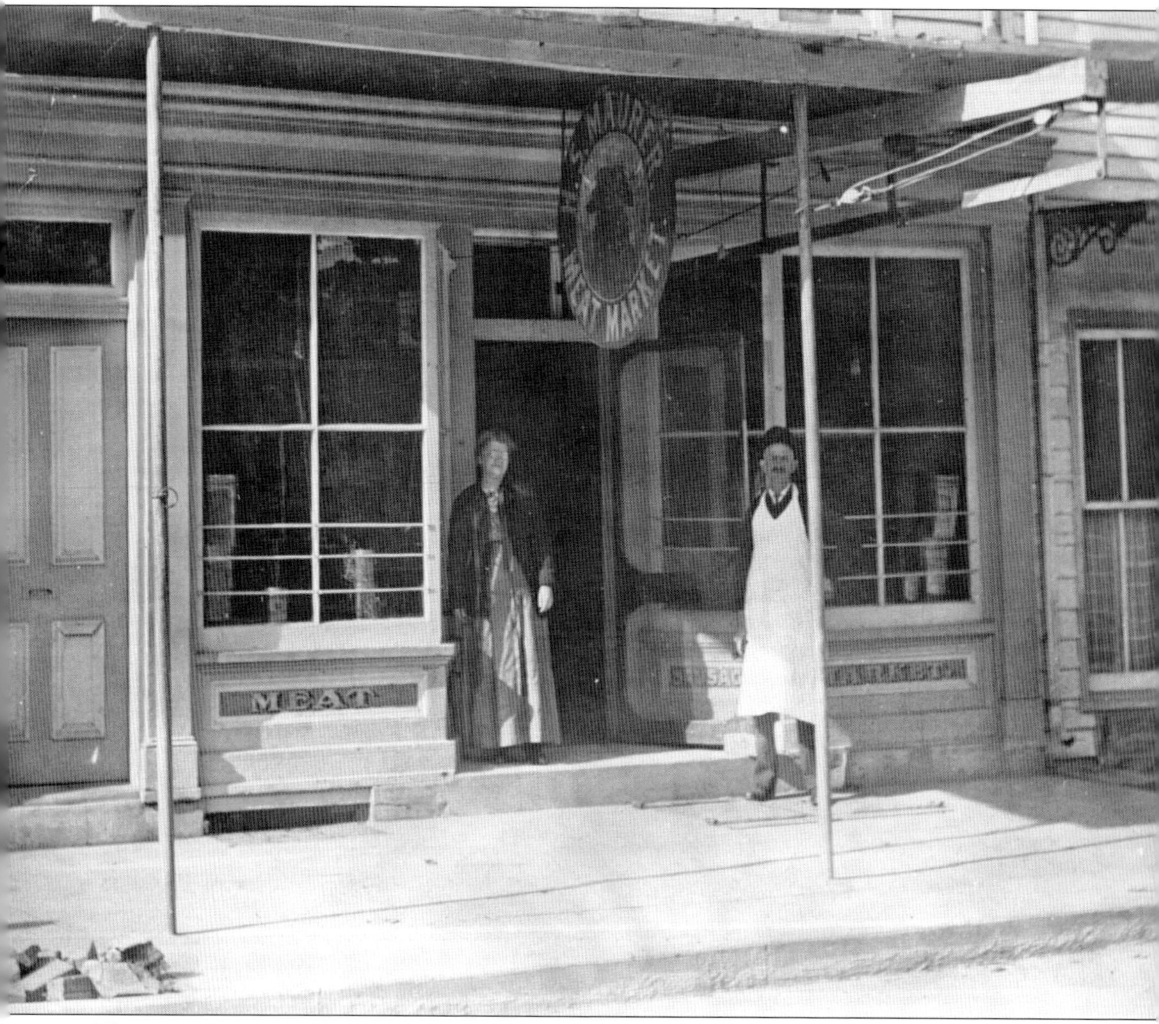

The Maurer Meat Market building has been owned by many Muncy residents. Beginning in 1885, Charles Maurer, a resident of Glade Run, established the meat market in Muncy. In 1965, while the building was undergoing renovation for the Byerly Meat Market, Harry Byerly found an old tintype of Henry Maurer, Charles's son and a previous owner. Maurer had sold the building to Dave Brass, who then sold out to Byerly. In 1939, Byerly purchased a sort of "meat mobile," selling meat from house to house, an investment the *Luminary* touted as "modern in all its appointments." (Courtesy of Bill Ritter.)

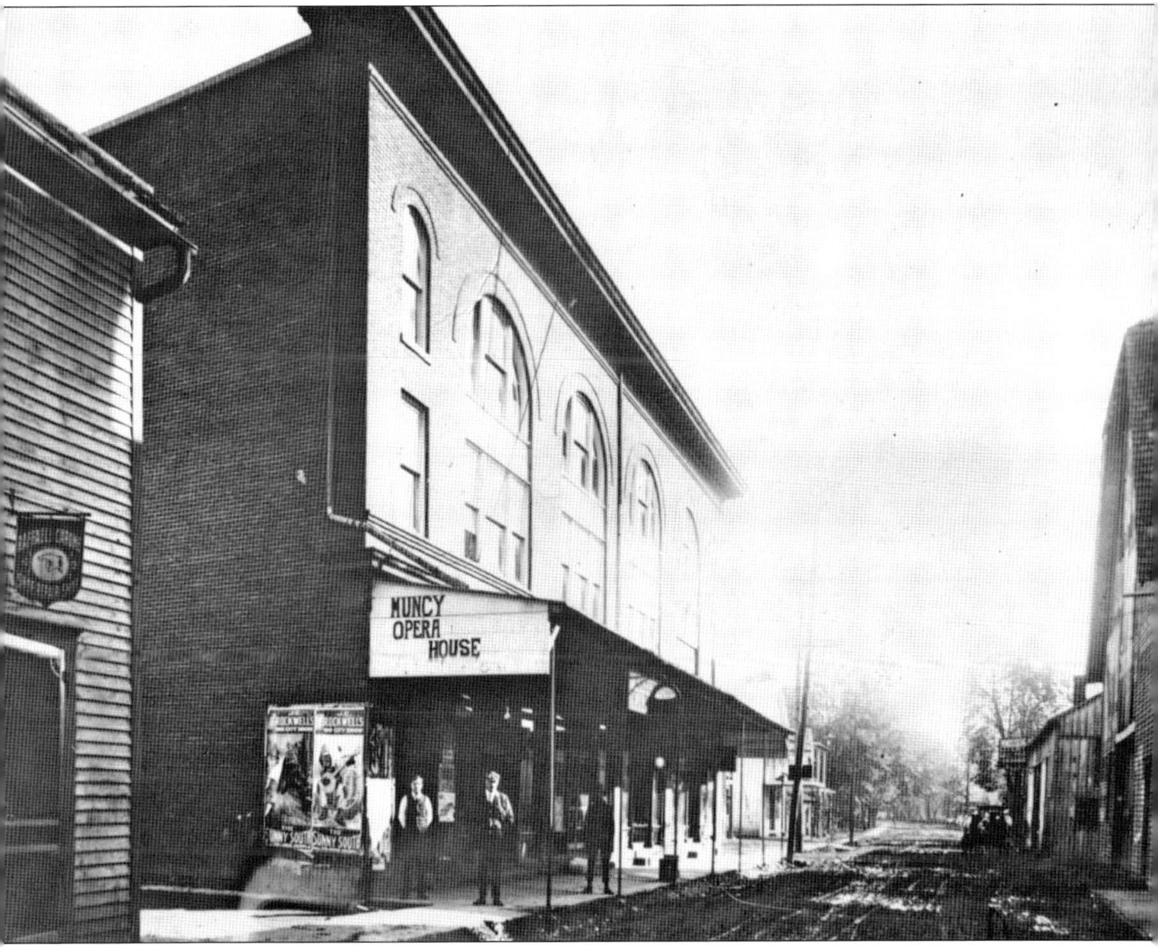

The Muncy Opera House was very active in the early part of the 20th century, with performances primarily consisting of photoplays, a theatrical play that has been filmed to be shown as a movie. Performances included European war pictures, Geraldine Farrar in *Maria Rosa*, and even a young woman from California advertised as a "mentalist." The building was also used as a meetinghouse: a mass meeting to discuss food control rules and the need for food conservation was held here during World War I. Today, the opera house looks to reestablish its connections to the community, as it is being considered for the Muncy Resiliency Project, which looks to show other communities how to reincorporate aging infrastructure. (Courtesy of the Muncy Historical Society.)

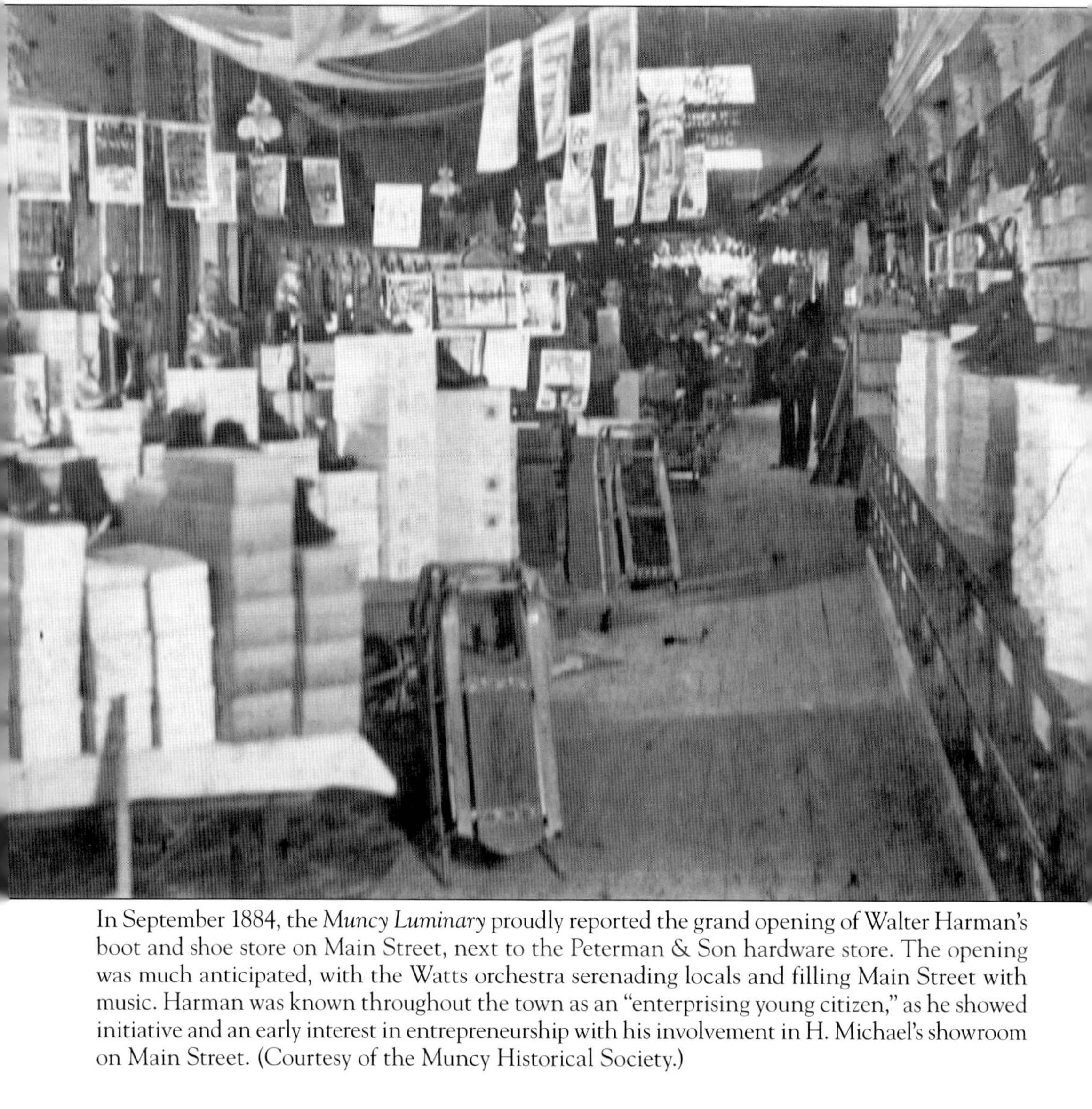

In September 1884, the *Muncy Luminary* proudly reported the grand opening of Walter Harman's boot and shoe store on Main Street, next to the Peterman & Son hardware store. The opening was much anticipated, with the Watts orchestra serenading locals and filling Main Street with music. Harman was known throughout the town as an "enterprising young citizen," as he showed initiative and an early interest in entrepreneurship with his involvement in H. Michael's showroom on Main Street. (Courtesy of the Muncy Historical Society.)

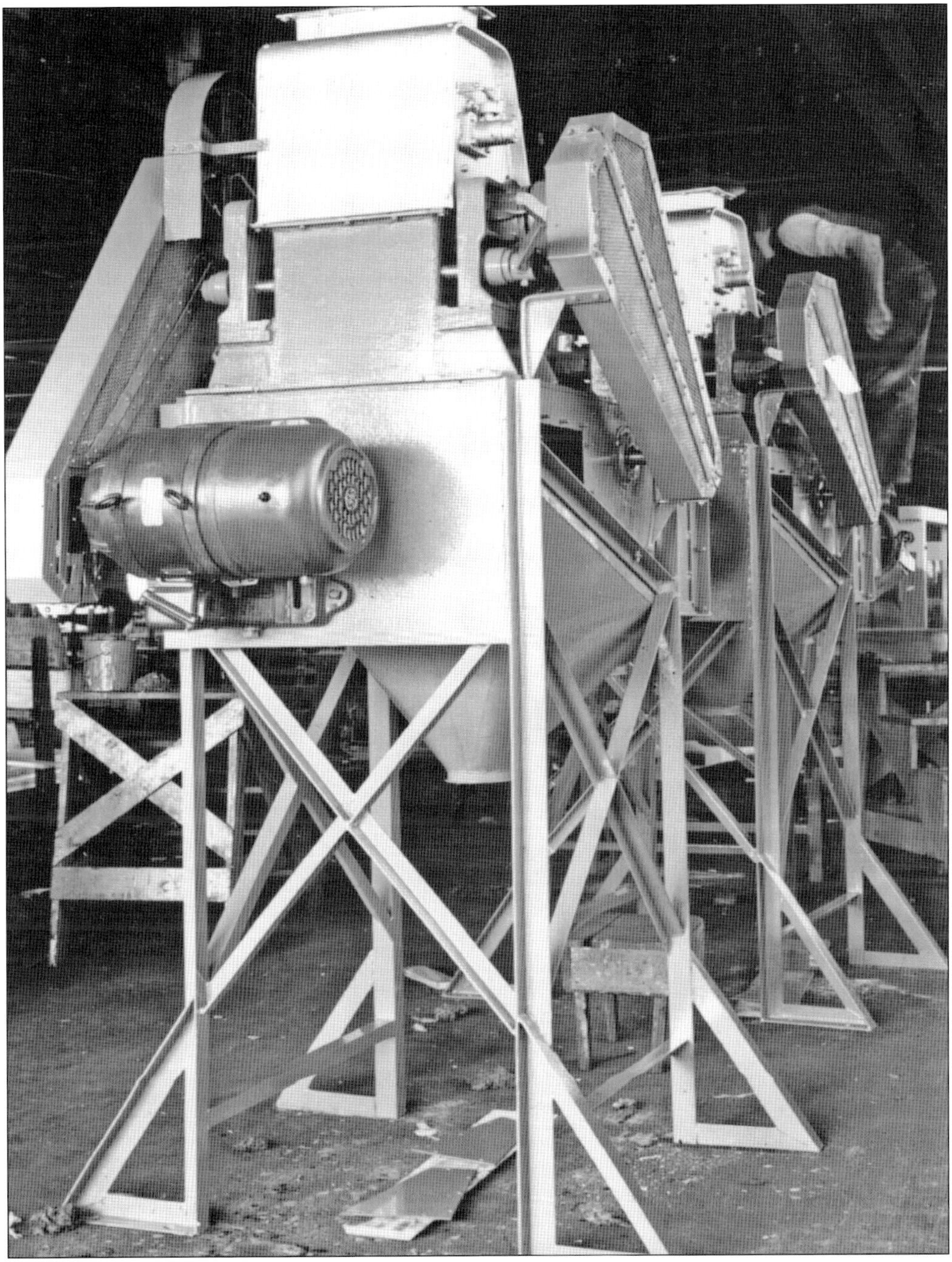

This photograph shows an employee working on a piece of machinery in the Sprout & Waldron factory sometime after the 1960 flood. Although there have been several name and ownership changes during its existence, according to current ownership, the business can trace its roots back to two companies: Sprout & Waldron, which was founded in 1866, and the Bauer Brothers Company, which was founded in 1878. Machinery like this came into use in 1932, when the company shifted its focus from coal and wood to the feed industry. (Courtesy of the Muncy Historical Society.)

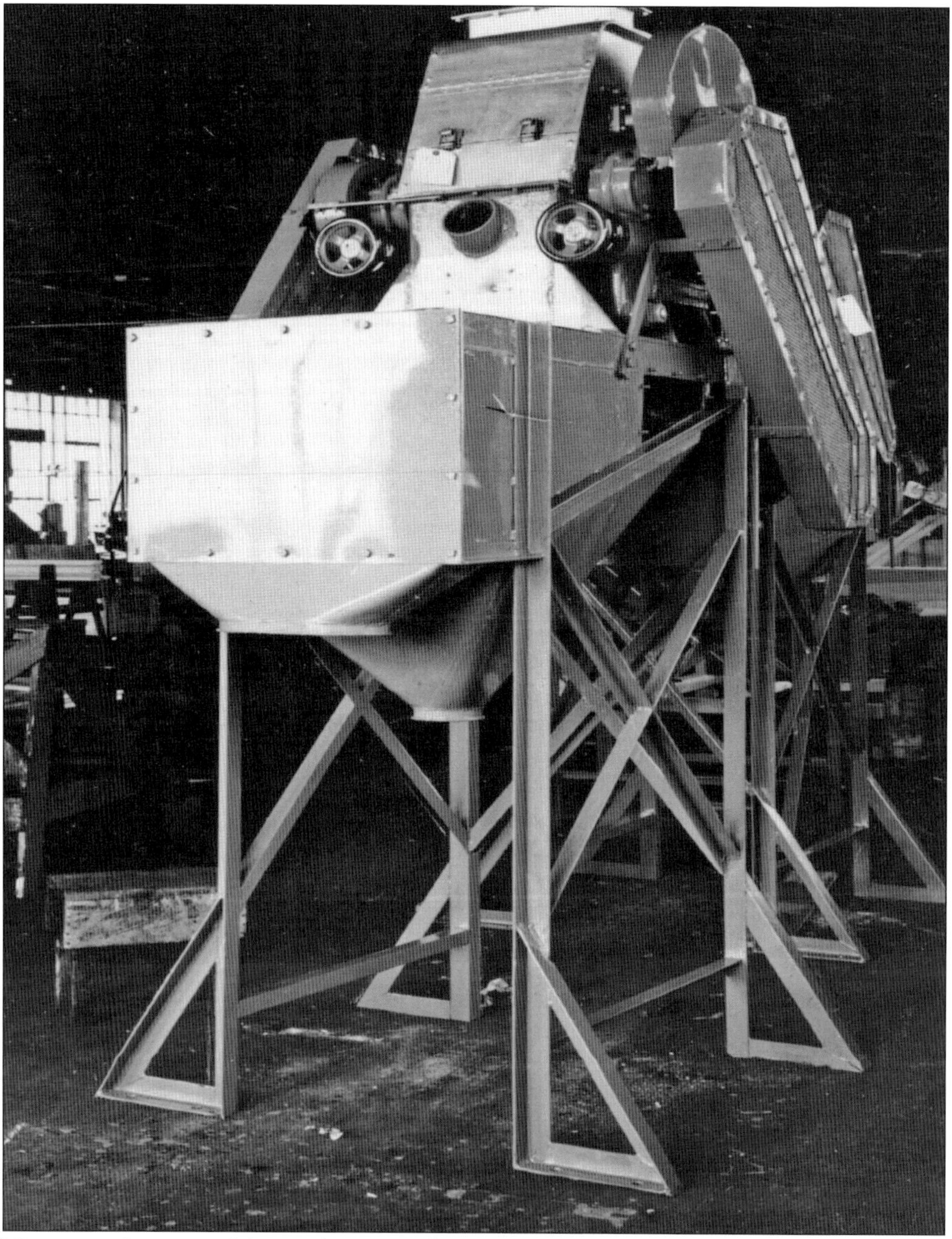

This is another view of the machinery used by Sprout & Waldron in the 1960s. The company was purchased in 1990 by the Andritz Group, which deals in feed and industrial machinery as well as biomass processing and other processing industries. The company has offices in Muncy, Denmark, the Netherlands, Germany, France, the United Kingdom, Brazil, Mexico, Chile, Colombia, Vietnam, India, and China. (Courtesy of the Muncy Historical Society.)

Six

Fortunate Ones
Military and Service in Muncy

If the ride of Rachel Silverthorne was any indicator, the tradition of loyalty and service to the United States shown by the people of Muncy would end up being unrivaled by any other place in rural America. And while nearby Williamsport may serve today as the molder of young men and the American spirit of service and participation with the Little League World Series, Muncy's legacy is rooted more in the blood, sweat, and tears that make sacrifice for America the hallowed, honored tradition that it is. Muncy has sent at least one of its children to service in every major conflict in the history of the United States, and the list of dead and maimed is staggering for such a small town.

To limit the service of those in Muncy to military action would be shortsighted, however. The Muncy Police Department and the Keystone Hook and Ladder Company have served the area through 22 floods since 1936, to say nothing of crime prevention, justice, and the innumerable fires that have plagued the area since its inception. Civic groups such as the Muncy Professional and Business Association, the Muncy Rotary, Muncy Veterans of Foreign Wars Post 3428, Muncy Lodge 299 of the Free and Accepted Masons, and many Boy and Girl Scout troops throughout its history have sought to instill a sense of pride and accomplishment in the locals.

Not all heroes wear capes, and not every hero's story takes place on the battlefield. Muncy's teachers, politicians, druggists, and athletes have all done their parts to make the community proud, and the pictures that follow put this sense of civic pride and duty on full display. This sense of honor and duty is one that is consistently passed down from one generation to the next in the area, and those that follow the forebearers of the community do everything in their power to ensure the service of Muncy's past is honored by the work and deeds of Muncy's present. Their stories will one day add to the legend and stories presented here.

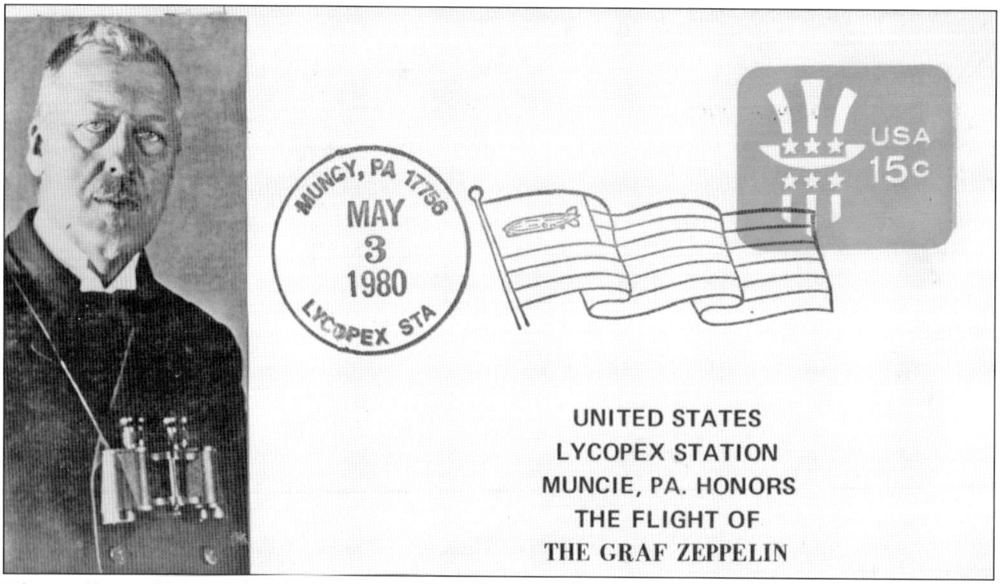

The spelling of Muncy has been a complicated and varied topic. This example shows one of the many ways the town's name was spelled, often a result of whether the speller was Dutch, English, French, or Irish. Additional variations depended on the education level of the writer, as other possible spellings have included Monsey, Muncey, Munsey, Munsee, Minsi, Munci, Muncee, Muncie, and Munzey. Originally, the name was derived from a tribe of Delaware Indians, the Munsees, who carried their linguistic imprint all the way to Indiana with the town of Muncie. (Author's collection.)

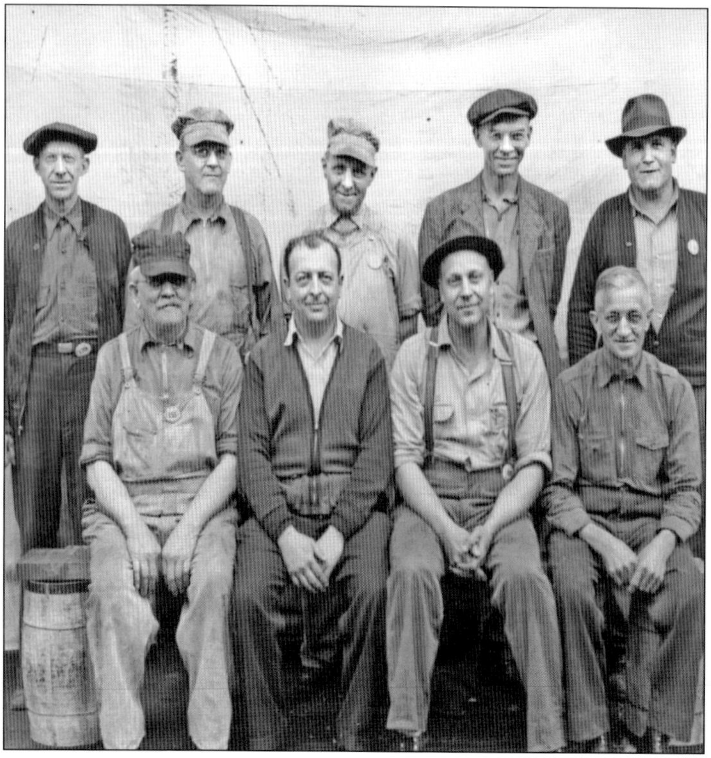

Shown here are the shop supervisors at the Sprout & Waldron factory in March 1942, when the factory had ramped up production to assist in the war effort. From left to right are (first row) Tom Hess, Ralph Feigles, Jim Hitesman, and Charles Frey; (second row) Frank Berger, Ray Voneida, Fred Murray, Walter "Salty" Gottschall, and Foster Klingerman. Not pictured is Harry Gundrum. Sprout & Waldron primarily manufactured equipment for the pulp and paper industries. (Courtesy of the Muncy Historical Society.)

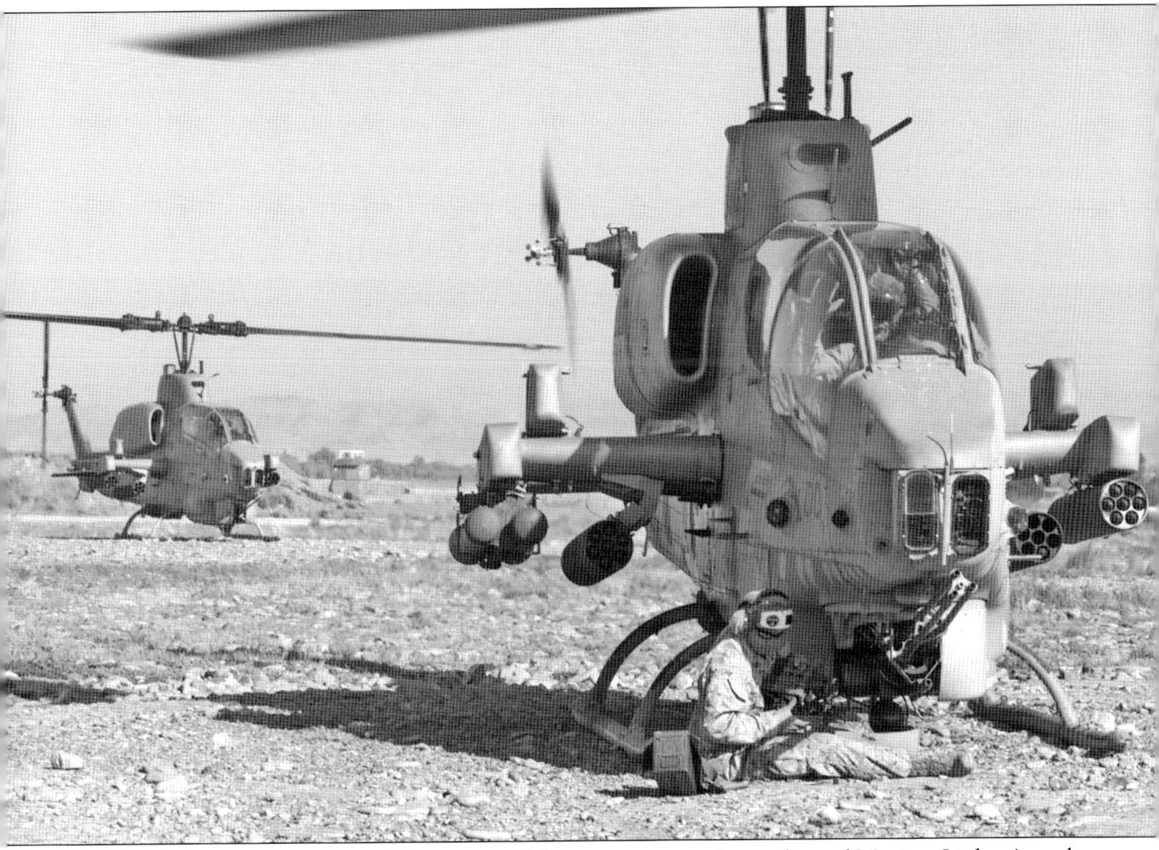

Shown here is S.Sgt. Daniel Demuro, a Muncy native and member of Marine Light Attack Helicopter Squadron 773, during the war in Afghanistan in 2004. Staff Sergeant Demuro is one of a long line of veterans from Muncy to have served the United States overseas; in fact, Muncy has been represented in every war from the French and Indian War to current military operations around the world. In this photograph, Staff Sergeant Demuro is repairing the 20-millimeter nose cannon of an AH-1W Super Cobra while on Forward Operating Base Salerno, Afghanistan. This photograph was taken by S.Sgt. Rusty Baker. (Courtesy of the Library of Congress.)

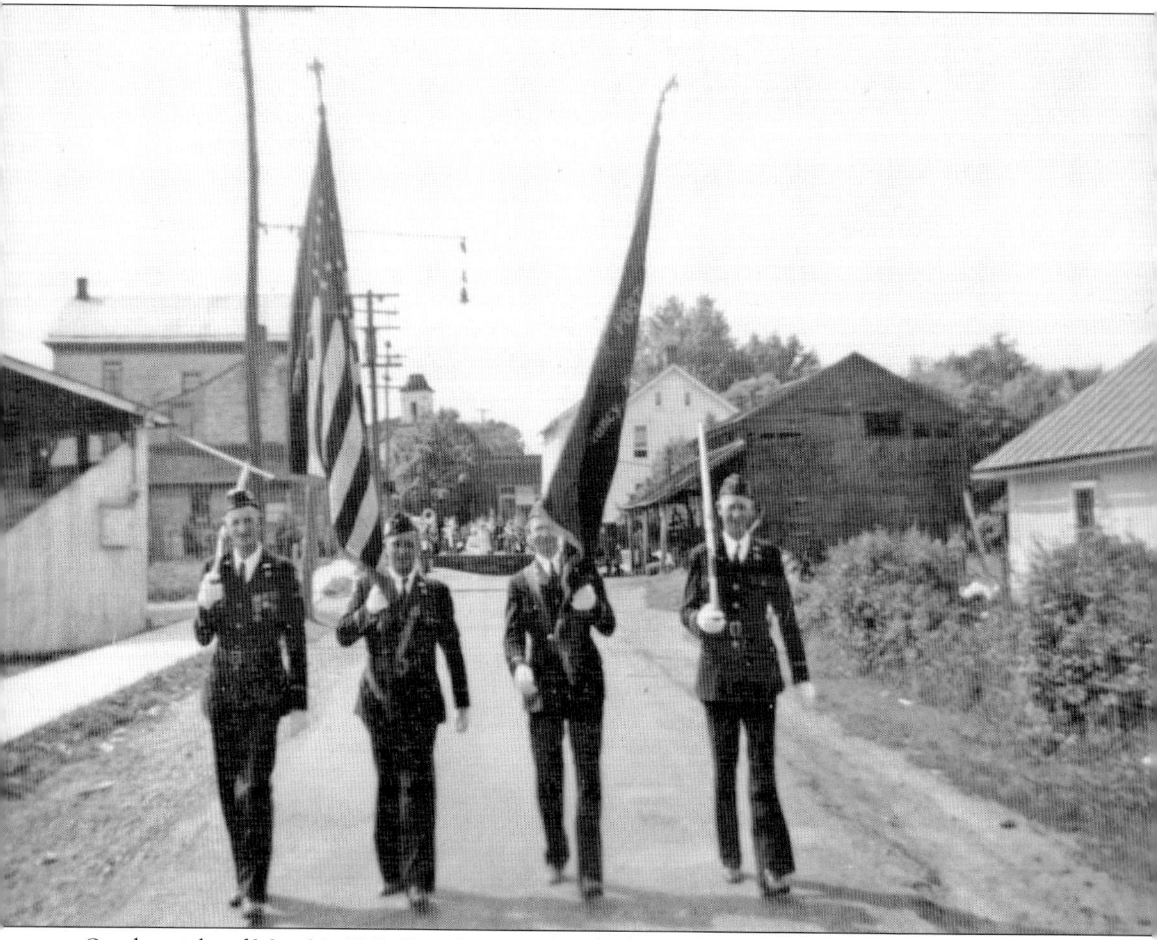

On the night of May 30, 1942, British troops bombed Cologne, bringing World War II inside of Germany for the first time. With the war persisting, Memorial Day would have been especially meaningful to residents of the United States. The following day, May 31, the Muncy Color Guard proudly walked in the Memorial Day Parade in Turbotville. Home to hundreds of war veterans, Muncy remains a vibrant town on Memorial Day—local students visit the cemetery to honor veterans with flags, the Lions Club celebrates with a barbecue, and local veterans continue to walk in the Memorial Day Parade. (Courtesy of the Muncy Historical Society.)

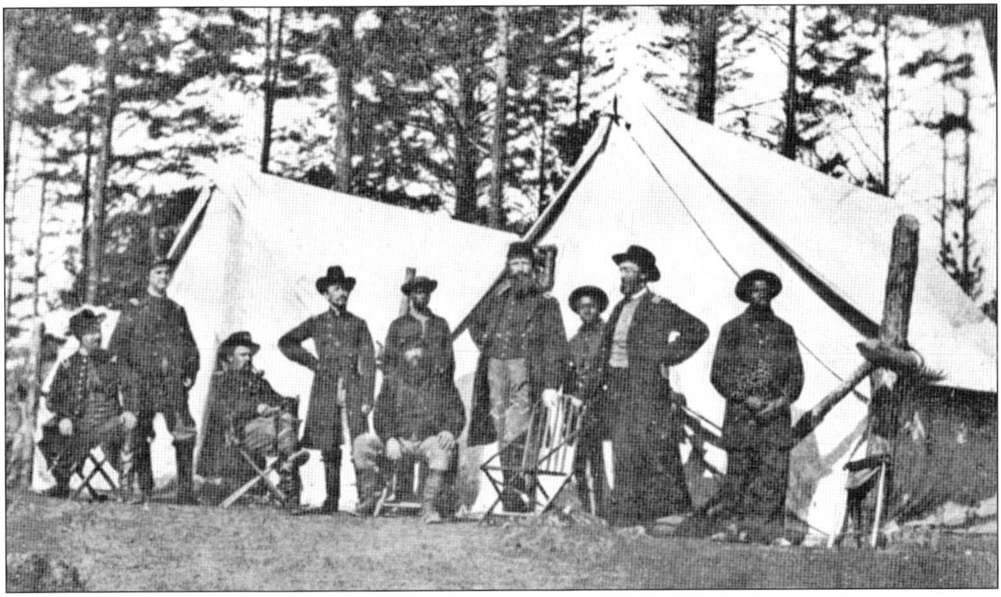

The 131st Pennsylvania Volunteers are encamped near Muncy during the Civil War. The group formed near Harrisburg in August 1862 and spent nine months contributing to the Union war effort before being mustered out on May 23, 1863. They participated in three battles: Antietam, Fredericksburg, and Chancellorsville. The group suffered 83 deaths during the war, although more men died due to disease than battle. (Author's collection.)

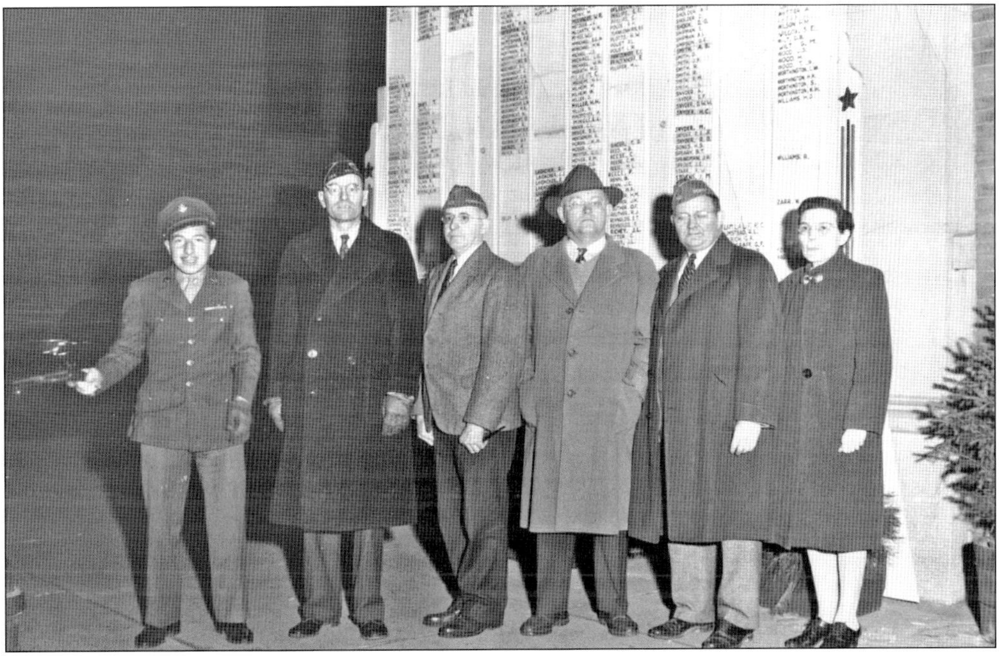

On January 1, 1945, the Germans initiated Operation Bodenplatte, an attempt to recover air superiority against Allied forces. On the same day, this image was taken of Muncy service representatives. From left to right are Angelo Butera, John Hagerman, Bill Wolf, Pete Link, Bob Mitchel, and Mae Reed. World War II would come to an end in September of this year. (Courtesy of the Muncy Historical Society.)

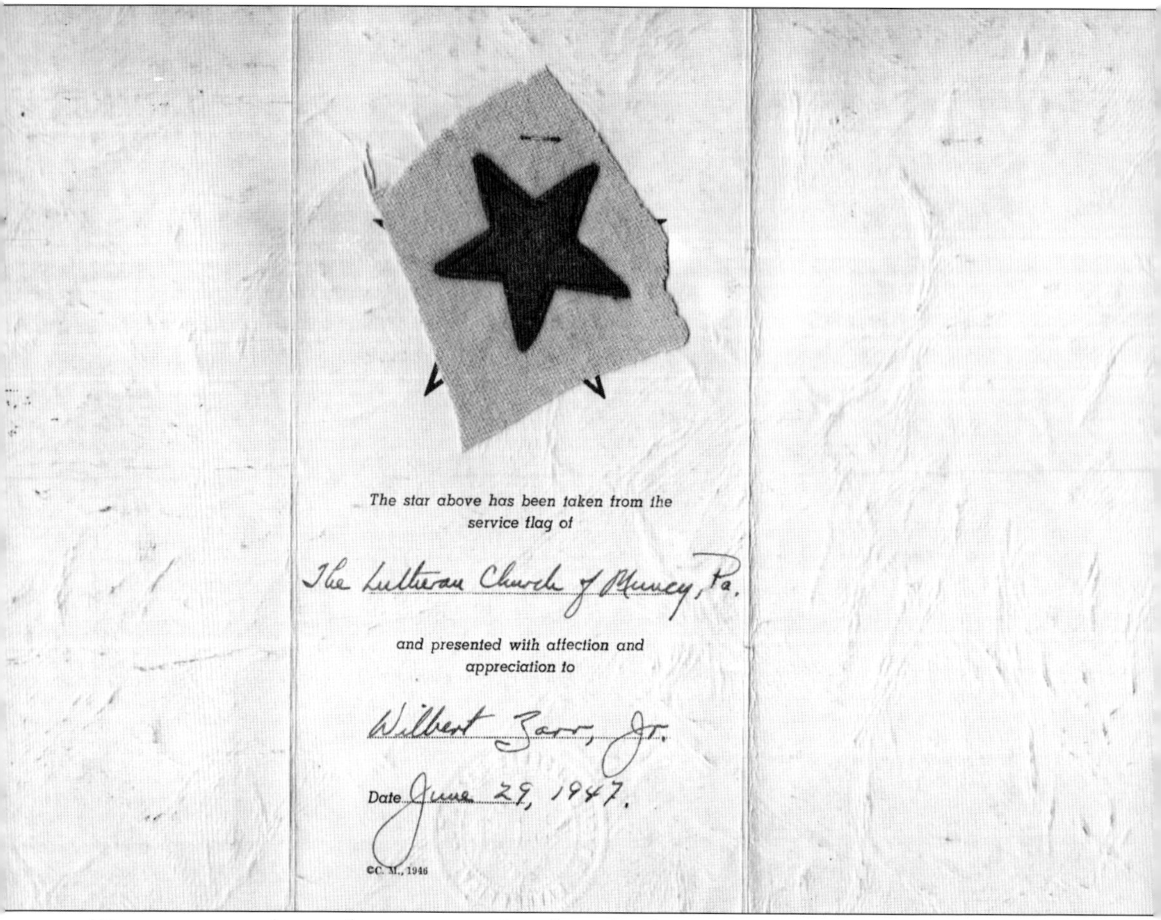
The star above has been taken from the service flag of

The Lutheran Church of Muncy, Pa.

and presented with affection and appreciation to

Wilbert Barr, Jr.

Date June 29, 1947.

©C. M., 1946

This star is one of many from a service flag, flown by the families of soldiers in various conflicts to signify the number and status of family members participating in the conflict. A blue star stood for a soldier, and a gold one stood for a soldier who had passed away. The churches of Muncy took it a step further, with a blue star for each member of their congregations. When a soldier returned, his star was removed and presented to him. This star belonged to World War II vet Wilbert Barr Jr., a member of the Lutheran church. (Courtesy of the Muncy Historical Society.)

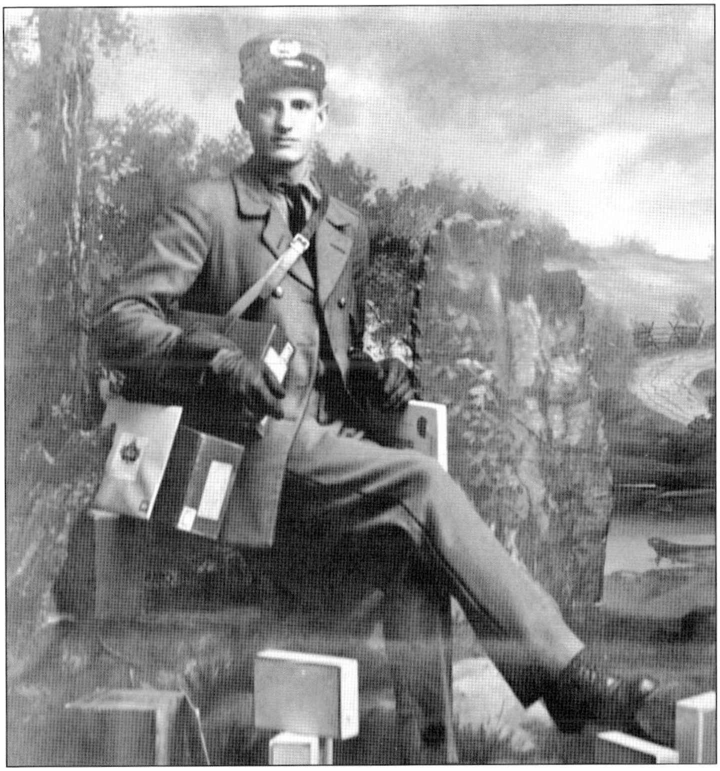

Beginning in 1912, Brady Snyder was employed as the parcel post carrier of the Muncy Post Office. In 1917, he started training with the Army at Camp Hancock. Before leaving, he received two testimonials regarding his fine service and a safety razor outfit from the postmaster. His activities frequently made the news, with the *Luminary* reporting in April 1913 that his horse became frightened at a newspaper blowing toward him and ran the streets of Muncy until it was captured by Bud Gortner. (Courtesy of the Muncy Historical Society.)

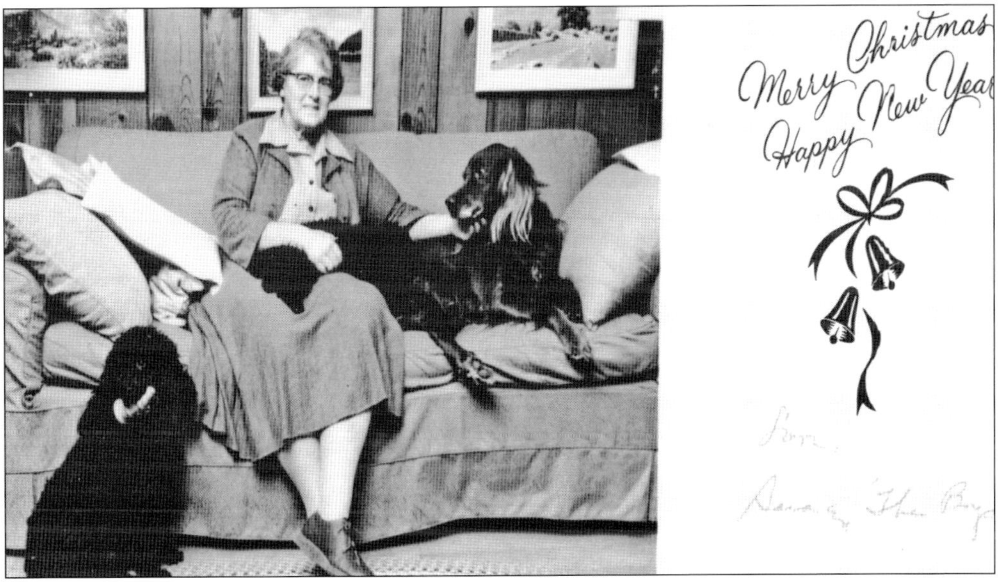

This photographic postcard shows Dr. Sara Anna Hall with her three pooches, who were, without a doubt, very good boys. Dr. Hall served as a doctor and saw the Sprout family move into a home that she had vacated. The back of this Christmas card reads, "Dear Jessie (McMichael), Supper Sunday night Dec. 30th at 6 P.M. Hope the weather is somewhat better by then. (Anna). Dr. Sara Hall." (Courtesy of the Muncy Historical Society.)

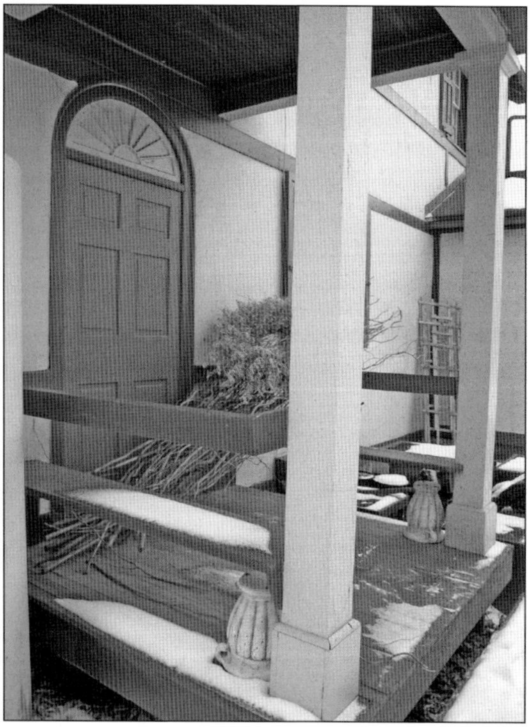

This fake door is on the McCarty-Wertman house. In the process of protecting slaves from sadistic masters and runaway slave patrols, homes such as the McCarty-Wertmans' would include some extreme elements. These included underground passages, hidden cellars, and, in this case, a fake door to throw off anyone who might try to enter the house without the acknowledgement of the owners. Such measures ensured the liberation of those who had fled. (Courtesy of the Muncy Historical Society.)

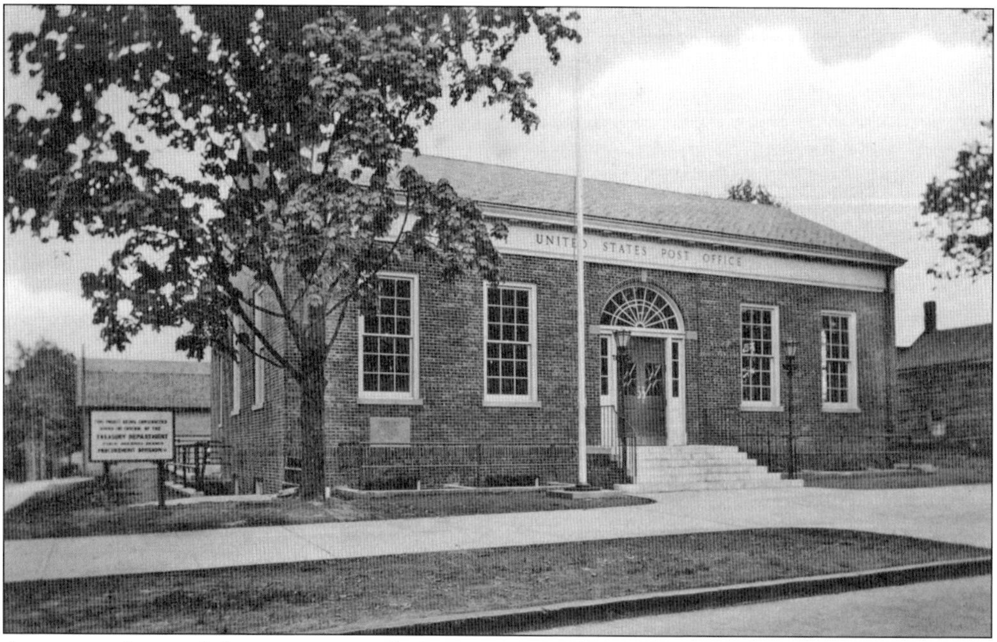

An essential part of the community, the Muncy Post Office celebrates over 200 years of service. The post office was first established in 1800, with Henry Shoemaker serving as the town's first postmaster. By 1905, business had increased so much as to elevate the post office to second class, which created new titles of assistant postmaster and clerk. In May 1967, the post office delivered its last mail by train. A structural memory of years past, the post office today still retains its fallout shelter. (Courtesy of the Muncy Historical Society.)

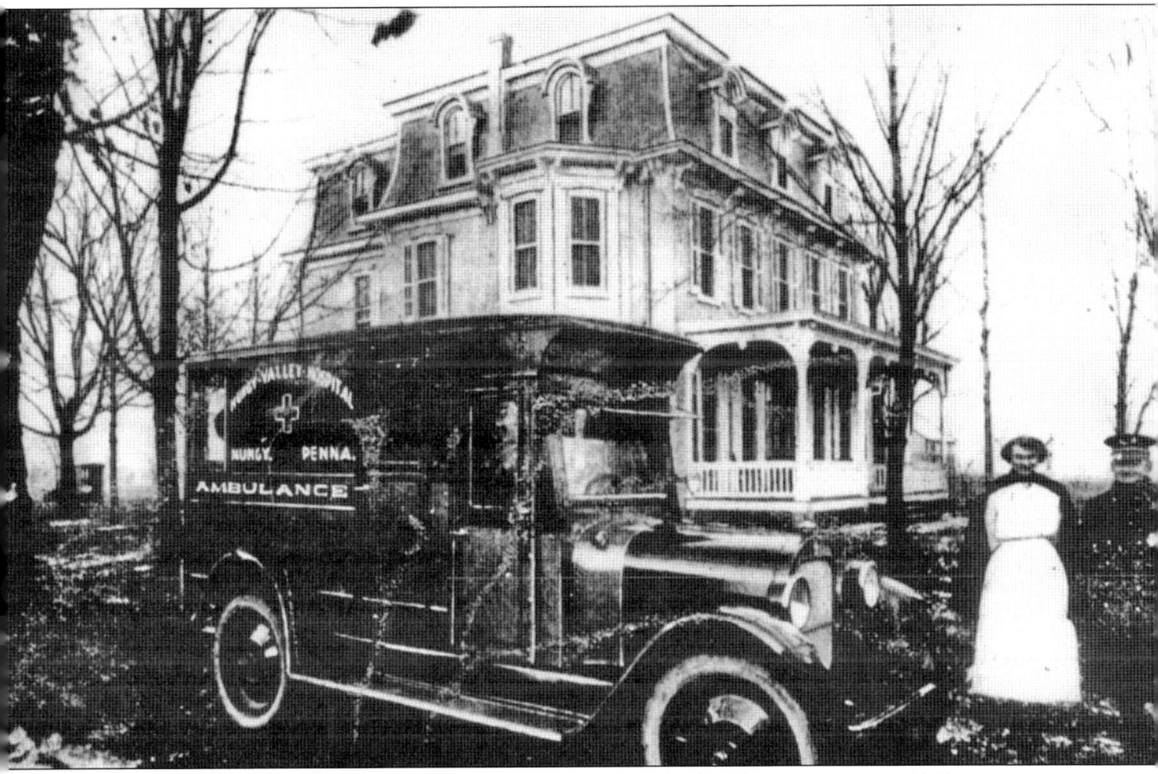

Though the Muncy Valley Hospital officially opened to the local community in 1923, its origins began in 1920 with the collaboration of doctors from the surrounding towns, including Dr. George Metzger, Dr. A.P. Hull, Dr. Alvin Poust, Dr. D.E. Kiess, Dr. Charles D. Voorhees, Dr. T.T. Gilmore, Dr. H.F. Baker, and Dr. T.K. Wood. The hospital was originally the Noble Mansion, home of the "Merchant Prince of Muncy," Ernest Noble. With the renovation of the Noble home, the Muncy Valley Hospital made health services much more accessible, as the closest hospital at the time was 12 miles from Muncy. (Courtesy of Bill Ritter.)

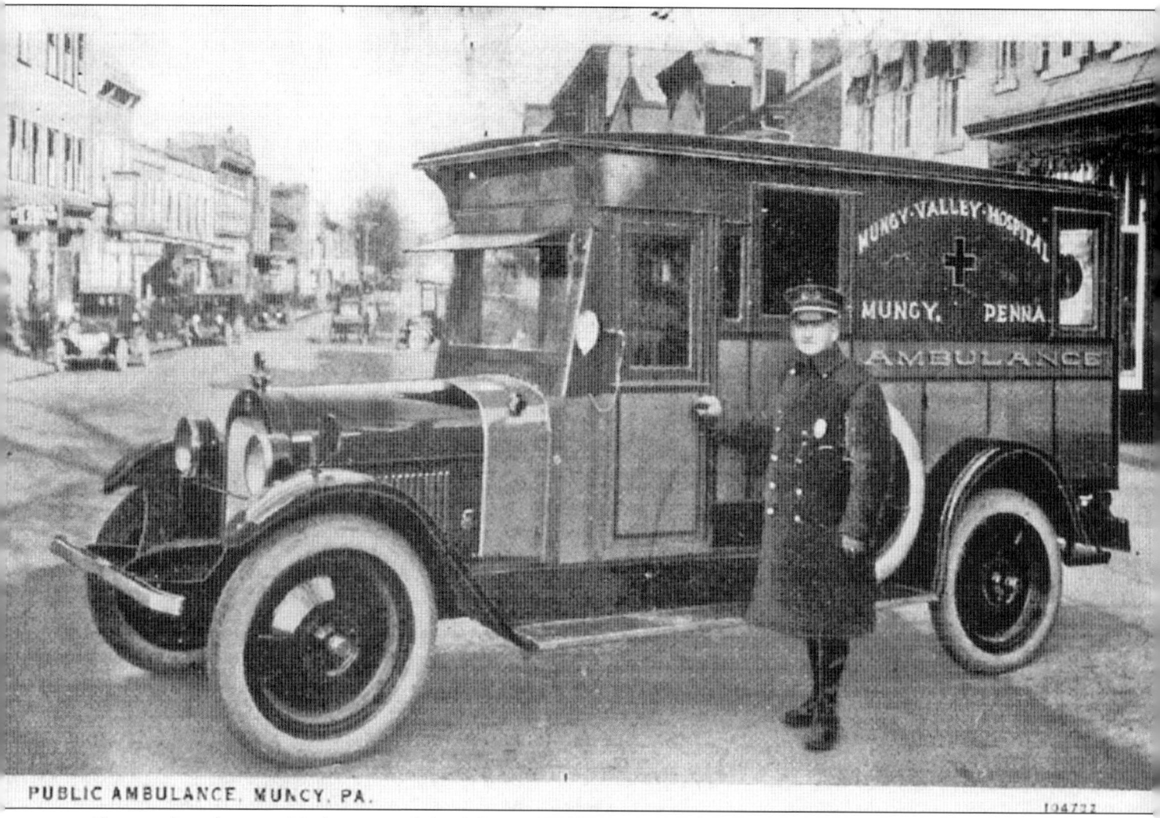

Soon after the establishment of the Muncy Valley Hospital, public funding enabled the addition of a modern ambulance. Designed and built by local Arthur Fisher, the vehicle was equipped with a first aid kit, hot and cold water, and a pulmotor, a device that provided oxygen to patients. In the early 20th century, the closest hospital was in Williamsport, over 12 miles away. Bad roads contributed to tough traveling, so physicians from the surrounding area banded together to provide a closer option for health services. (Courtesy of Bill Ritter.)

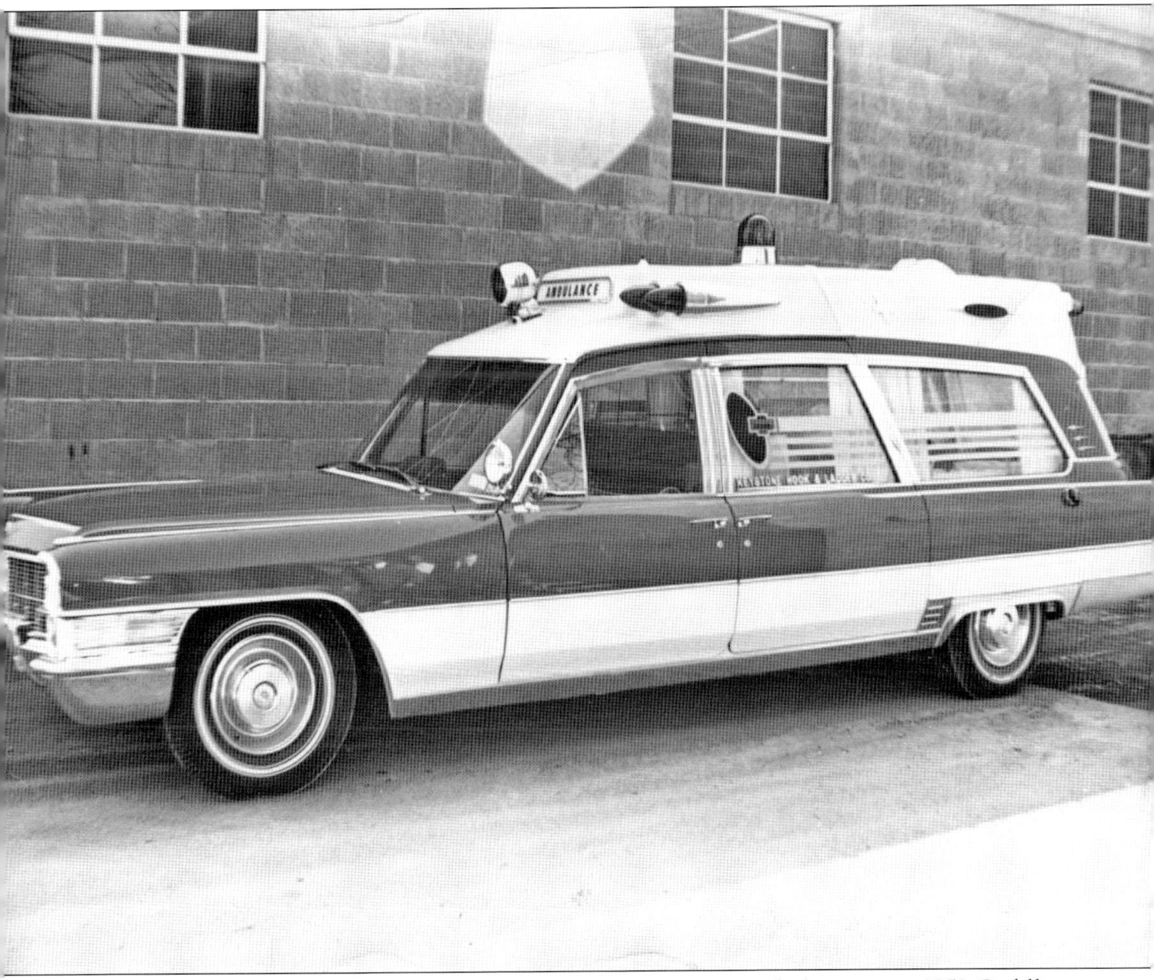

Shown here at the Keystone Hook and Ladder Company is an ambulance on a 1959 Cadillac professional chassis, built for the car manufacturer by the Miller-Meteor Company. This is the same model that Ivan Reitman used for the Ecto-1 in the 1984 blockbuster film *Ghostbusters*. The vehicle features a roll-out bed for fast patient transport and is powered by a Cadillac V-8 engine. While the vehicle could perform the duties of both an ambulance and a hearse, advances in technology and new federal regulations limited such vehicles to the latter in 1979. (Courtesy of the Muncy Historical Society.)

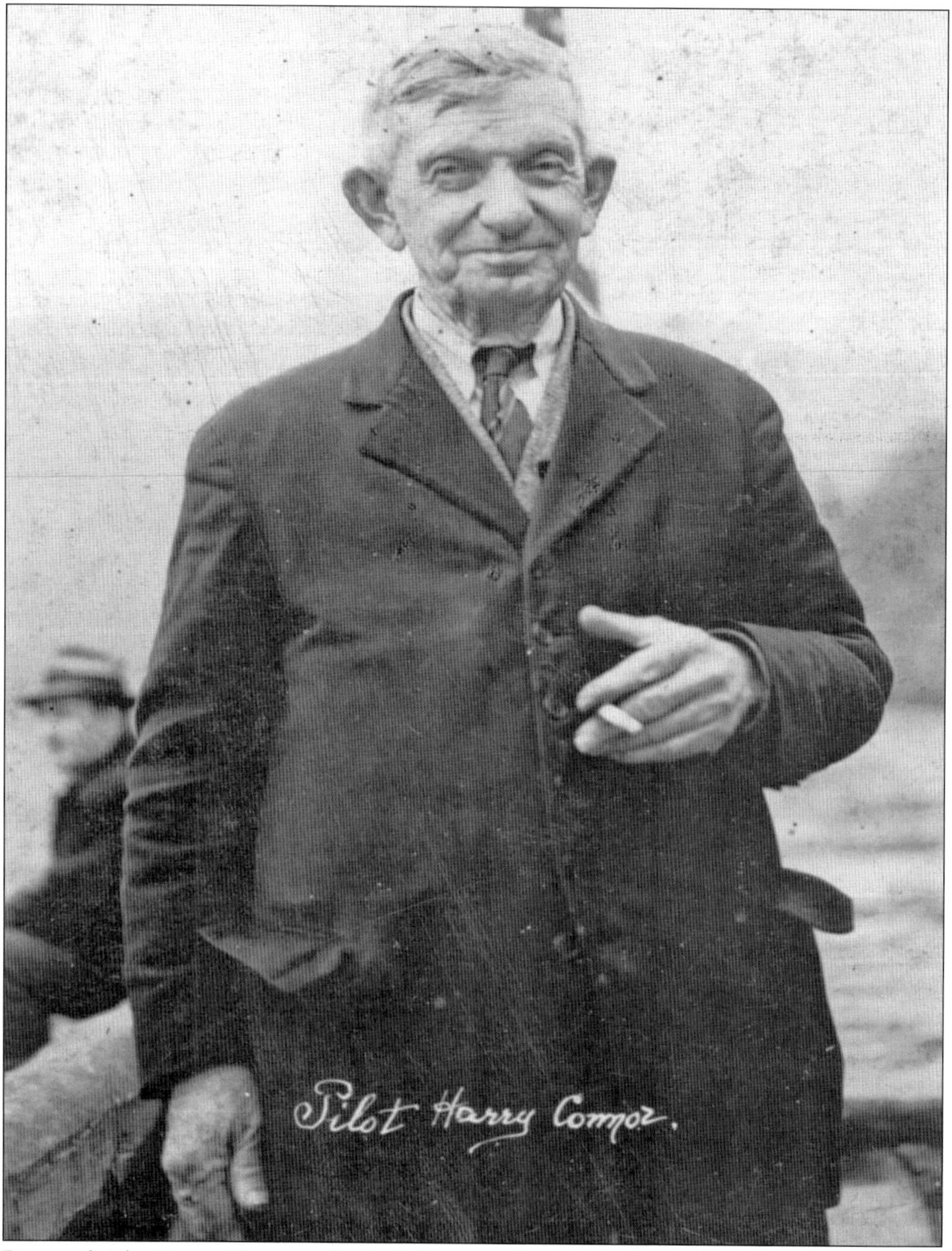

River raft pilot Henry Connor, who had 50 years of experience, is seen a few hours before his demise at the clutches of the frigid waters of the Susquehanna River on March 14, 1938. What started as a living history lesson by brothers R. Dudley Tonkin of Tyrone and V. Ord Tonkin, who were loggers in the area, ended in disaster when their hand-constructed raft collided with the Reading Railroad Bridge next to what is now Muncy Heritage Park. Six people died in addition to Connor: Montgomery's mayor, Dr. Charles Taylor; Universal cameraman Thomas Profitt; Harold Berringer; W.C. VanScoyoc; Malcolm McFarland; and Williard Holley. (Courtesy of the Muncy Historical Society.)

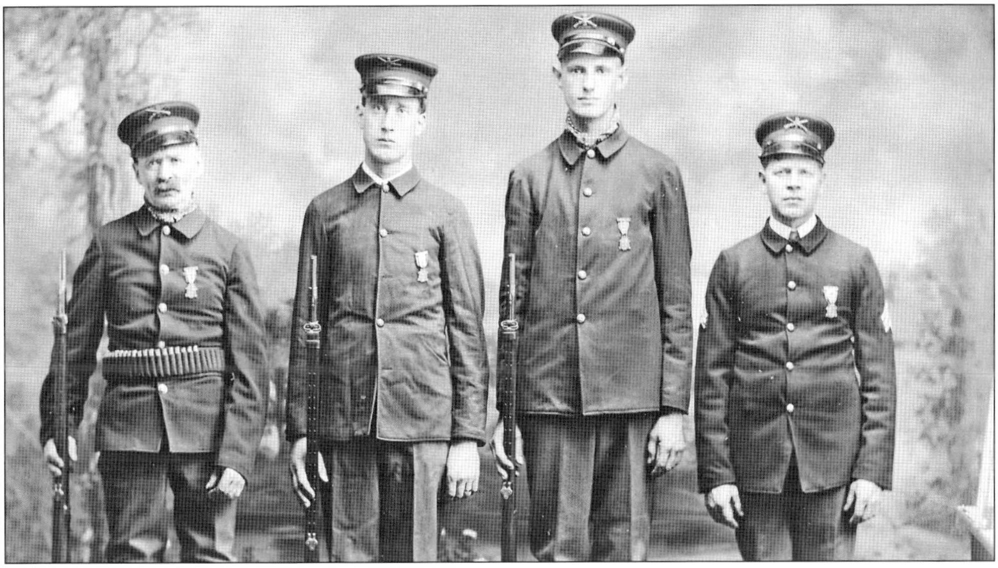

Given the history of violence in the lore of the US Postal Service (shootings by postal employees in Edmond, Oklahoma, in 1986; Ridgewood, New Jersey, in 1991; Royal Oak, Michigan, in 1991; Dearborn, Michigan, in 1993; Dana Point, California, in 1993; Goleta, California, in 2006; and Baker City, Oregon, in 2006), it is unsettling, indeed, to see former postmaster Brady Snyder and his employees decked out in enough arms and ammunition to invade a small country. Yet given the circumstances that made mail delivery a dangerous job, it was deemed necessary. (Courtesy of the Muncy Historical Society.)

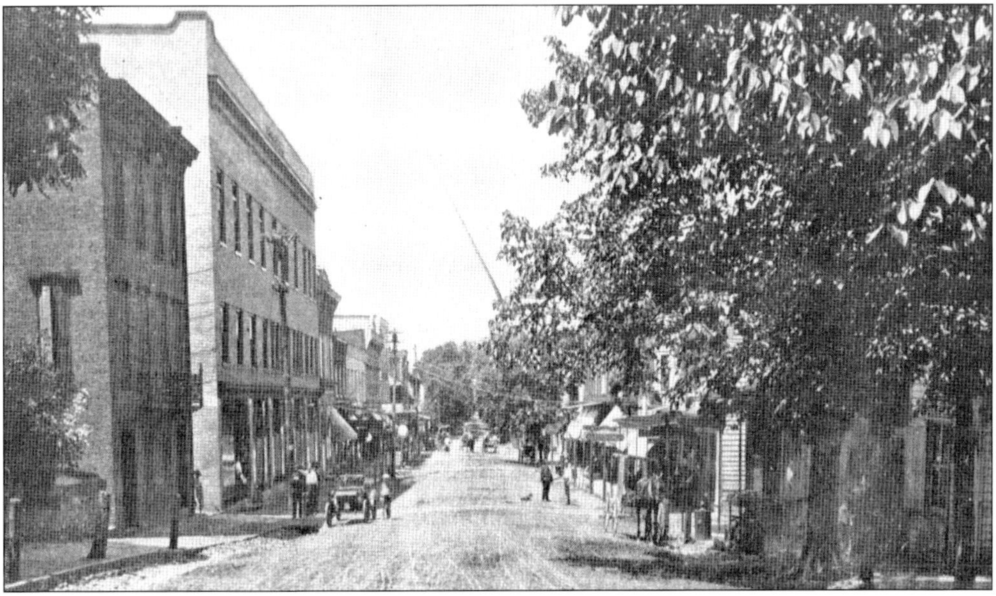

This postcard was published in Muncy by druggist C.W. Harter, who ran a franchise of Rexall Pharmacies, a chain founded in Boston in 1903 that now serves as one of Canada's largest pharmacy chains. Rexall lives on in the United States, as Dollar General Stores (with locations on Pennsylvania 405 and Washington Street in Muncy) uses the name to market vitamins, supplements, and other health-care products. Harter was responsible for distributing much-needed treatments during illness outbreaks, including the diphtheria outbreak of 1918. (Courtesy of Bill Ritter.)

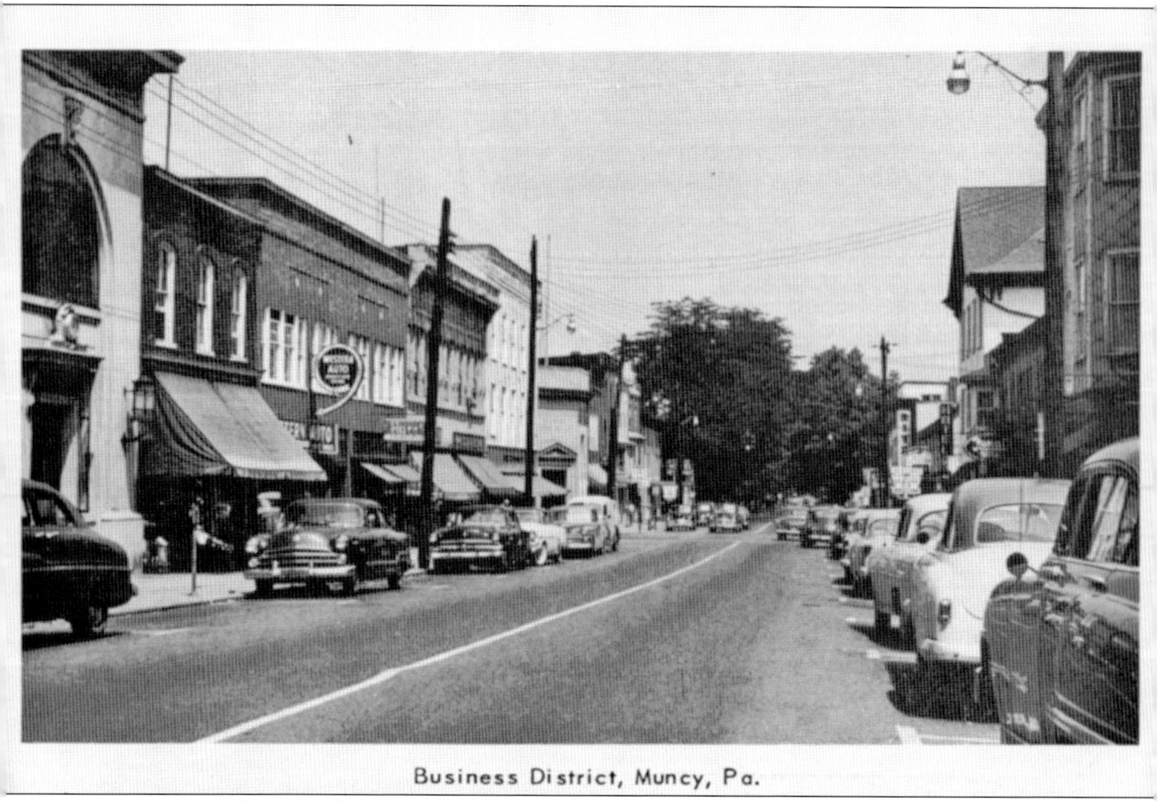

This postcard shows the business district in the 1950s. Local business interests are represented today by the Williamsport–Lycoming County Chamber of Commerce. The chamber has been around for 131 years and has served as the primary fulcrum for expansion of business and capitalist interests in the Susquehanna River valley and Lycoming County in general. It operates the Lycoming County Visitors Bureau and the Leadership Lycoming program. (Courtesy of Bill Ritter.)

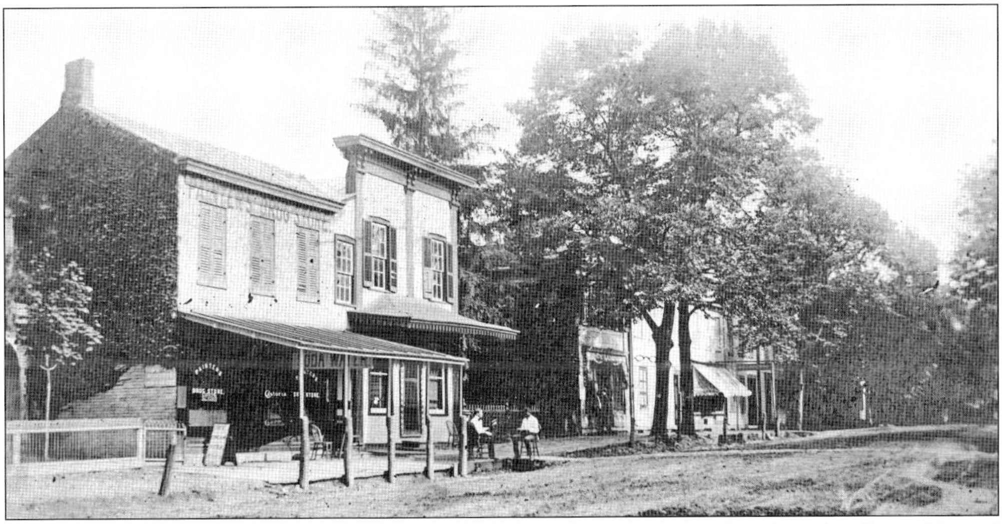

This photograph shows Painter's Drug Store in Muncy. The Painter brothers (William P.I. and George L.I.) founded the *Muncy Luminary*, today the 12th-oldest continuously published newspaper in the United States. While William withdrew from the publishing business in 1846 to focus full-time on his drugstore, George became a titan of early Muncy, serving terms as postmaster, trumpeter for the Muncy Band, president of the Muncy Cemetery Association, and owner of a book and stationery store. (Courtesy of the Muncy Historical Society.)

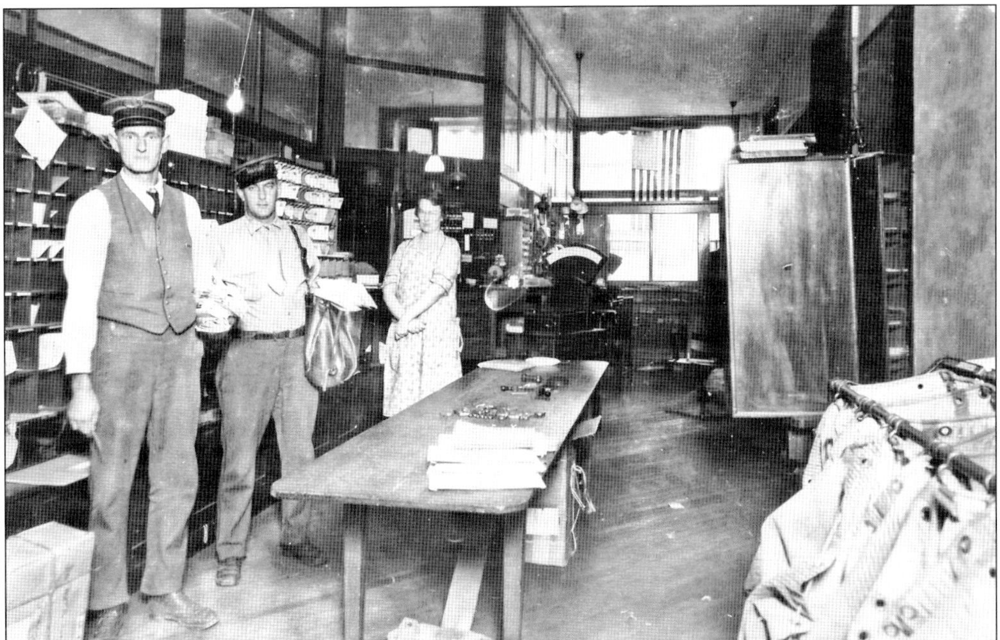

This turn-of-the-century image shows Brady Snyder and his motley band of mail clerks hard at work sorting mail. By 1926, the post office started keeping records of how much mail was sent, with a peak of over five billion separate postcards in 1997. This mail was scattered far and wide, as the post office has recorded as many as 157 million delivery points, which were serviced by over 800,000 postal employees at different points in the postal system's history. (Courtesy of the Muncy Historical Society.)

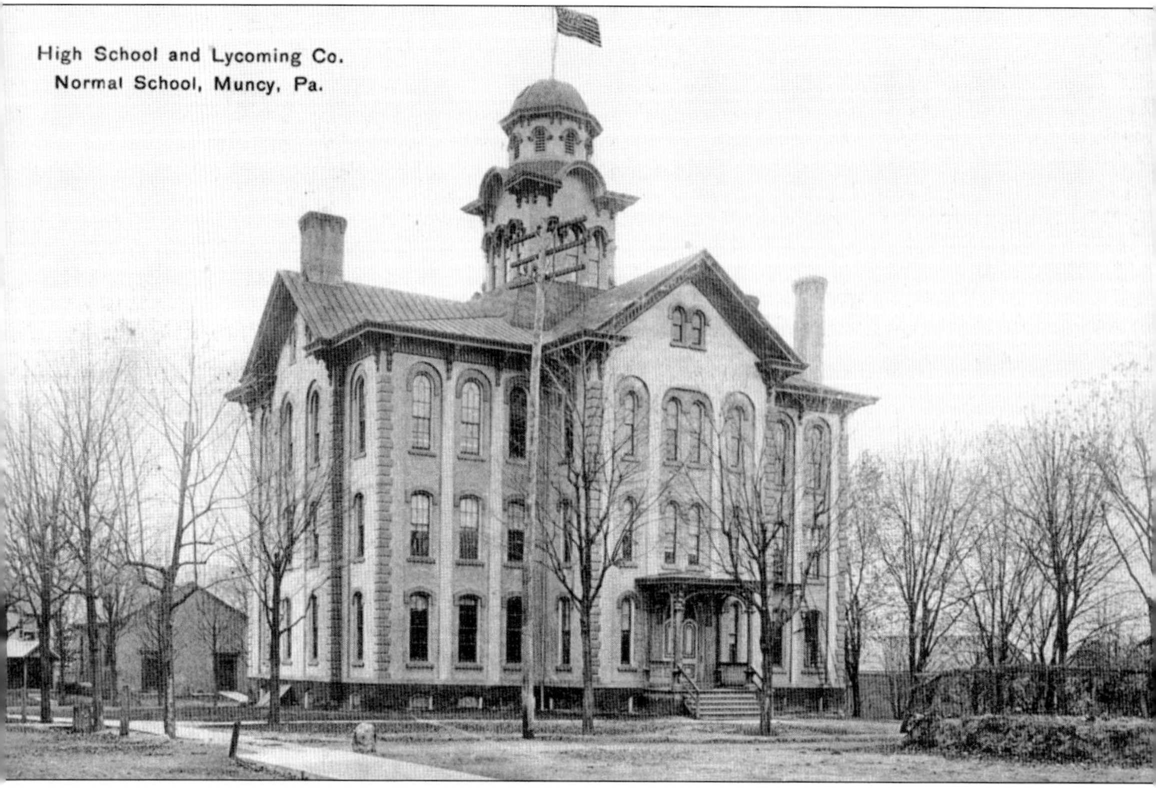

Although known as the Muncy Normal School, by the 1913–1914 school year, the institution had been renamed the Lycoming County Normal School. By this point, the school had been served by 11 different principals, 21 active professors, faculty, and lecturers, and a five-man board of trustees. The graduating class had grown to 45 students: 44 from the Keystone State and one from the Empire State (New York). There were 241 students in total enrolled. (Courtesy of the Muncy Historical Society.)

Seven

You're Gonna Go Far, Kid
The People of Muncy

The most striking aspect about Muncy resides not in its photographic landscapes or the winding country roads but rather in the people who call this town home. For generations, Muncy residents, whether from generations of local inhabitants or newly moved, have left an indelible mark on the area. Individual personalities shine in local artwork, community groups, and even the landscape itself.

A nexus for community activity, the Muncy school system has given local students and families an outlet for athletics, volunteerism, art, and intellectual growth. In a town situated only miles from the home of the Little League World Series, sports continue to be an essential part of local life. From football games evoking scenes from *Friday Night Lights* to winning the shoe from crosstown rival Montgomery, athletics serve as a uniting force among community members young and old alike.

Numerous types of material texts help to preserve the memory of past residents. An interesting and artistic marker of the past, CB radio cards were popular in Muncy among amateur radio members. These cards, though not in use anymore, leave personalized memories of past Muncy residents. Postcards sent to relatives and friends showcase points of pride for locals and emphasize the ordinary aspects of daily life that are quintessentially Muncy. Perhaps one of the most influential aspects of the town, the landscape has a huge role in daily life and recreation. Local businesses have been inextricably tied to the land. The railroad industry intersected with mining, and the lumber boom of Williamsport was felt by many residents and local businesses. On the weekends, many locals retreat into nature, taking up fishing, hunting, and hiking.

At its core, the history of Muncy is one that is vitally rooted in its residents. Individual interests and talents have created a beautiful community that unites around similar attachments to its history and landscape. As the years progress, Muncy residents will continue to find their identities largely connected to their home in Main Street, USA.

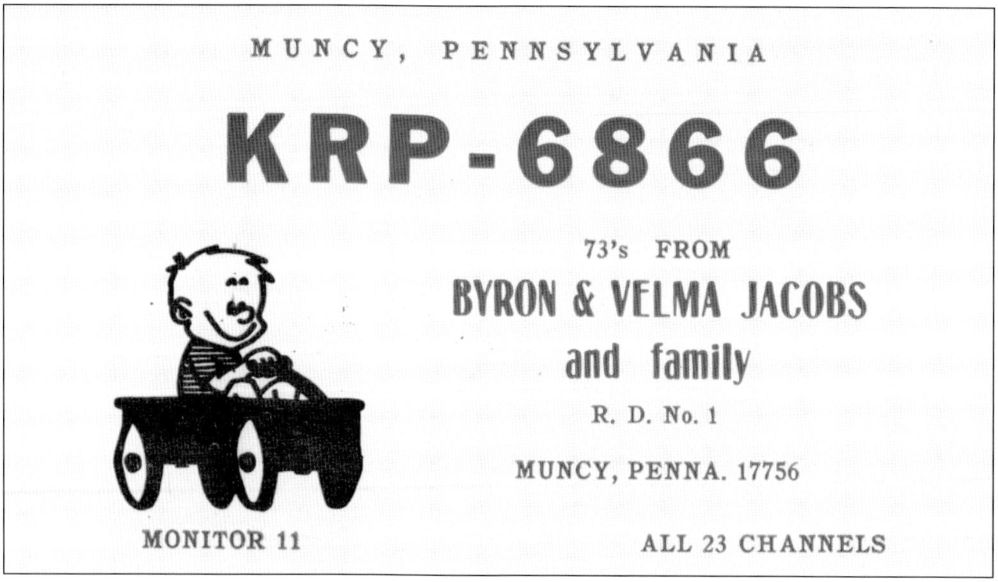

This CB radio card is one of many that survive from the Muncy area from the 1950s to the 1970s. Amateur CB radio is still popular in America, with over 830,000 registered private radio frequencies in use. This card, featuring a character plagiarized from one of the popular *Peanuts* comic strips, advertises KRP-6866, a private channel operated by Byron and Velma Jacobs. Byron was born on February 18, 1918, in Jordan Township, Lycoming County. He died in Muncy on February 3, 1995. Velma was born on November 8, 1920, and passed away in Muncy on October 9, 1996. (Author's collection.)

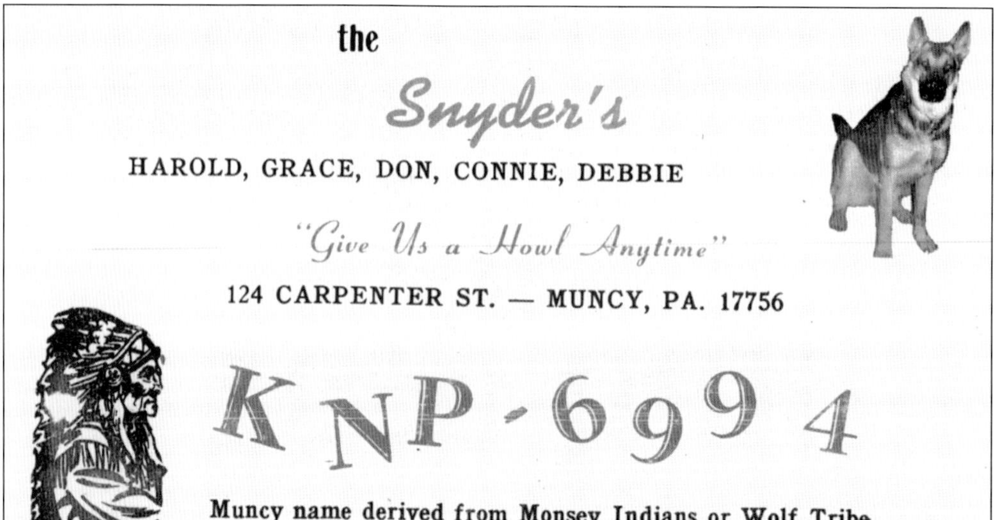

This CB radio card shows KNP-6998, the family channel of Harold, Grace, Don, Connie, and Debbie Snyder, formerly broadcasting from 124 Carpenter Street in Muncy. Harold and Grace were married for 66 years before his death on June 13, 2013. Grace would live to the age of 89, passing away peacefully on March 26, 2016, at the Susquehanna Health Skilled Nursing and Rehabilitation Center in Muncy. Don still lives in Muncy; Connie and her husband, Brad Beals, live in Jersey Shore; and Debbie and her husband, Leonard Klees, live in Pennsdale. (Author's collection.)

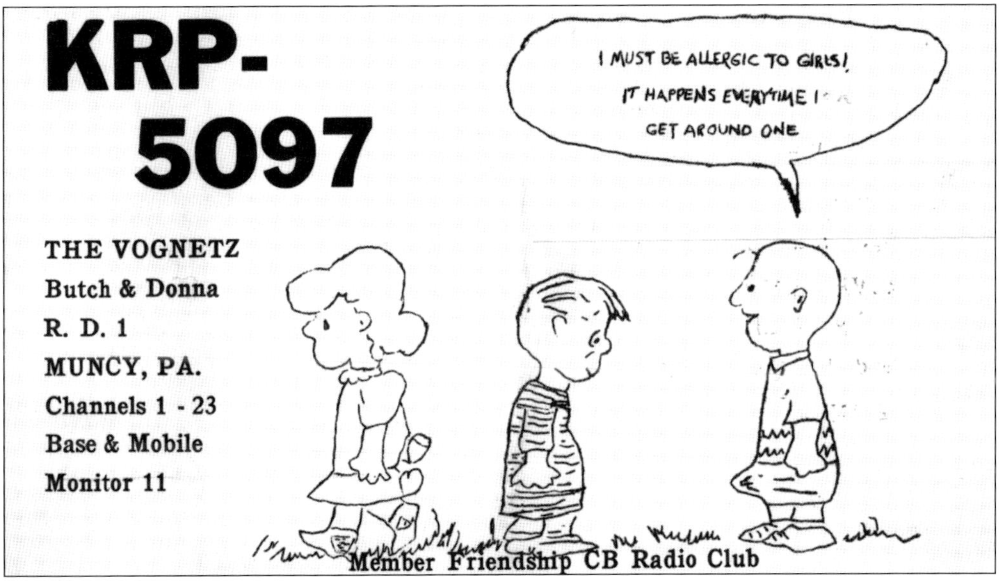

This card, using *Peanuts* characters, shows the information for KRP-5097, the CB radio channel for Dewain "Butch" and Donna Vognetz. Butch was born on December 31, 1945, and passed away at his home on February 17, 2009. He worked for the Andritz feed company for 30 years and was married for 42 years. His roots in amateur radio ran deep, as his station was a member of the Friendship CB Radio Club. He also served as a Scoutmaster and Little League coach and was a member of the Fairview Church of the Nazarene in Muncy. (Author's collection.)

This CB radio card features America's national bird, the bald eagle, decorated with patriotic symbolism. The channel, KPQ-0591, was run by Donald A. and Mary E. Mincemoyer. Donald was born on October 3, 1909, in Lycoming County. He served during World War II as a member of the 198th Infantry, Company B. Don died on November 19, 1984, and is interred at Twin Hills Memorial Park in Fairfield Township. Mary E. Mincemoyer was born in 1911 and perished sometime before 2009. Their house at 12 Bruner Street is Muncy is still standing as a one-bedroom home. (Author's collection.)

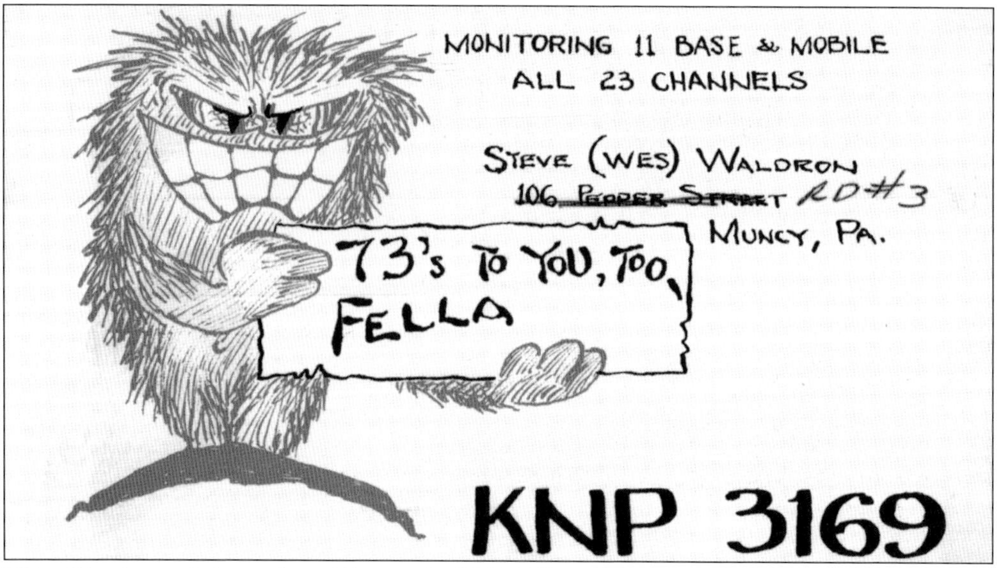

This CB radio card shows the call letters for KNP-3169, a channel run by S. Wesley Waldron, one of the pioneers of the Muncy amateur radio movement. Waldron's equipment was enough for him to reach Illinois in the west, Nashville in the south, Rhode Island in the north, and fishermen off the Atlantic Seaboard. After his discharge from the military, Waldron's activities in amateur radio were limited to a CB set he kept in his truck. Today, Waldron is retired, although he spends time lobbying as the liaison of United Bowhunters of Pennsylvania. (Author's collection.)

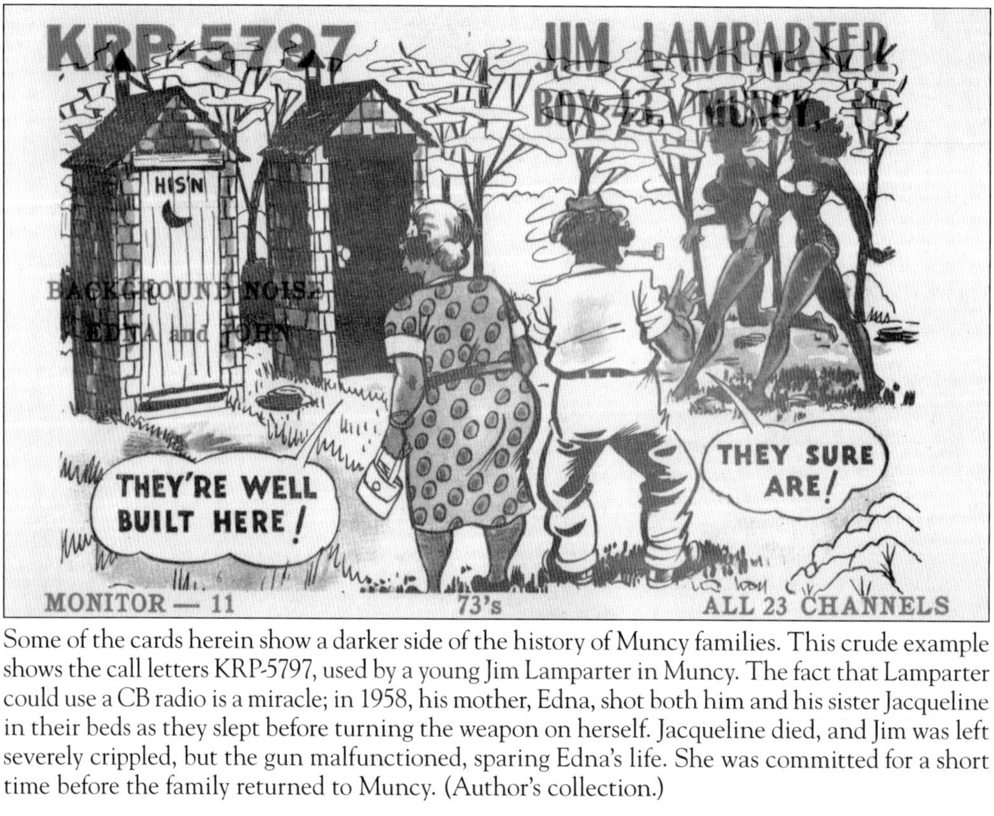

Some of the cards herein show a darker side of the history of Muncy families. This crude example shows the call letters KRP-5797, used by a young Jim Lamparter in Muncy. The fact that Lamparter could use a CB radio is a miracle; in 1958, his mother, Edna, shot both him and his sister Jacqueline in their beds as they slept before turning the weapon on herself. Jacqueline died, and Jim was left severely crippled, but the gun malfunctioned, sparing Edna's life. She was committed for a short time before the family returned to Muncy. (Author's collection.)

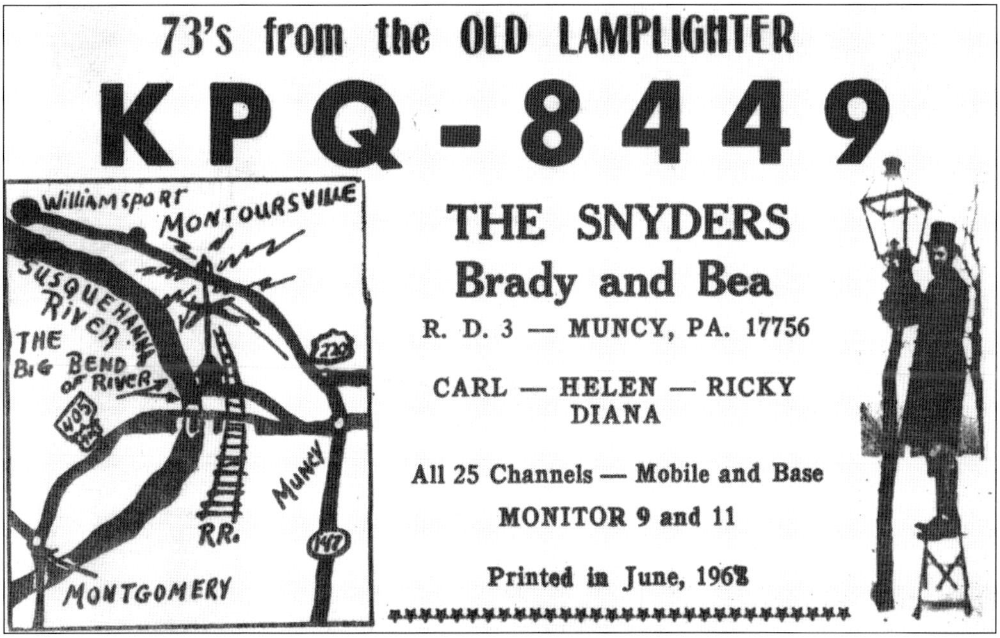

This card is fascinating not for the location or the call letter of the operators but for the history behind the property pictured. In 1976, Muncy resident Claire Kepner and her two children (10-year-old Tammy and 10-month-old Tommy) were murdered. Per Ricky Snyder and two others, the murders were committed in part by local handyman Milton Scarborough. The tale, however, was concocted under the influence of drugs, and Ricky recanted his testimony, despite the threat of prosecution, in 1980. It would be another 33 years before the work of Centurion Ministries freed Scarborough in 2013. (Author's collection.)

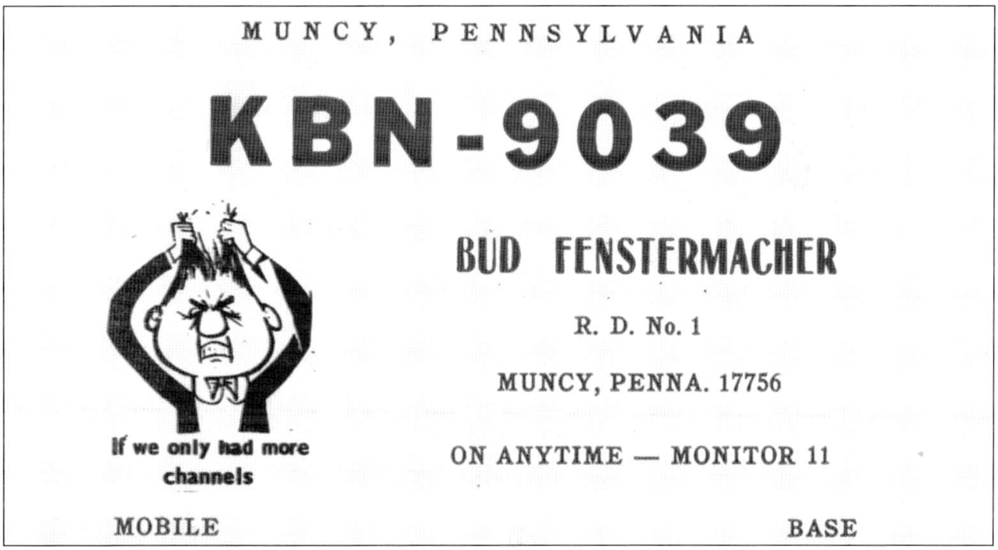

This card, which aptly shows the frustration the CB radio community has with signal and equipment issues, belongs to lifelong Muncy resident Sylvan "Bud" Fenstermacher. Fenstermacher is a 1954 graduate of Muncy High School and still participates in CB radio in the area, although he has since relocated to Picture Rocks, Pennsylvania, a tiny hamlet of just 693 people less than 15 minutes northeast of Muncy. Bud is still active today at a spry 76. (Author's collection.)

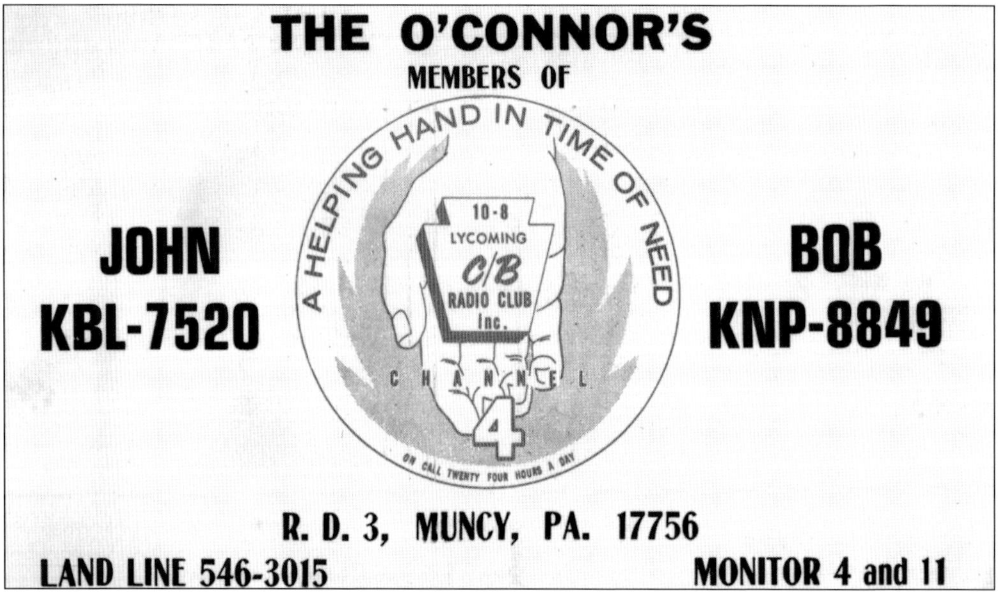

The community of CB radio operators served several purposes in the Muncy and Lycoming County area, as displayed by this card from the O'Connor brothers. They were a part of the Helping Hands CB club, which, like many clubs across the United States, put its skills and equipment to use in a time of need, such as during a disaster or aiding emergency response services. One current club in Muncy is the Bald Eagle Repeater Association, which operates under the call letters KB3HLL and holds regular meetings for CB operators in Muncy. (Author's collection.)

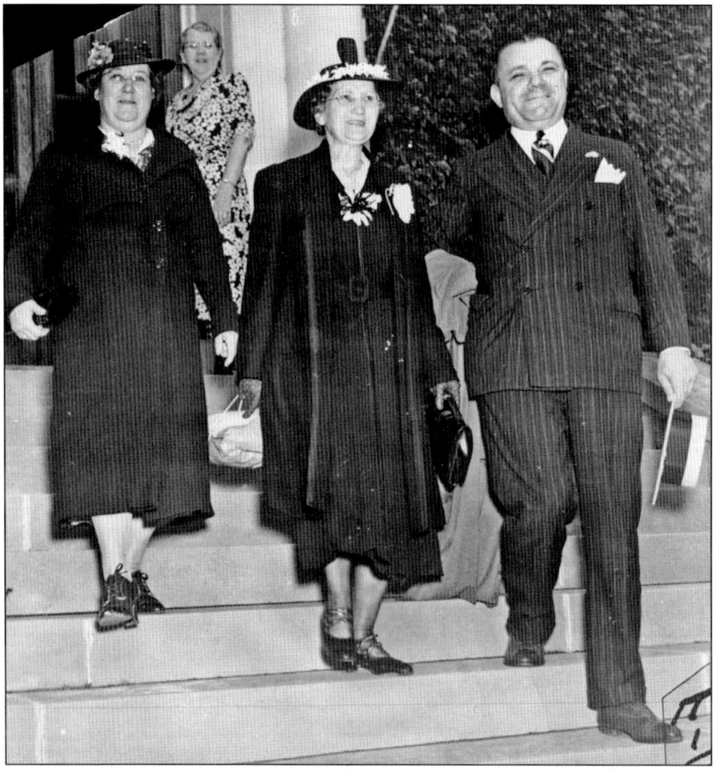

Frieda Trost (center) of Philadelphia is released from the Muncy prison after serving a 26-year sentence. Known as "the woman without tears," she was convicted in 1912 of poisoning her husband with arsenic a week after their marriage. Initially, Trost was sentenced to the gallows, but she received a commuted sentence that, after seven appeals, resulted in her release on June 3, 1938. Pictured with her are Albertine Birr, a member of the Philadelphia Prison Society, and Trost's attorney, Michael J. Matta. (Author's collection.)

This was sent as a birthday card to Florence Craig in 1910. Born in 1892, Florence was celebrating her 18th birthday and preparing to take her final exams in school when she received this postcard from Lloyd M. of Linden. Florence was the daughter of John (47) and Verina Craig (39), who owned their own farm in Muncy. (Author's collection.)

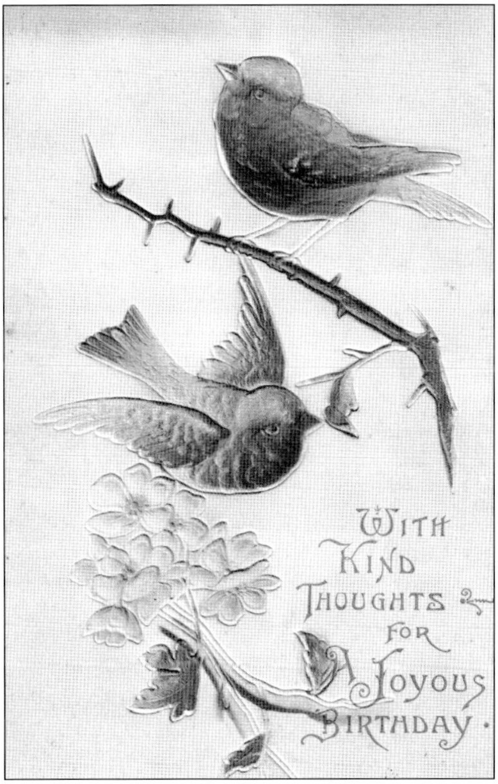

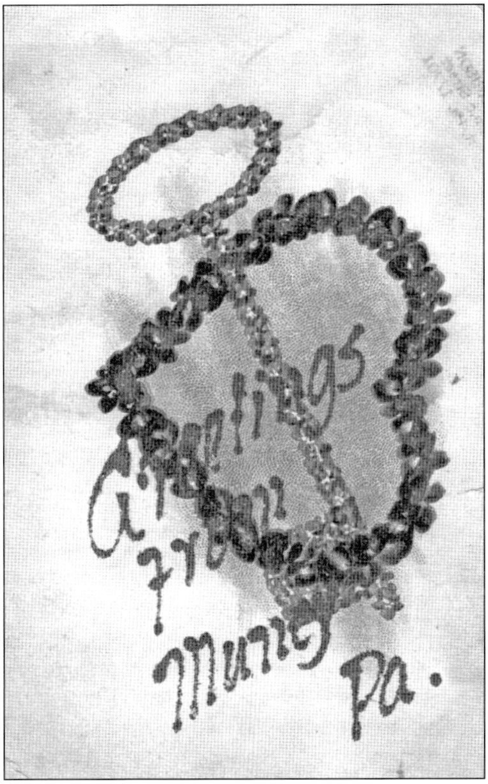

This greeting card was sent by Nancy Hall to her sister. Born in 1869, Nancy married Eber W. Hall in 1890, and together they had three daughters—Enna, Florence, and Nellie Hall. Her husband worked as a laborer on Buss Farm in Muncy. (Author's collection.)

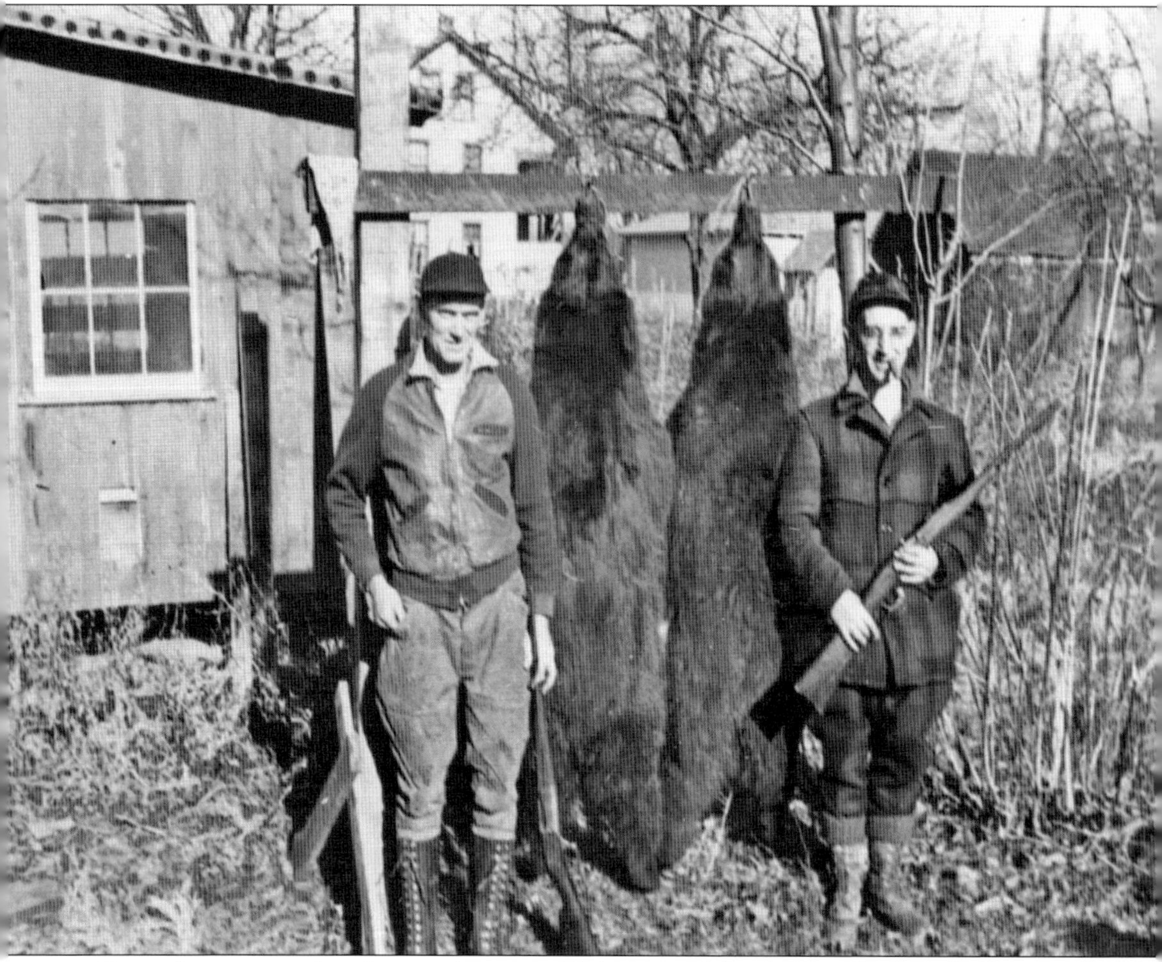

Shown here are two bear hunters from around the turn of the century in Muncy. While there is no information about the hunters themselves with the photograph, bear hunting was and continues to be a popular sport in the Muncy area and the Keystone State. In 2016, more bears were slaughtered in Lycoming during bear-hunting season (243) than in any other county in Pennsylvania. In 2016, the state saw its fifth-largest bear harvest on record; 3,529 total bears were killed. While in early times such hunts were needed to protect people, crops, and livestock, today, such hunts exist purely for sport. (Courtesy of the Muncy Historical Society.)

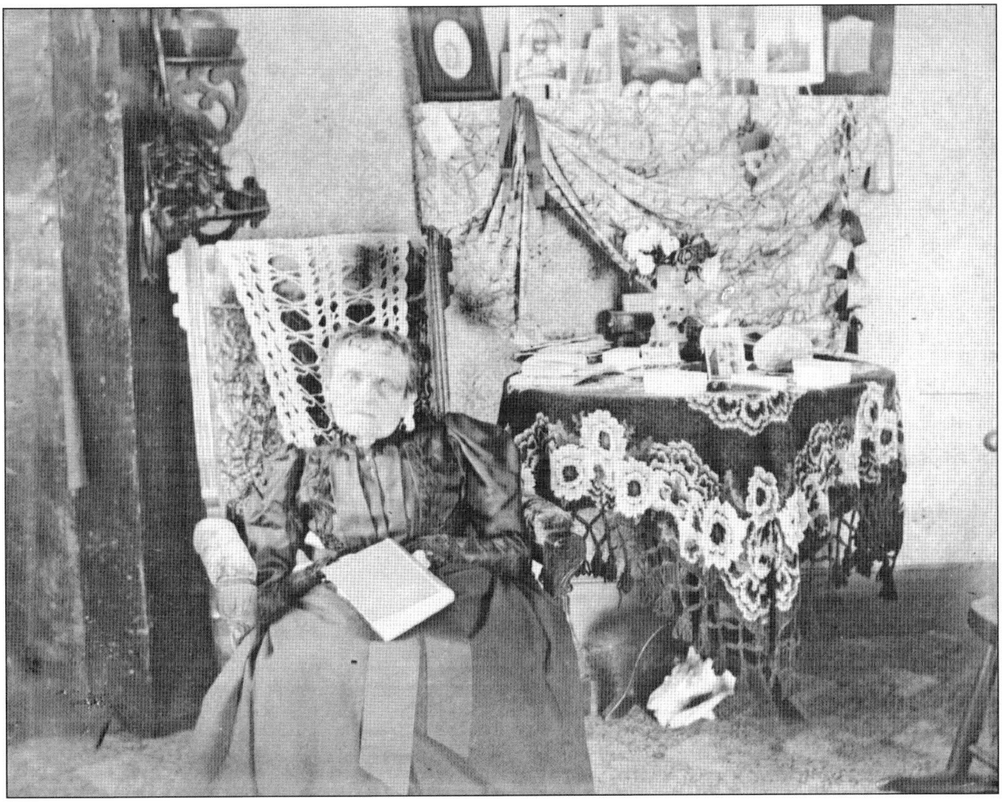

In a macabre scene normally associated with the Victorian era, here is the dead body of Cassie Fredricks, a Muncy citizen near the turn of the century. The writing on the back of the photograph reads, "Cassie Fredricks in her tiny house on the present site of Roy Sprout's home. Found one morning dead on her hearth from burns. Chas Golden made it his room for a while." Not even the specter of death, it seems, can prevent a home from being used. (Courtesy of the Muncy Historical Society.)

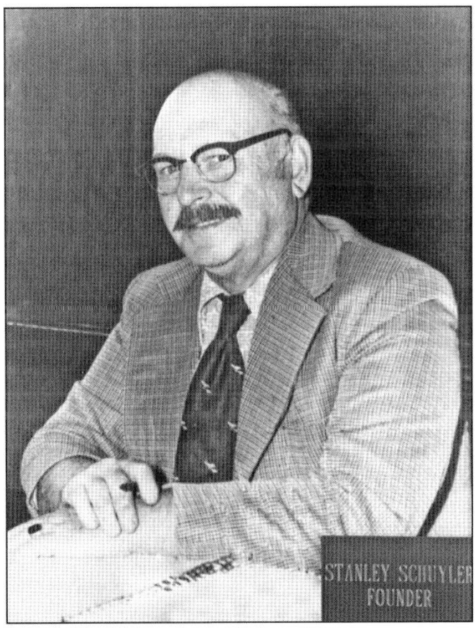

This is one of the most beloved figures in Muncy sports history, Stan Schuyler. A graduate of Bloomsburg Teachers College in 1939, Stan came to Muncy, and in addition to teaching at the high school, he coached football for 17 years and wrestling for 10 and was also athletic director for 10 years. He wrestled as a heavyweight at Bloomsburg College. Today, Muncy High School's football field bears his name, and as an honor for his service and for founding the hall of fame, he remains the only non-Muncy graduate to ever be enshrined. (Author's collection.)

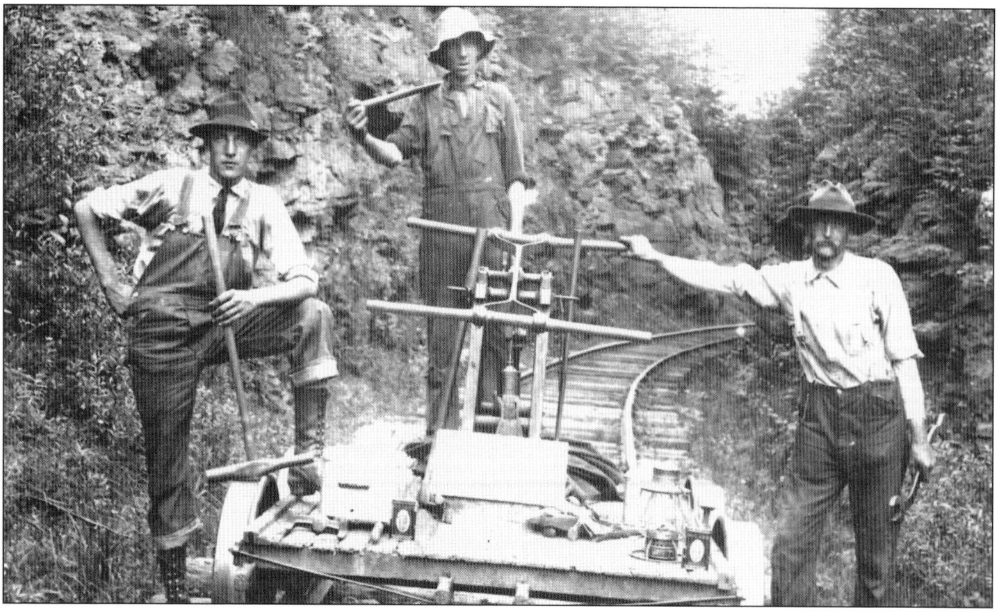

Given the extensive use of coal in the Pocono Mountains, both for personal heating and industrial use, an image such as this one of a trio of unidentified miners standing on their railcar is not uncommon. This photograph was found in the collection of legendary local Benjamin Franklin Merrill. Carts such as this were used in the early days of the railroad. Handcars were manual train carts used by two men pumping in a see-saw motion to propel the car forwards. (Courtesy of Janet Woodside Shoemaker.)

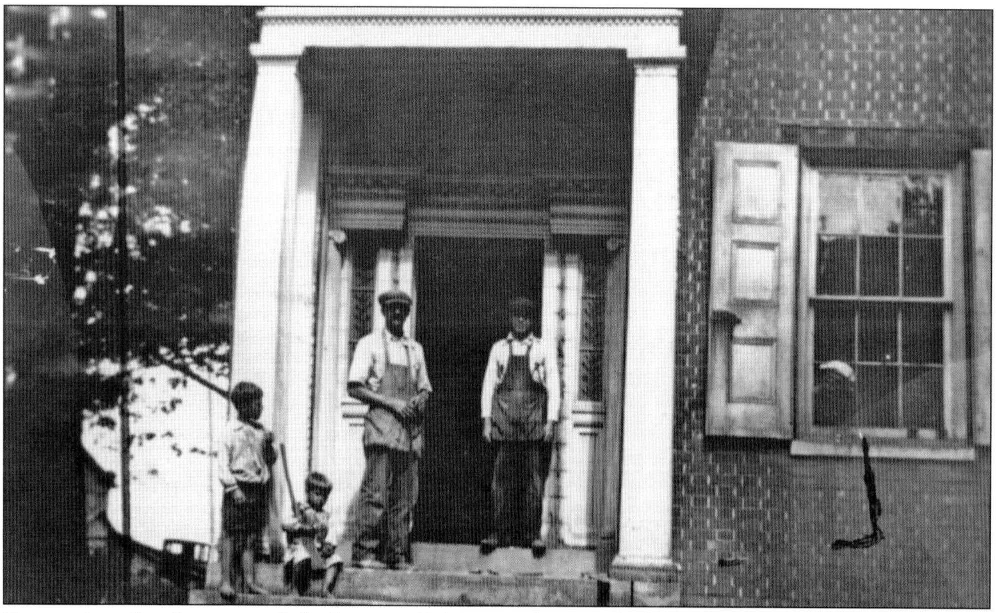

Pictured in the doorway of the home of T. Kenneth Wood, these two unidentified carpenters show pride in their handiwork. There is a long-standing tradition of fine door work in the history of Muncy, and this example appears to be no different. The back of the photograph reads "2 Carpenters just after his columns have been removed. T Kennedy Wood, Muncy PA." The children in the photograph are unidentified. (Courtesy of the Muncy Historical Society.)

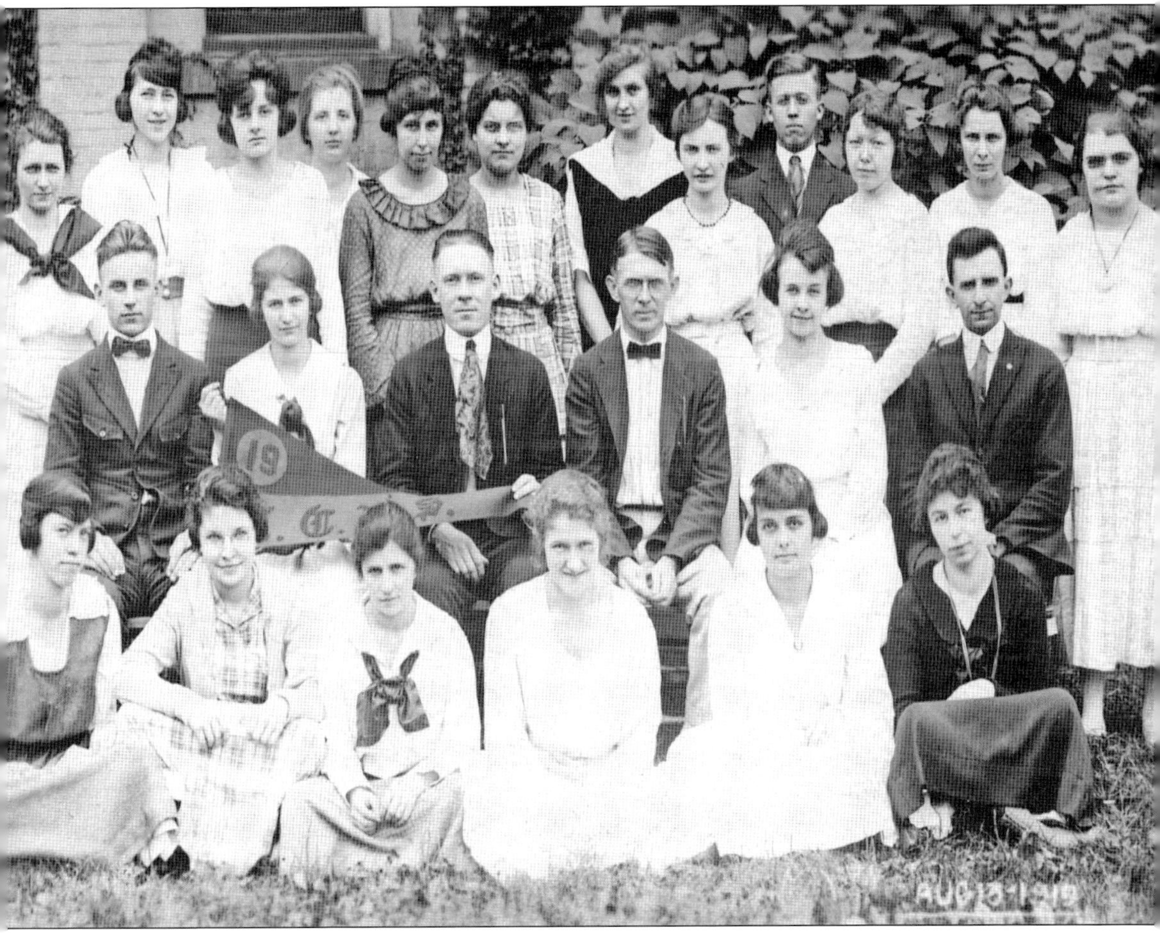

The Lycoming County Normal School was opened in Muncy in 1870 and prepared students for careers in teaching. The class of 1919 includes, from left to right, (first row) Vera Montaque, Frances Stevenson, Mary Strunk, Charity Lowe, Henrietta Moyer, and Irene Grady; (second row) Charles Reese, Rebecca Crist, Willis Moore, Prof. S.B. Dunlap, Geraldine Smith, and Dewey Knight; (third row) Marian Vanderbilt, Miriam Decker, Mary Gardner, Margaret Hurr, Theresa King, Marion Faque, Alverta Seeley, Lucy Barbour, Earl Houseknecht, Letty Roller, Elise Keller, and Mary Evans. (Courtesy of the Muncy Historical Society.)

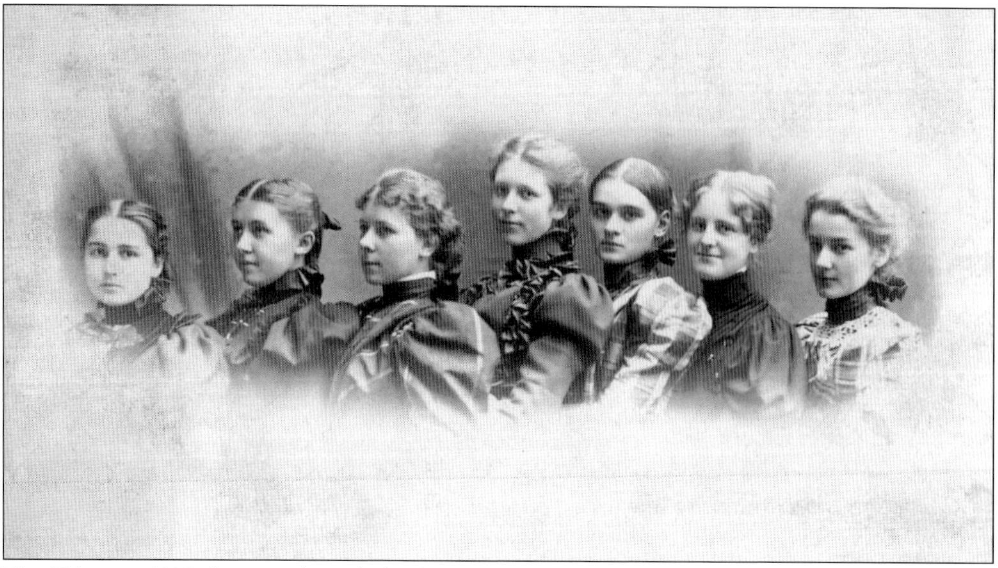

This February 1898 photograph, with the dramatic title *We Are Seven*, shows seven pupils of Muncy's Shawmut School, a small postsecondary institution. From left to right are Dorothy Lunt Gray, Carrie Louise Fairbanks, Maude A. Johnston, Clara Sydney Andrews, Rosetta Schuyler Montgomery, Mildred Cordelia Davis, and Nellie Bird Luthers. (Courtesy of the Muncy Historical Society.)

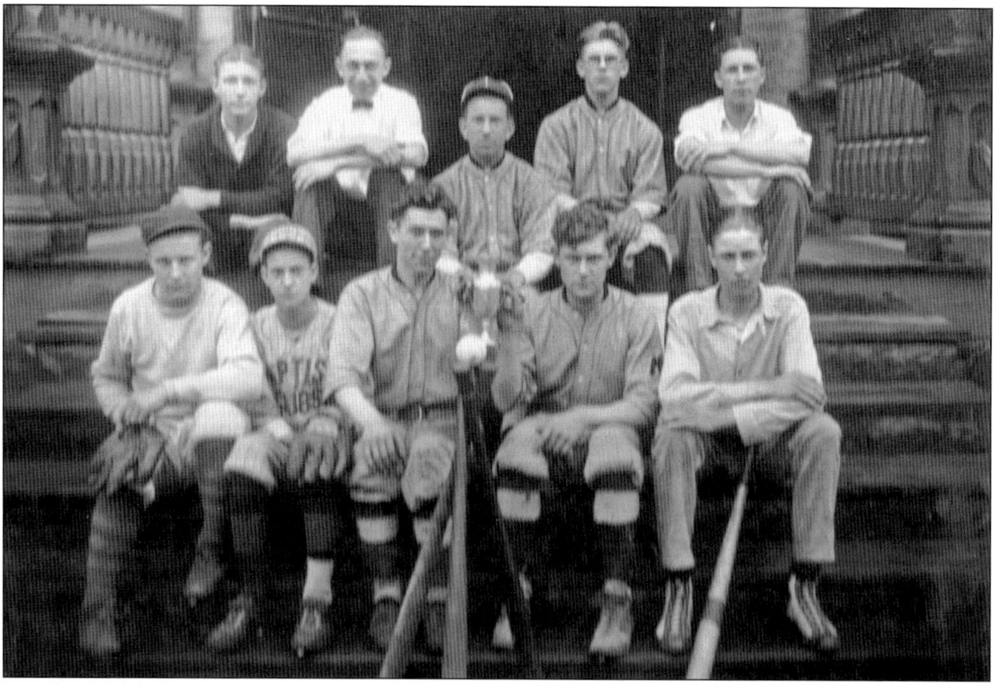

Members of the Muncy High School baseball team in 1926 are, from left to right, (first row) Clay Lee, Don Rohm, Amos Smith, Harold Deeter, and Jim Hitesman; (second row) Roy Moyer, Don Campbell, Meredith Gardner, Spike Frey, and Leonard Hill. The Muncy players were fortunate enough to win a championship, and they display the trophy in the foreground. In the major leagues, the St. Louis Cardinals beat the New York Yankees to win the World Series. (Courtesy of the Muncy Historical Society.)

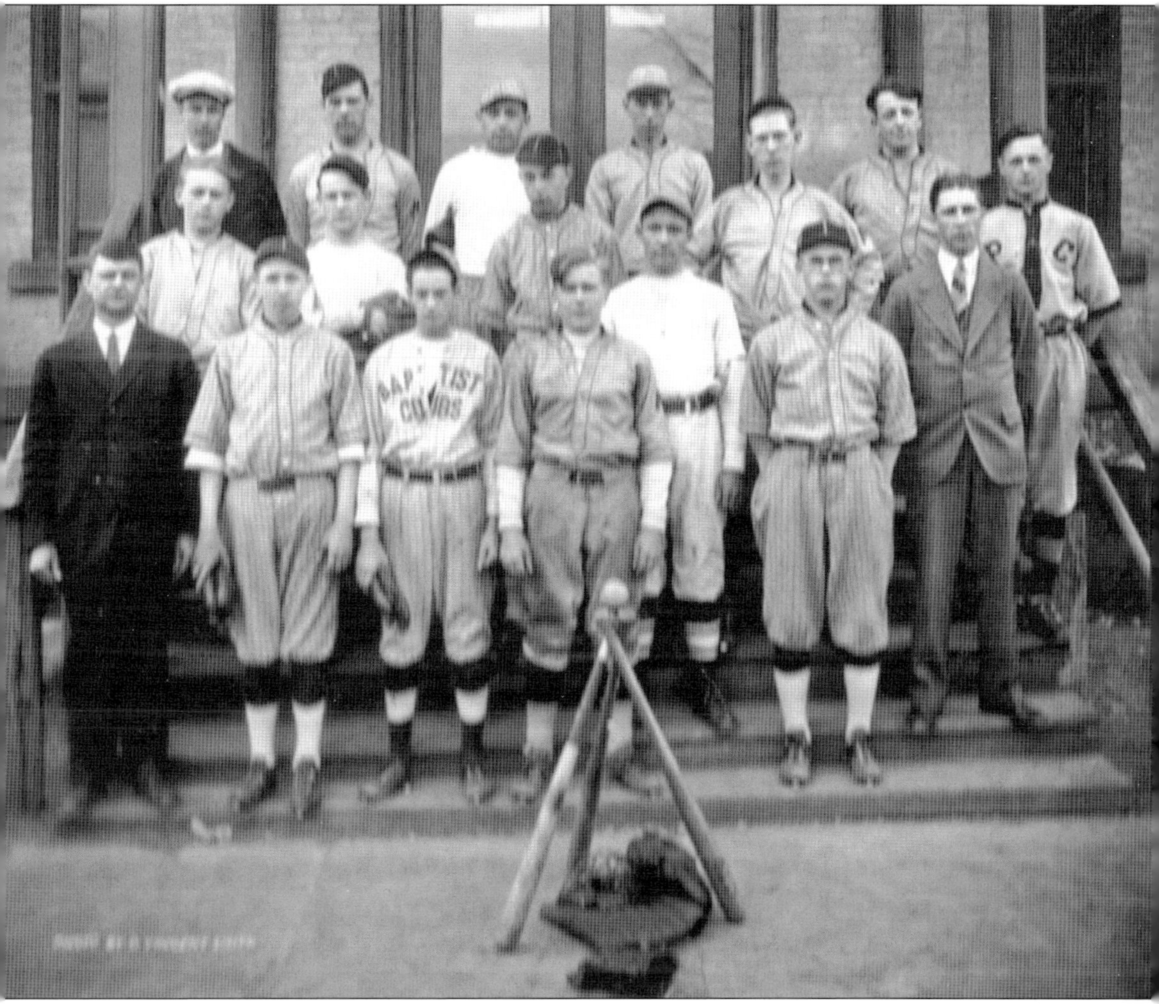

Shown here is the 1927 champion Baptist baseball team. From left to right are (first row) Amos Gruber, Max Edmonds, Don Rohm, Harold Brown, and Spike Frey; (second row) Mark Hester, Clay Lee, Kenneth Dunlap, Roy Moyer, and Leonard Hill; (third row) Jim Hitesman, Andy Anderson, Harold Koons, Warren McCarty, Jim Wagner, Ralph Feigles, and Grant Sline. That year's World Series was won by the New York Yankees. Dubbed "Murderers' Row," the 1927 Yankees are considered one of the greatest teams in baseball history. (Courtesy of the Muncy Historical Society.)

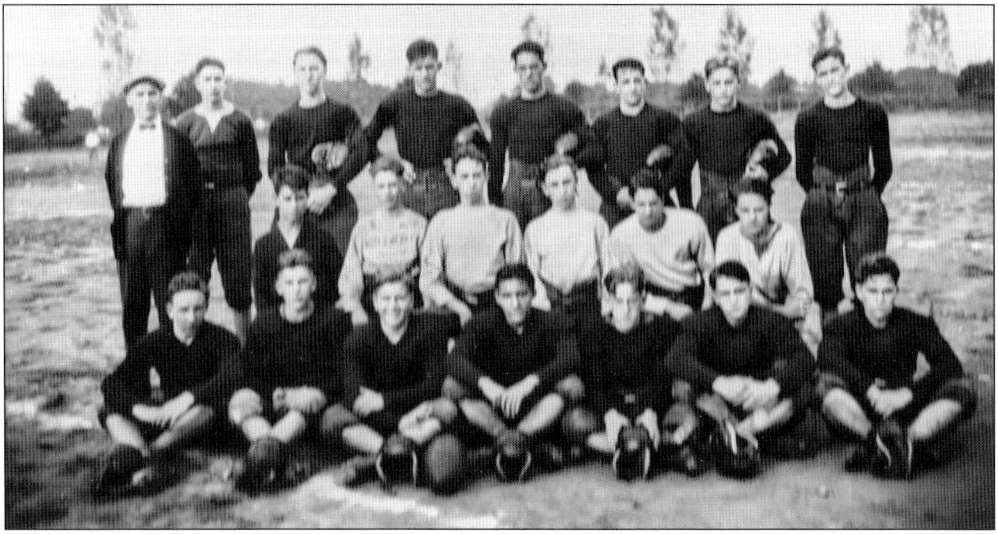

This photograph shows the 1927 Muncy High School football team. From left to right are (first row) Fred Stolz, Spike Frey, Harold Brown, Roy Moyer, Gene Stolz, Kim Worthington, and Paul Long; (second row) Jim Rager, Clay Berger, Emerson Frautz, Harold Feigles, Don Rohm, and Fred Blankslee; (third row) Ernie Braut, Don Bardo, William Barthow, Max Schoch, Andy Anderson, Ralph Feigles, Mark Hester, and Ray Long. In the pre–Super Bowl era, the New York Giants were the 1927 NFL champions. (Courtesy of the Muncy Historical Society.)

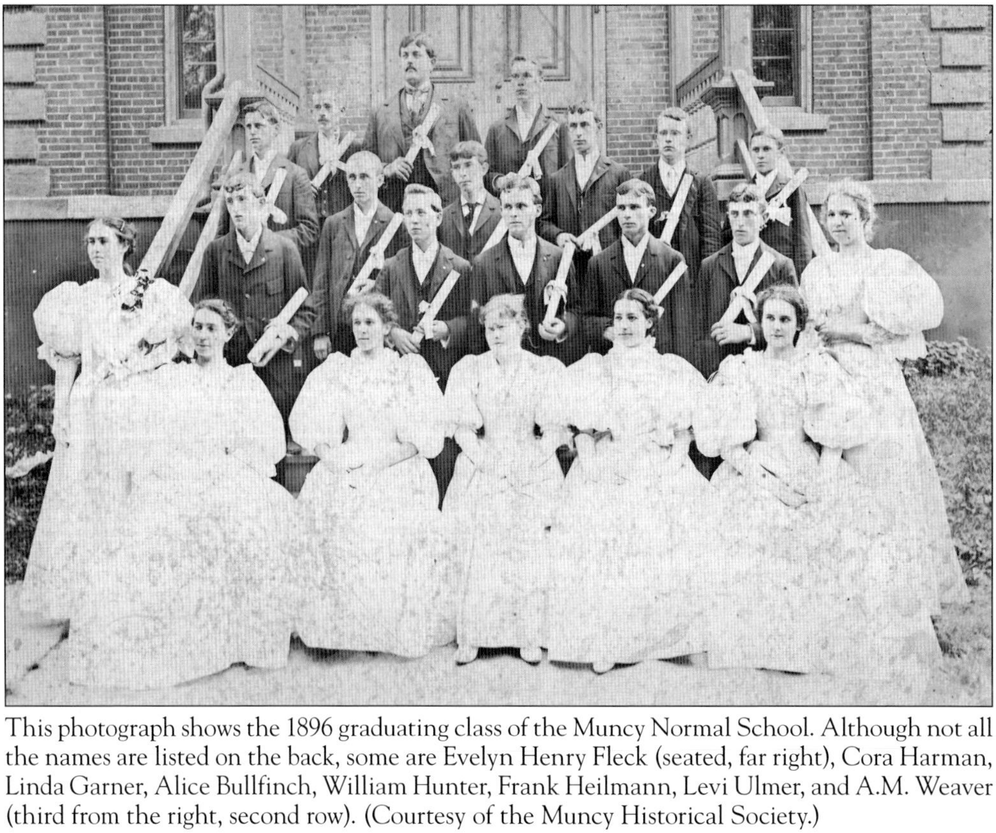

This photograph shows the 1896 graduating class of the Muncy Normal School. Although not all the names are listed on the back, some are Evelyn Henry Fleck (seated, far right), Cora Harman, Linda Garner, Alice Bullfinch, William Hunter, Frank Heilmann, Levi Ulmer, and A.M. Weaver (third from the right, second row). (Courtesy of the Muncy Historical Society.)

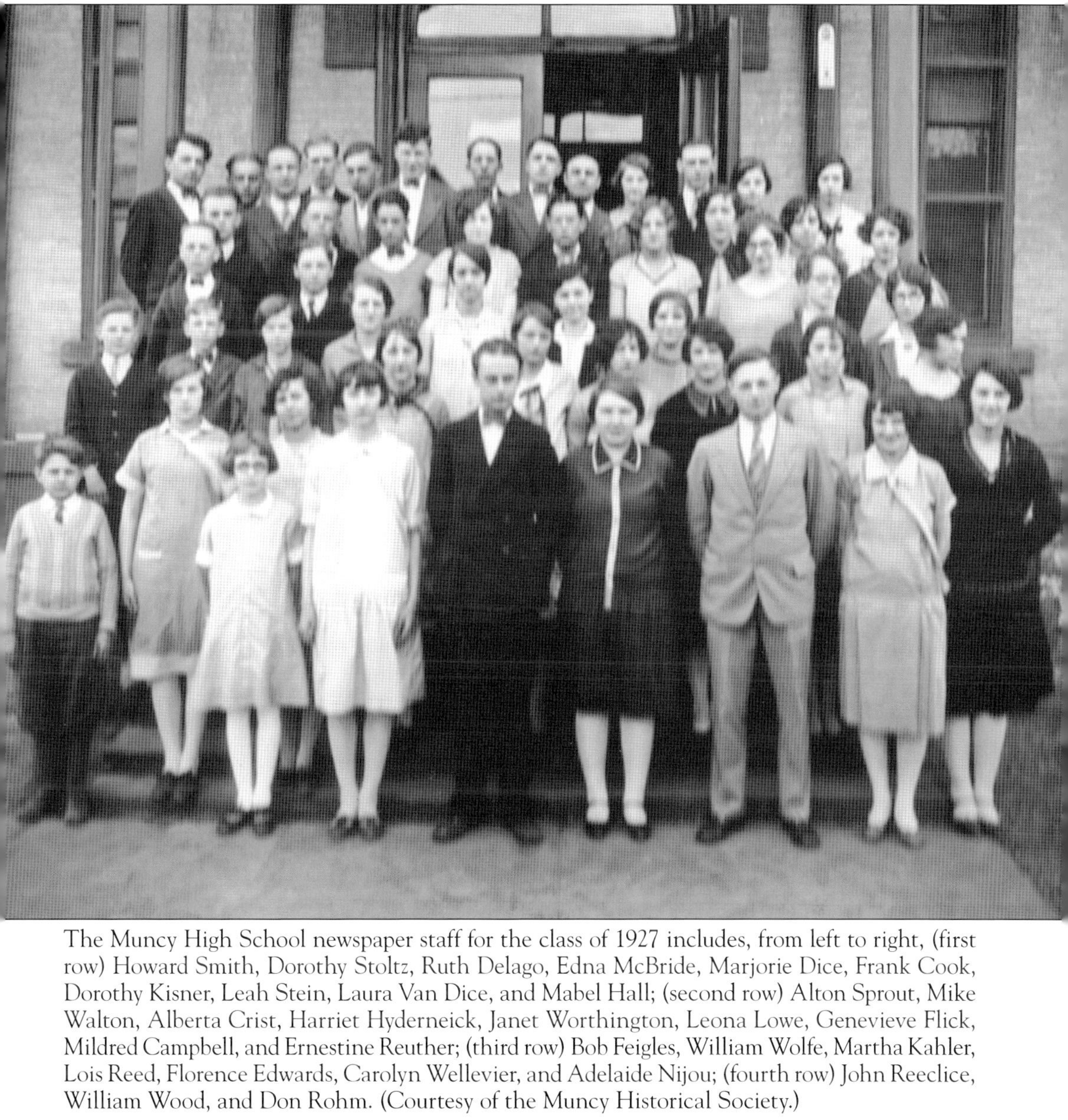

The Muncy High School newspaper staff for the class of 1927 includes, from left to right, (first row) Howard Smith, Dorothy Stoltz, Ruth Delago, Edna McBride, Marjorie Dice, Frank Cook, Dorothy Kisner, Leah Stein, Laura Van Dice, and Mabel Hall; (second row) Alton Sprout, Mike Walton, Alberta Crist, Harriet Hyderneick, Janet Worthington, Leona Lowe, Genevieve Flick, Mildred Campbell, and Ernestine Reuther; (third row) Bob Feigles, William Wolfe, Martha Kahler, Lois Reed, Florence Edwards, Carolyn Wellevier, and Adelaide Nijou; (fourth row) John Reeclice, William Wood, and Don Rohm. (Courtesy of the Muncy Historical Society.)

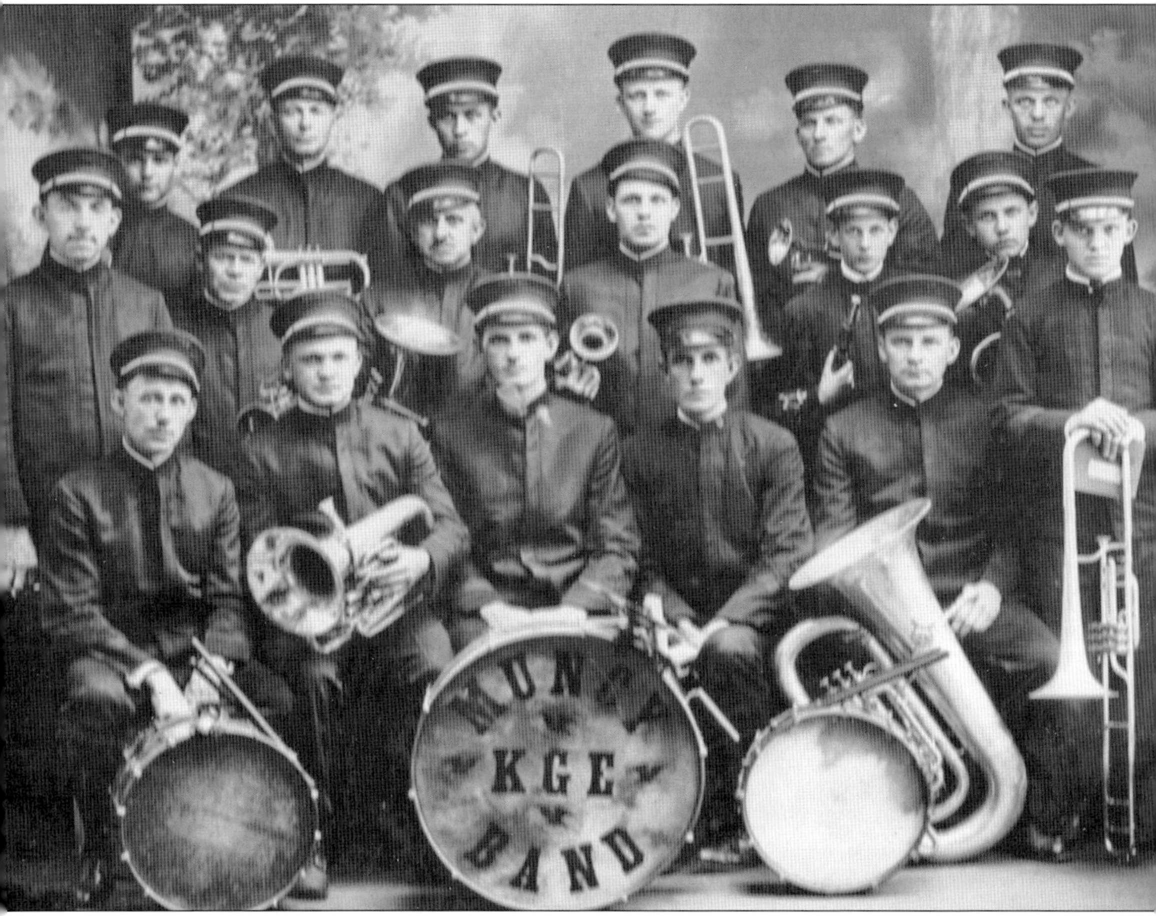

Although this image shows the Muncy KGE Band it all its glory, it gives little information about the circumstances behind its production. On the back are a date (Christmas, 1913) and obituaries for two of its possible members: Harvey J. Artley, who died at his home on Water Street on Christmas Day 1934, at the age of 64; and William Taylor, who died in his home in Lyndonville, New York, on January 15, 1933, at the age of 46. The cause of death for each is given as a lingering illness, an unfortunate legacy for this band. (Courtesy of the Muncy Historical Society.)

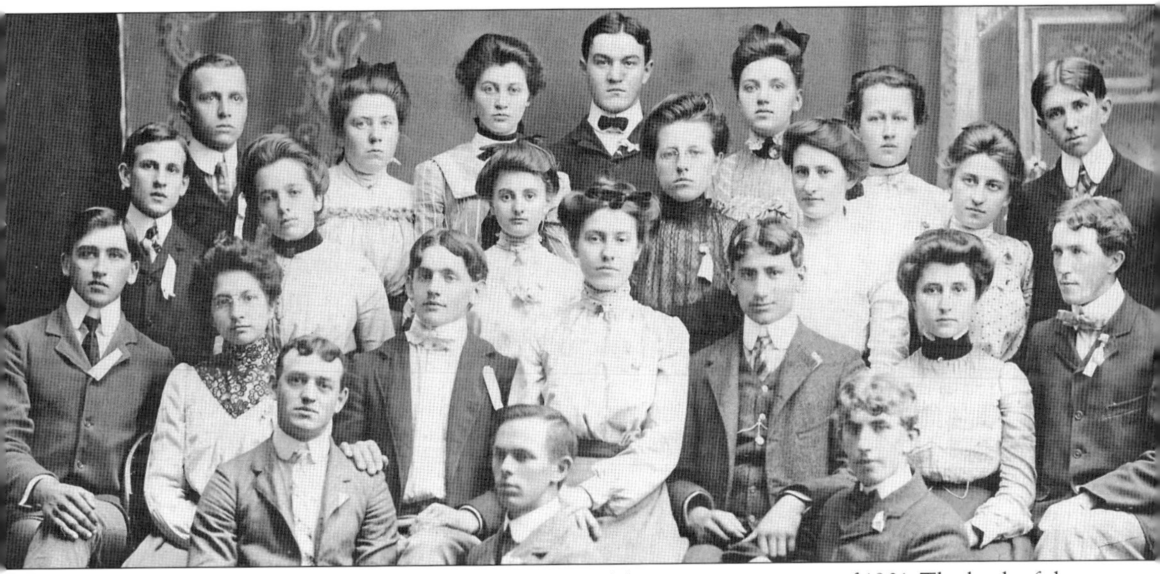

The Muncy Normal School class of 1902 is pictured during its junior year of 1901. The back of the photograph lists the following class members (not in order): Henry Packard, Elfie Braun, Jennie Boyle, Walter Bertin, Eleanor Dawson, Mary Farr, Creighton Turner, W.M. Lochameyer, Miriam Shafer, Helen Ware, Pauline Hain, Rosetta Kuntz, Lila Williamson, John Lamb, Emma Dervick, Oliver Coates, Laura Weaver, Ray Jarrett, Katie Frick, Bob Foresman, Ray Coppes, Emory Myers, and Arthur Tomlinson. (Courtesy of the Muncy Historical Society.)

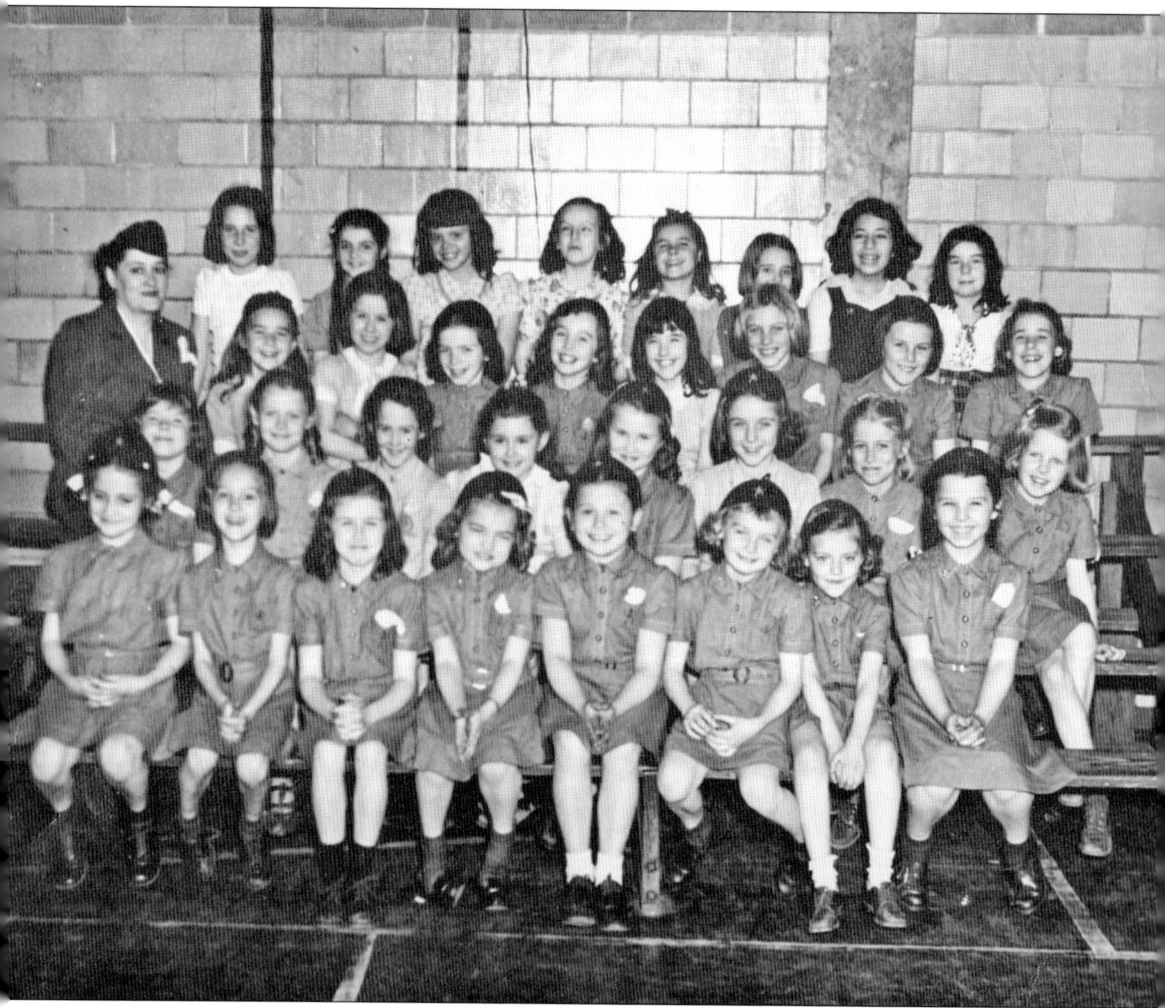

This is one of the many Girl Scout troops to serve in Muncy since 1912. In this undated image, some of the girls in Scout leader Mrs. C. Goodenow's troop include Connie Cummings, Gail Neufer, Mary Lee Warish, Lois Ann Greenberg, Joanne Houseknecht, Shirley Feigles, Arua Jo Hilner, Jean Holtzapple, Susan Brown, Ann Sensemes, Norma Jean Murray, Lee Goodenow, Judy Honkle, Loretta Houseknicht, Barbara Kilgus, Patty Heller, Donna May Sheppard, and Beverly Parsons. This photograph was donated to the Muncy Historical Society by Loretta Winters. (Courtesy of the Muncy Historical Society.)

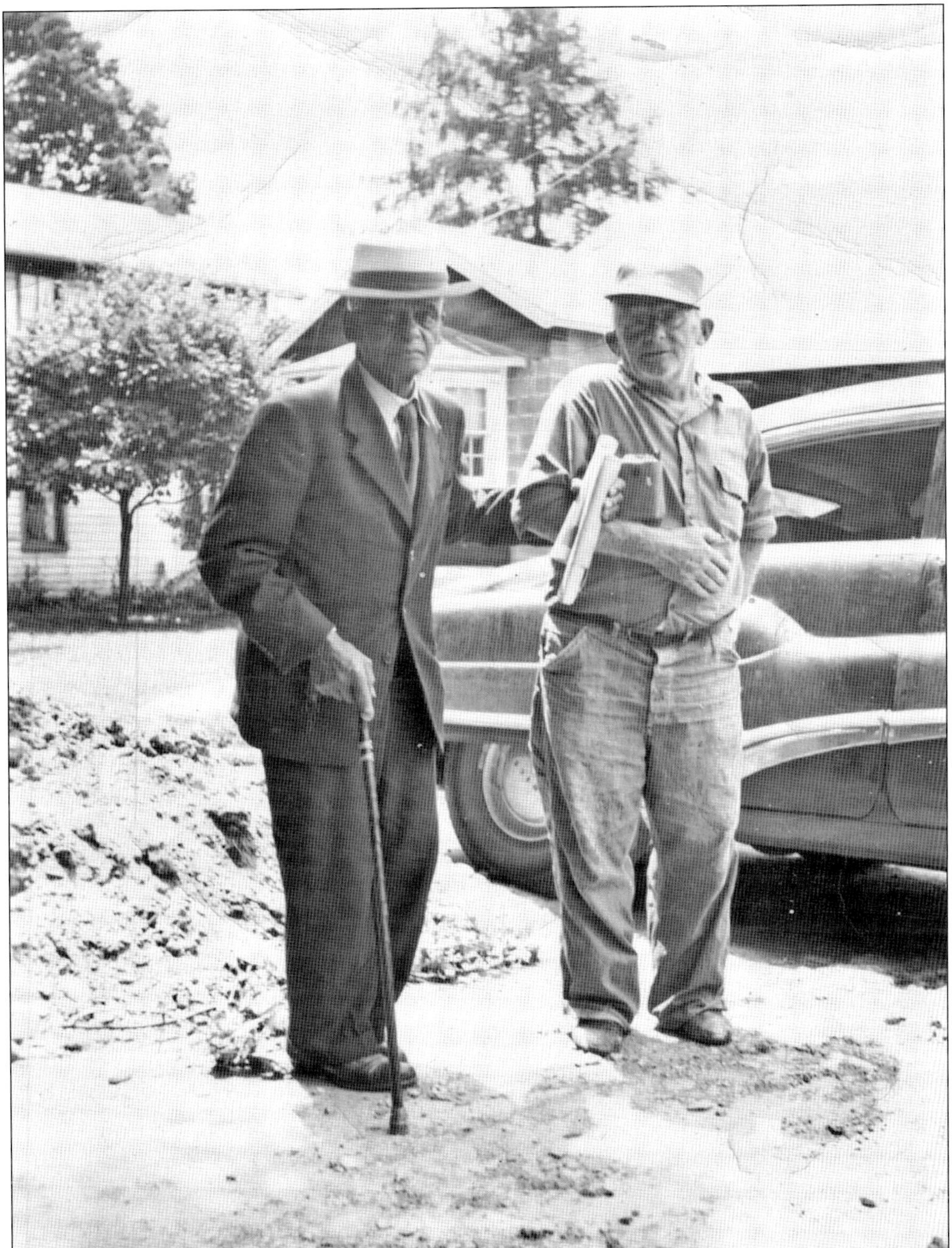

Shown in this undated photograph are Lee Kennedy (left) and Frank Brittian, both of Muncy. Kennedy was the high school custodian at Muncy throughout the 1940s and 1950s. Brittian has a few traces in the area: According to the 1940 census, he was born in 1888, was married to Florence, and claimed four children—Thomas, Delphia, Evelyn, and Dorothy. Evelyn, according to local news sources, underwent a successful operation for appendicitis on February 4, 1938, and the Brittians entertained the Hill family during the week of April 9, 1953. (Courtesy of the Muncy Historical Society.)

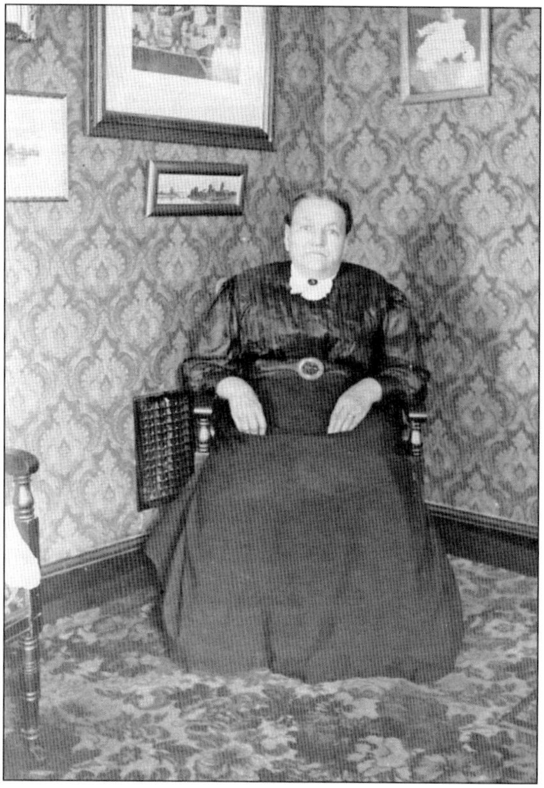

Shown here is Grace Hauger in 1903 at the age of 58, the product of a hard life that began in Germany in 1845. She is listed in census records in 1900 as an immigrant widow whose occupation is "farmer" and whose first language is German. Hauger did not learn English until she immigrated to the United States at the age of 25, in the last year of the Civil War. After the war, she settled down in Muncy and raised a family that included at least five children: twins Frank and Harry, Jennie, Tessie, and Carl. The census of 1900 claims at least five more, although they were no longer a part of the household. According to the information on the back of the photograph, Hauger survived until at least 1903. (Courtesy of the Muncy Historical Society.)

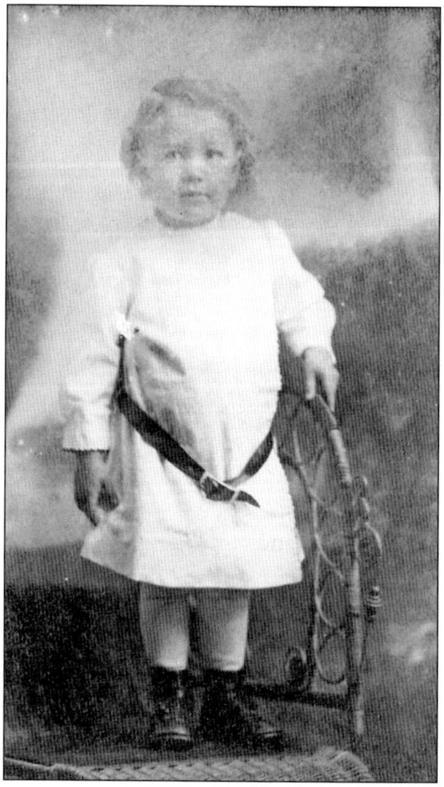

Although the identity of this child is unknown, the picture is from around 1900. Also at question is the gender of the child, given the standards of the day for hair and the proper time for a male child to wear pants. Clues, mainly the child's belt, point to it being male. The photographer was John Reed, who had been married to Martha for six years at the time of the 1900 census. (Courtesy of the Muncy Historical Society.)

Eight

Country Roads, Take Me Home
The Streets of Muncy

Adages like "there's no place like home" exist for a reason. Of course, the fondness people experience for their hometowns gives root to this idealistic thought, but to say that is the only reason would dismiss very practical reasons behind these words. If one were to find an interest in cartography, a secondary meaning behind these words would come to light. Each little hamlet in America is laid out differently from the next, with both aesthetic and logical considerations at play.

Muncy is no different. Its layout partly pays homage to Pennsylvania's founder, William Penn (who was a big fan of grid patterns, with no idea of the horrors of gridlock that would follow): the central grid of the town is its heartbeat, with Main, Washington, Penn, and Market Streets hosting the businesses and the houses of worship that Muncy's people hold dear. The town is also fed by many state and federal highways, with I-80 and I-180 and Highways 405, 220, and 147, among others, winding like veins through the Pennsylvania countryside, bringing the lifeblood of travel and commerce to the Muncy core.

Alongside such giant pathways are small alleys, walking trails, bridges, and even train tracks that move people and industry in and out of the area. One even has to view the Susquehanna River as a road in this context, as it provides many of the same functions. Dotting these streets are the homes and businesses that Muncy and its people pulled out of the muck and clay over 250 years ago. These paths allow Muncy to bring in those who look to find a place to call home and send out the best and the brightest into the world with a hope that they leave as great a mark on America as they have on Muncy.

Muncy, for all intents and purposes, is Main Street America: a place where the values of the past and the hopes of the future intersect.

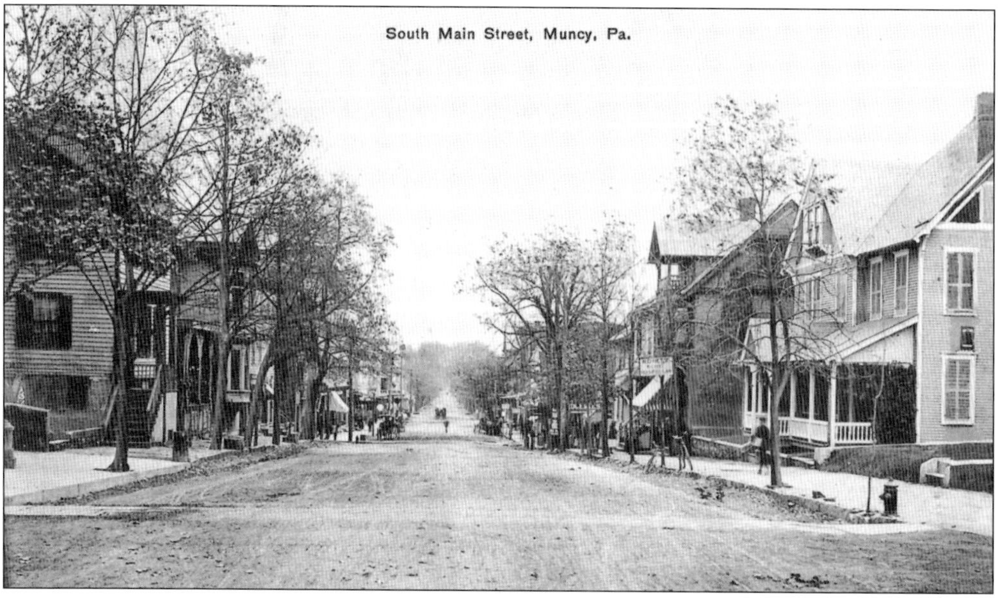

After meeting with North Main Street at Water Street, South Main Street intersects High and Penn Streets, Church Alley, Lafayette, Pepper, and New Streets, South Alley, Lincoln Street, Riddell Lane, Quarry Road, and Rose Hill Road before terminating at the intersection of T-862 and Susquehanna Trail. Along its route, one can find the Inn at Shuttle Hill, Hope Community Church, Muncy Bank & Trust, Grenoble Funeral Home, the post office, the Muncy Area Volunteer Fire Company, Orlando's Restaurant, and at 200 South Main Street, the childhood home of coauthor Maggie S. Rymsza. (Author's collection.)

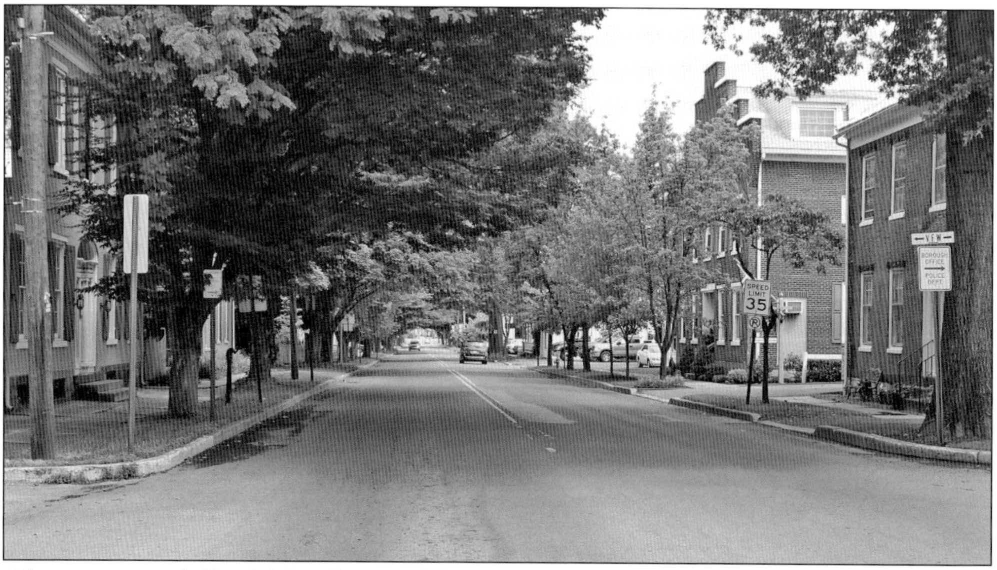

After meeting with South Main Street at Water Street, North Main Street intersects Noble Alley, Brady, Grant, and East Mechanic Streets, Glade Run, and Muncy Creek before merging into John Brady Drive. Along its route, one can find Frosty Beverages, Tommy's Bar and Grill, Fort Brady Hotel, the Muncy Historical Society, Pic Brothers Auto Sales, Galen R. Betzer Funeral Services, Brelsford Motors and Equipment, Muncy Quilts, and several residential homes, some dating back to the settling of the area. (Author's collection.)

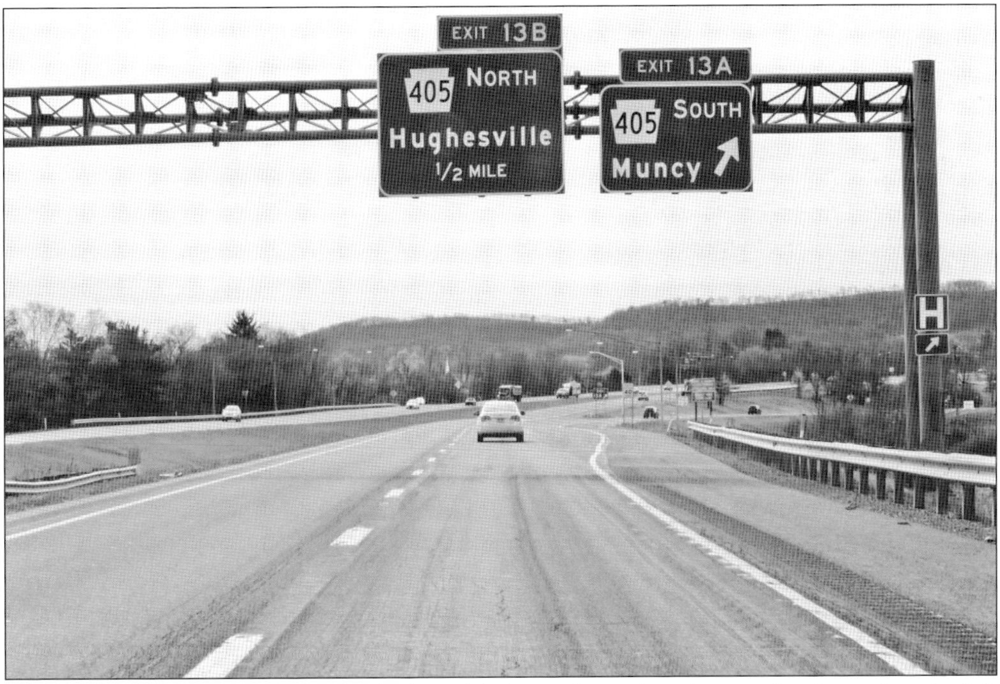

Although it began life as a five-mile plank road (a dirt and gravel road covered with wooden planks), Pennsylvania 405 has moved far beyond connecting the towns of Muncy and Hughesville. Today, it is a 27-mile connector highway administered by the Pennsylvania Department of Transportation. Shown here at the Muncy exit, it crosses Pennsylvania 147 near Lewisburg and Interstate 80 before terminating at US Highway 220 in Hughesville. (Author's collection.)

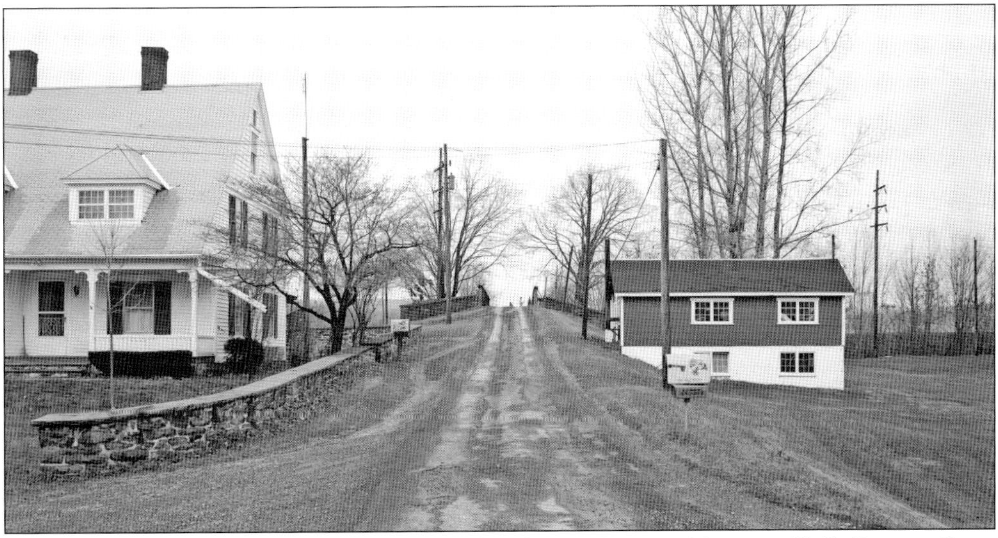

Shown here is the Reading–Halls Station Bridge along US 220 in Muncy at Halls Station. Once a train bridge, this was one of three built by Reading engineer Richard B. Osborne (1815–1899). The bridge was 69 feet long with 48 panels in total. The compression beams on the side formed an X pattern and allowed the bridge to give under the great weight of the train. The bridge is still in place, although it now serves solely as a farm bridge and is located on private property. (Courtesy of the Library of Congress.)

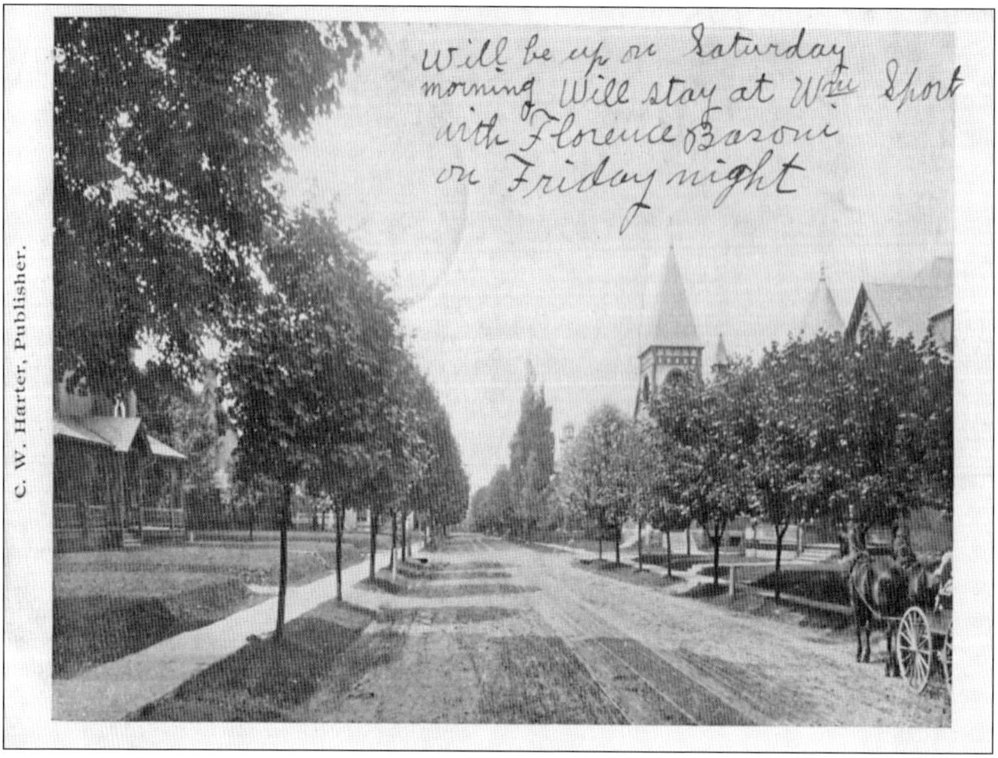

Shown at its intersection with Market Street, Penn Street is one of the largest homes of industry in the Muncy Valley. Starting in the west, the street intersects Railroad, Smith, Painter, and Sherman Streets, Dehaas Alley, Market Street, McCarty Alley, Main Street, Green Alley, Washington Street, and Glade Run before terminating at State Route 2055. Along its route, one can find the Muncy Cemetery, Muncy Presbyterian Church, St. Andrew's Lutheran Church, Muncy Baptist Church, Muncy High School, and the Sprout Company. (Courtesy of Bill Ritter.)

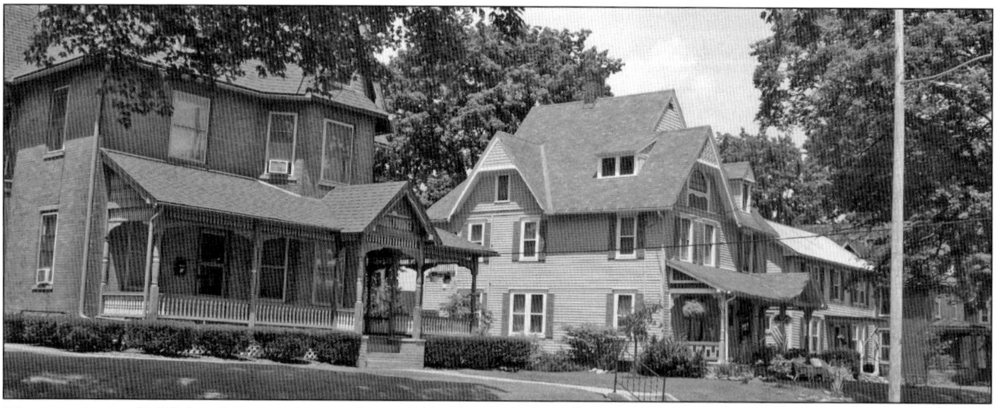

Consisting of 298 buildings, some dating back to 1798, the Muncy Historic District was added to the National Register of Historic Places on July 3, 1980. Notable buildings include St. Andrew's Lutheran Church, Muncy Presbyterian Church, the William McCarty Residence, the Walton-Weaver Residence, the Gray-Bodine Residence, the Clapp-Muncy Historical Society Building, Jacob E. Cooke Row Houses, the Clapp-Smith Building, the Rankin-Brindle Building, the Lloyd Building, the Lycoming County Mutual Fire Insurance Building, the Fahnestock-Petrikin Building, Muncy Valley House, and the D.O. Snyder Building. (Author's collection.)

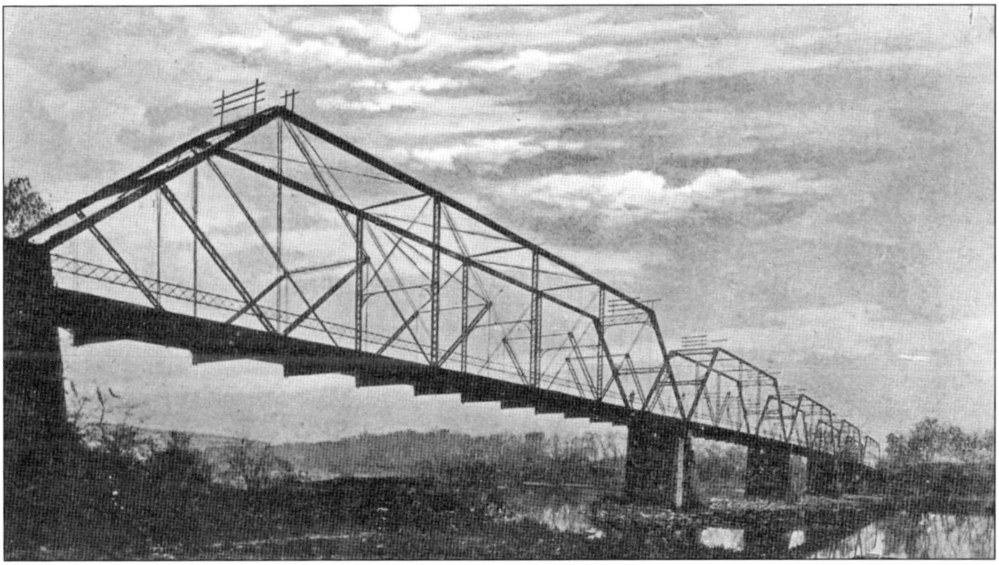

Shown spanning the Susquehanna River at night, this is the original bridge that connected Muncy to Montgomery. Unlike the steel beam design featured here, the current span is a simple column bridge updated to handle bearing loads and floods better. Bids are in place to add another bridge on Route 405 as a part of the Central Susquehanna Valley Transportation Project, which would connect Route 405 to Pennsylvania 147. The new bridge would lessen the amount of transportation on this bridge's descendant, although the project was placed on hold in 2005. (Author's collection.)

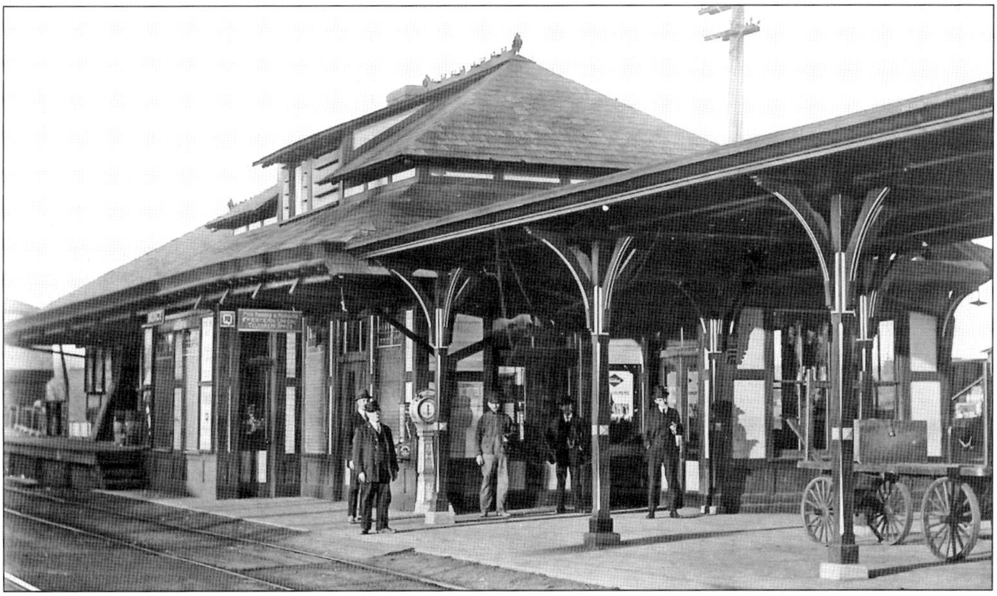

Although there is no longer commercial passenger train service to Muncy, the area did have several train stations during the 1800s and 1900s. The first was constructed in 1855 under the auspices of the Sunbury & Erie Railroad. The station pictured here was constructed by the Reading Railroad Company shortly after the Civil War. It would survive floods before being rebuilt in 1883 after the roof collapsed. Although all stations are gone from the area, rail service still plays a vital role in moving raw materials and manufactured goods from the valley. (Author's collection.)

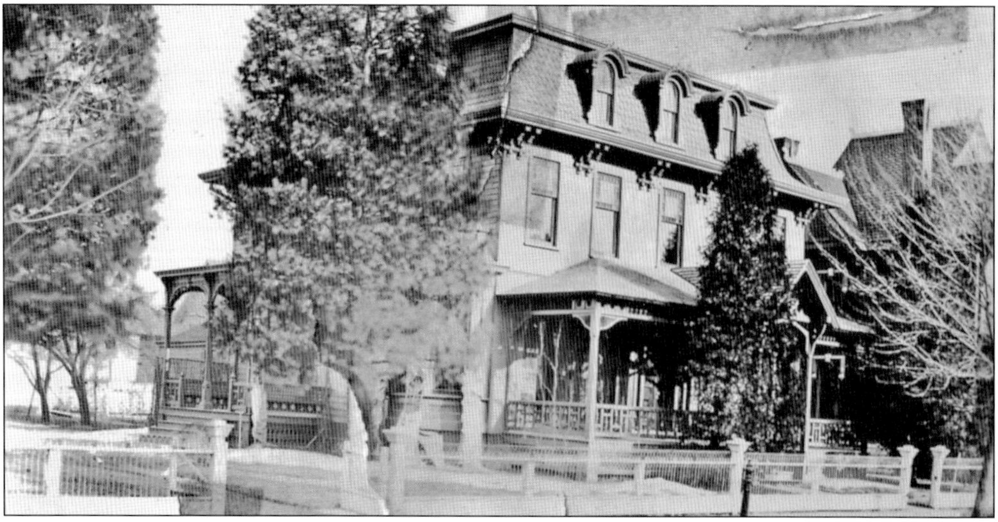

Today, the lot at 107–109 North Main Street hosts Pic Brothers Auto Sales, but it had a very different purpose at the beginning of the 20th century. The address initially hosted the home of L.S. Smith, who was responsible for the construction of the three-story brick building at the corner of Main and Water Streets. Smith's house was torn down in 1954 to make room for a gas station, which would later give way to the car dealership that stands there today. (Courtesy of the Muncy Historical Society.)

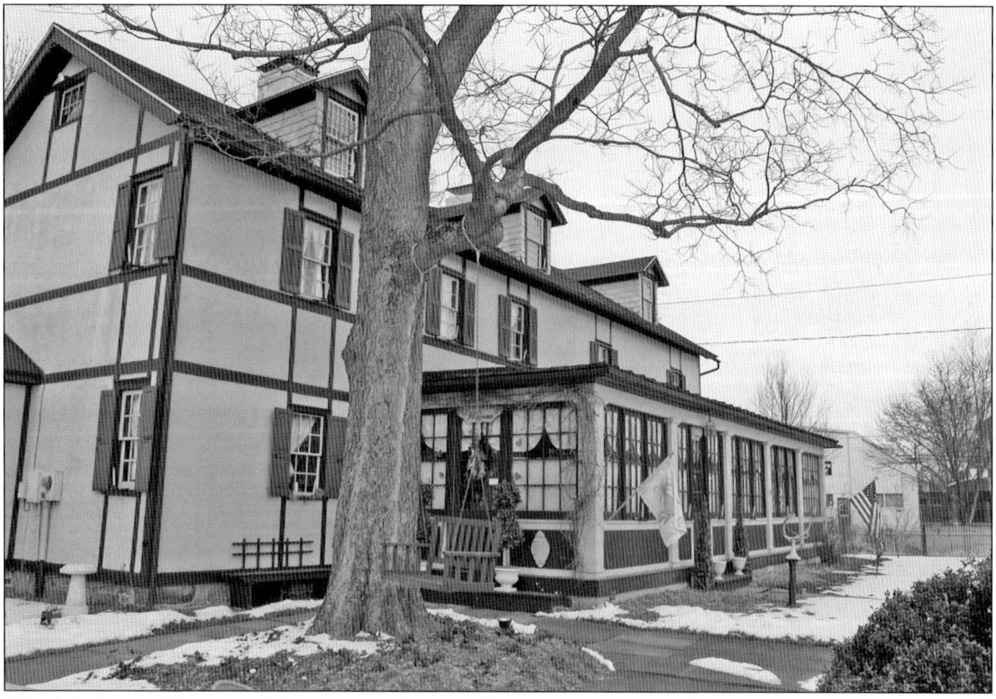

The McCarty-Wertman House is at 34 North Main Street in the heart of historic Muncy. Constructed during the Revolutionary period, this home has served several roles since its inception. William McCarty protected from one to five liberated slaves at a time, with the refugees usually being guarded by family members. (Courtesy of the Muncy Historical Society.)

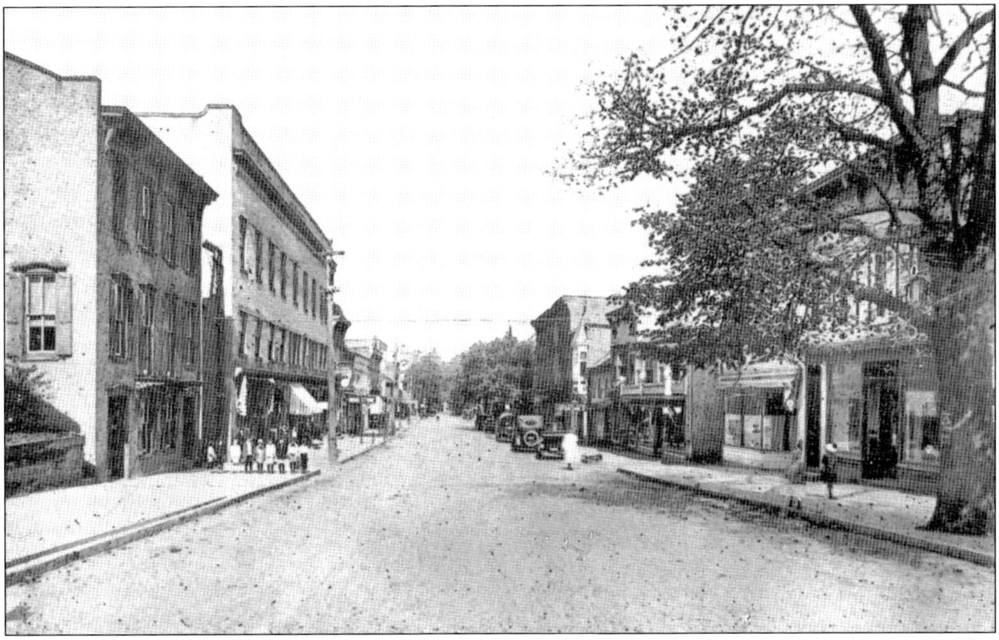

Main Street in Muncy is otherwise known as the heart of the Muncy Historical District. The district was added to the National Register of Historic Places in 1980. Dating back to 1798, the buildings represent Victorian, Georgian, and Federal architecture, among other styles. (Author's collection.)

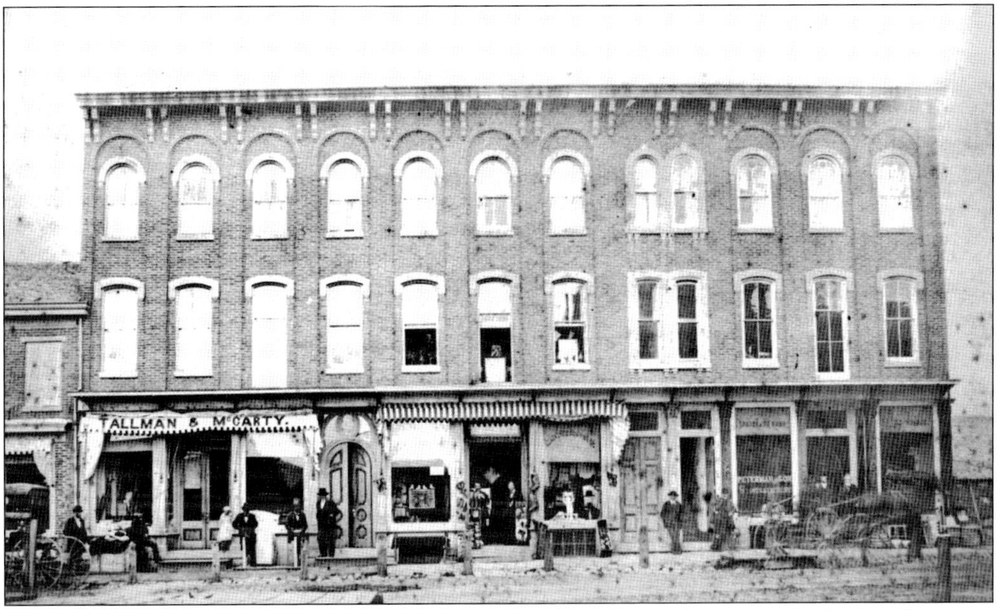

This photograph shows the business district in Muncy in 1876, a busy year for both village and nation. This was the 100th anniversary of the United States, an event that saw Susan B. Anthony give a speech in favor of universal suffrage in Philadelphia. The first baseball game recorded in Muncy took place on August 14 of that year, with Muncy defeating Williamsport 29–18. Also, a cow owned by farmer James Brass was discovered dead on August 31 on a side street in Muncy. The animal was struck by lightning. (Courtesy of the Muncy Historical Society.)

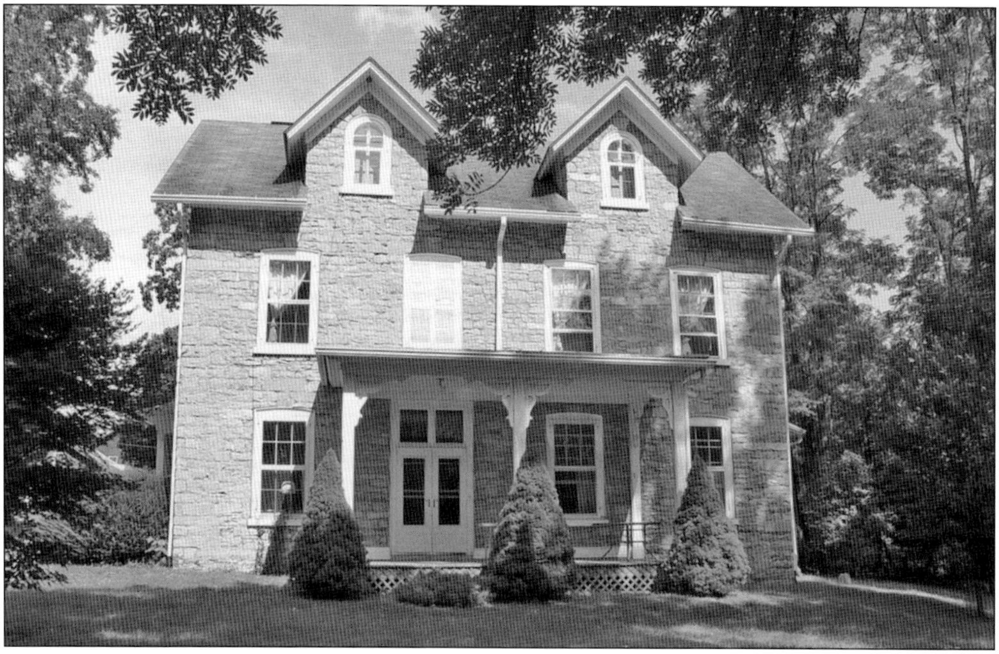

Formerly in Muncy but now in Pennsdale, Mount Equity was the home of local legend Mercy Ellis Cox. This house was built after 1806, when the will of William Ellis required and funded the construction of a suitable home for Mercy and their children. The stone-faced home was initially called the Cottage and was built on a plot of land near Wolf Run. Mercy lived and entertained in the house until her death in 1848. Her son Charles enlarged it to its current size in 1882. (Courtesy of the Muncy Historical Society.)

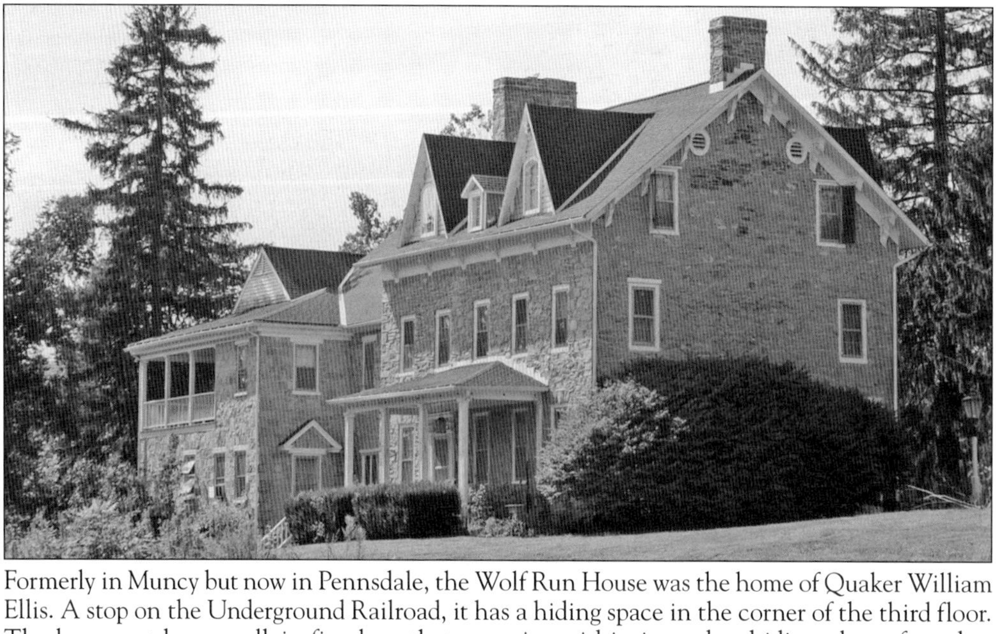

Formerly in Muncy but now in Pennsdale, the Wolf Run House was the home of Quaker William Ellis. A stop on the Underground Railroad, it has a hiding space in the corner of the third floor. The basement has a walk-in fireplace that contains within its arches hiding places for other runaways. Finally, there is a door, now bricked up, that led from the basement to a direct escape to the outside. (Courtesy of the Muncy Historical Society.)

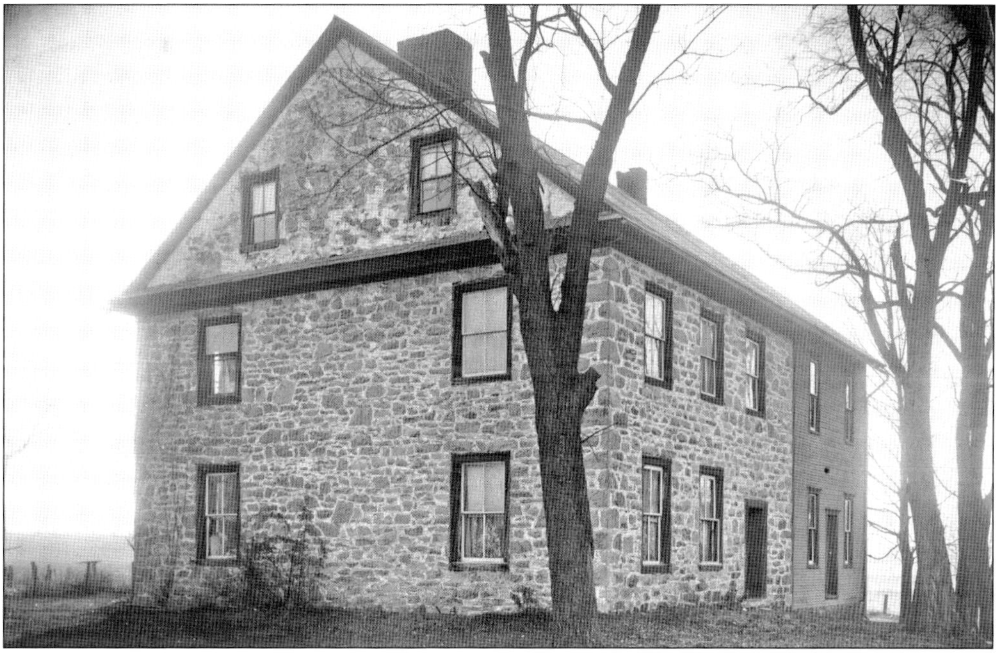

The John Adlum house, now in Pennsdale, was inspired by the Greek Revival movement. There were also influences of the Cape Cod and Colonial styles in this example, which was most likely built with local rock by the resident. Stone houses, although harder to heat, stood up better the damp, cold conditions of the Susquehanna River watershed and of Lycoming County. (Courtesy of the Muncy Historical Society.)

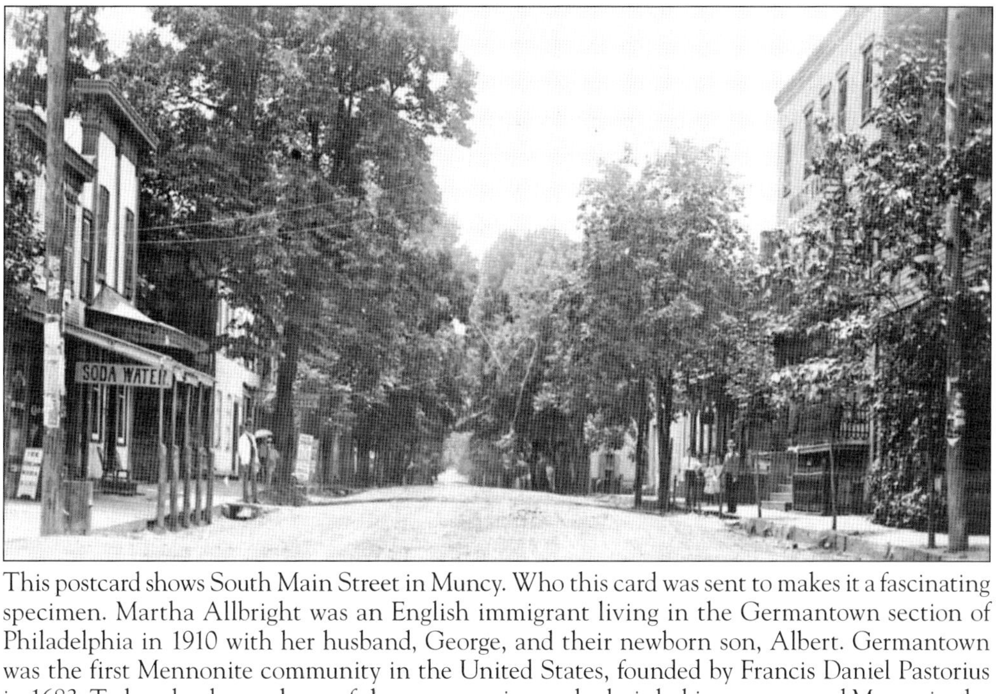

This postcard shows South Main Street in Muncy. Who this card was sent to makes it a fascinating specimen. Martha Allbright was an English immigrant living in the Germantown section of Philadelphia in 1910 with her husband, George, and their newborn son, Albert. Germantown was the first Mennonite community in the United States, founded by Francis Daniel Pastorius in 1683. Today, the descendants of that community no doubt inhabit areas around Muncy in the nearby communities of Watsonville and Trout Run. (Courtesy of Bill Ritter.)

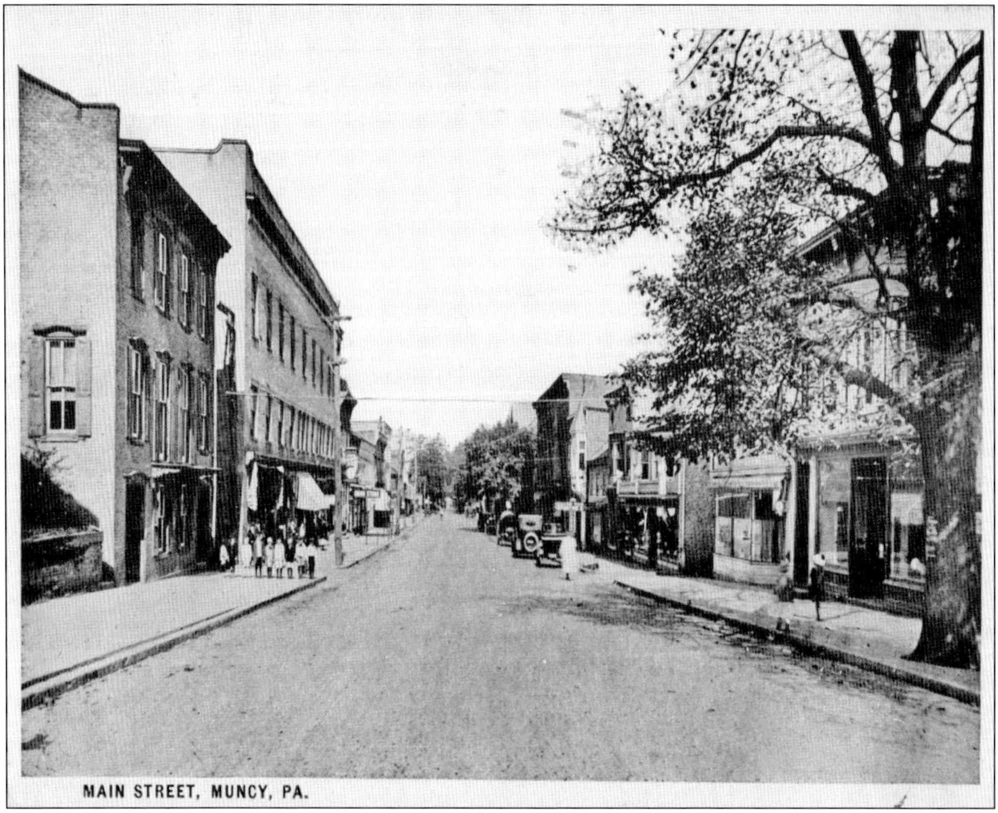

This postcard was sent on December 9, 1921, by George Haiser to his brother and sister in Mifflinburg. The sad message reads, "Dear Sister & Brother, I will try to write a few line to let you know me busy to work too much in shop at Muncy Pa. Yesterday I came home. Tomorrow I am going there again. I am sorry I can't go to you Christmas. I am tired. I feel bad cold cough. I must work every days. I am scare here no work. Write more soon. Your brother." (Courtesy of Bill Ritter.)

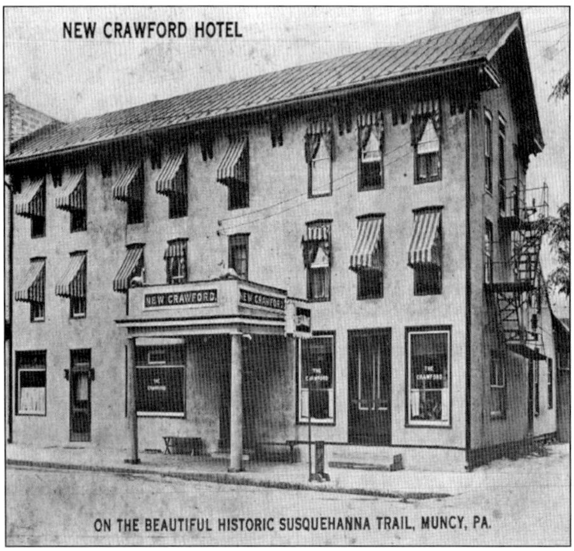

The Crawford Hotel, updated with a new porch, window awnings, and the removal of the addition (replaced with the brick building of another business), reopened as the New Crawford Hotel sometime after 1915. The hotel was closed to the public after a breakfast on March 24, 1913, as reported by the *Muncy Luminary*. Upon reopening, the hotel continued to be listed in theater guides in New York, Boston, and Philadelphia. (Courtesy of Bill Ritter.)

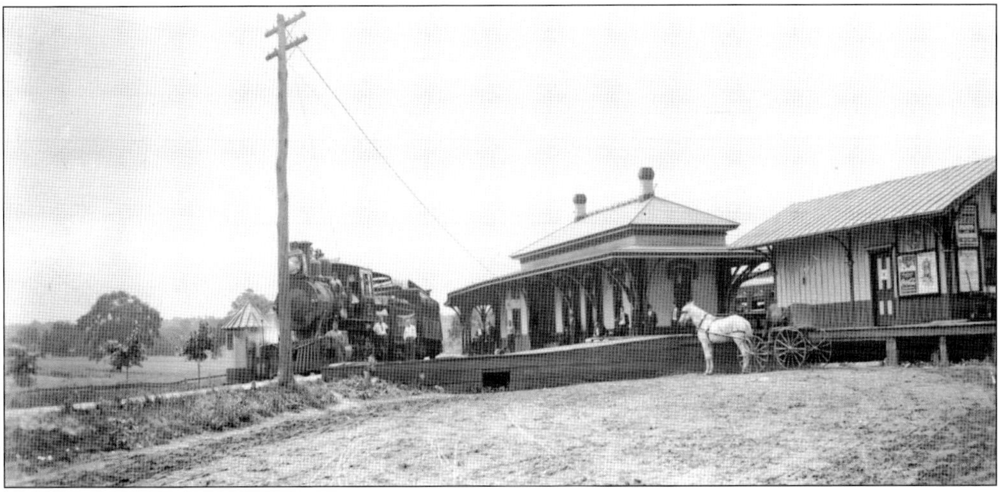

This railroad station was on West Penn Street across from the Keystone Company tracks and was a part of the Reading Railroad Company. In the early hours of June 8, 1939, locals gathered around the tracks to witness the train carrying King George VI and Queen Elizabeth of England from Niagara Falls to Washington, DC. Dozens of cars parked along the highway to witness the royal-blue-and-silver special. Sadly, the station was also the location of many local deaths, as travelers and residents were injured or killed during railroad accidents. (Courtesy of the Muncy Historical Society.)

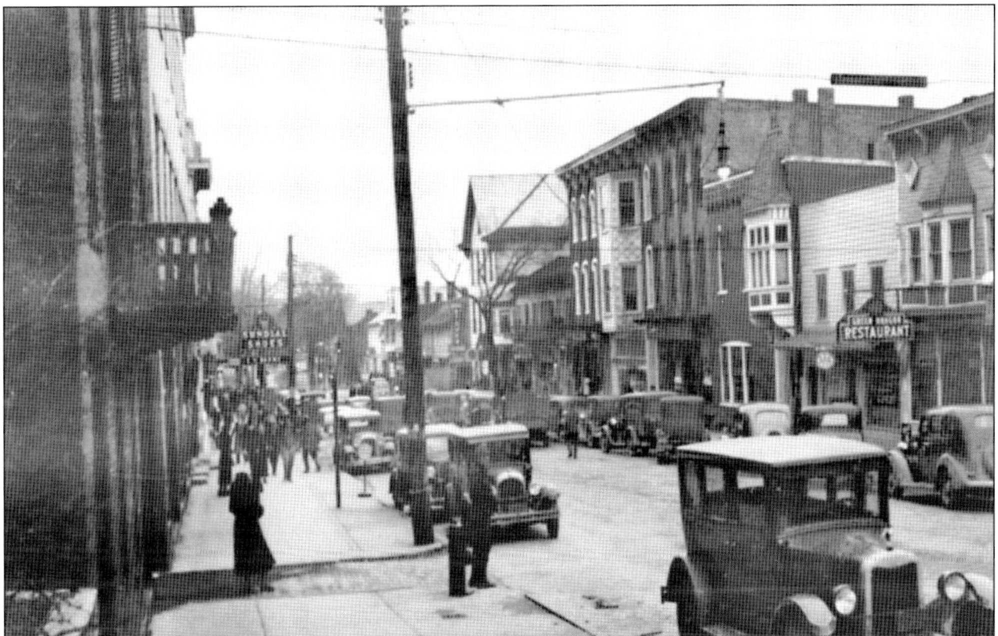

Taken during the 1930s, this photograph shows a bustling section of the Muncy business district. The 1930 census showed the second-largest increase in population in the town's history, a whopping 17.5 percent, which is second only to the staggering 49.5 percent increase that took place between the 1890 and 1900 censuses. Muncy's population boom seems to be behind it, as three of the last four censuses have shown population decreases, the sole exception in 1990 an increase of 2 people, or 0.1 percent. (Courtesy of the Muncy Historical Society.)

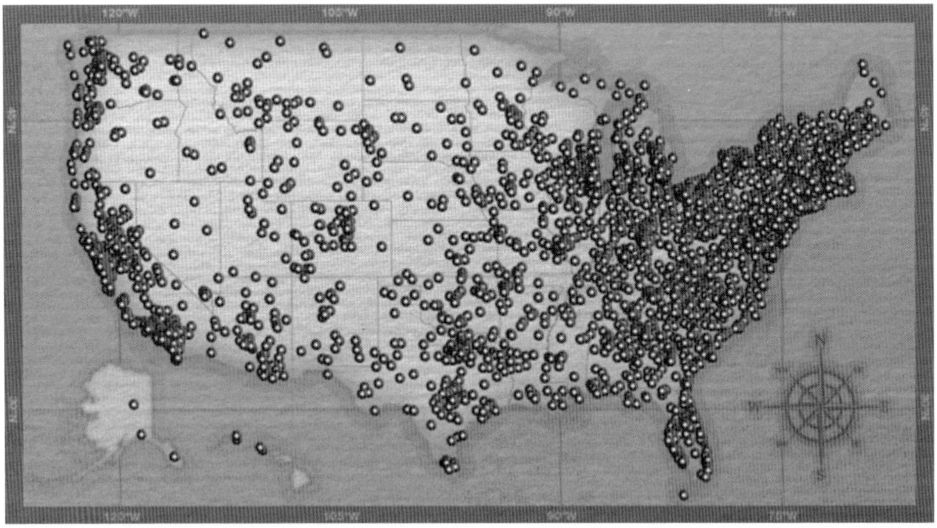